Constructing the Dynamo of Dixie

Constructing the Dynamo of Dixie

Race, Urban Planning, and Cosmopolitanism in Chattanooga, Tennessee

Courtney Elizabeth Knapp

The University of North Carolina Press CHAPEL HILL

This book was published with the assistance of the Authors Fund of the University of North Carolina Press.

The University of North Carolina Press has been a member of the Green Press Initiative since 2003.

Library of Congress Cataloging-in-Publication Data
Names: Knapp, Courtney Elizabeth, author.
Title: Constructing the dynamo of Dixie : race, urban planning, and cosmopolitanism in Chattanooga, Tennessee / Courtney Elizabeth Knapp.
Description: Chapel Hill : University of North Carolina Press, [2018] | Includes bibliographical references and index.
Identifiers: LCCN 2017041402 | ISBN 9781469637266 (cloth : alk. paper) | ISBN 9781469637273 (pbk : alk. paper) | ISBN 9781469637280 (ebook)
Subjects: LCSH: Chattanooga (Tenn.)—History. | City Planning—Tennessee—Chattanooga. | Chattanooga (Tenn.)—Race relations. | African Americans—Tennessee—Chattanooga—History.
Classification: LCC F444.C457 K63 2018 | DDC 976.8/82—dc23
LC record available at https://lccn.loc.gov/2017041402

Cover illustration: *Ascending Path* by Andres Hussey (author's photo, 2013)

Dedicated to the Knapp women:
Jessica, Sylvia, Gail, and Janice

Contents

Illustrations, Maps, and Tables

Acknowledgments

Anyone who has spent time with me over the past five years knows that this book was a collaborative labor of love that would not have been possible without the generous support of several dozen intelligent, committed individuals. A list of the community of friends and colleagues with whom I had the privilege to collaborate during my year of fieldwork in Chattanooga, Tennessee, could fill pages. Thanks first and foremost to the nearly fifty local "placemakers" who agreed to be interviewed for this project, and the more than one hundred participants of the Planning Free School. I want to particularly acknowledge Chattanooga Organized for Action (COA) organizers Perrin Lance, Michael and Keely Gilliland, Chris Brooks, and Megan Hollenbeck; and members of the Westside Community Association, Lincoln Park Neighborhood Association, and Glendale Neighborhood Association, especially Reverend Leroy and Ms. Gloria Griffith, the late Karl Epperson, Ms. Vannice Hughley and Ms. Tiffany Rankins, and Dr. Everlena Holmes. Thanks also to members of the Concerned Citizens for Justice (CCJ) for bringing an uncompromising revolutionary spirit to the streets of Chattanooga. Thank you to Idle No More! Chattanooga leaders William Boyd Nix, and Tamra and Micah Flores for inviting me to participate in your demonstrations and round dances; and, of course, a big shout out to the Occupy Chattanooga crew for helping out with the People's Park on Central Avenue. Big love, as well, to Lauren McEntire and the Idyll Dandy Arts (IDA) folx for becoming my queer comrades during the final weeks I lived in Tennessee.

I'd also like to thank staff at the Chattanooga Public Library for taking a risk with the Planning Free School and allowing eight workshops to evolve into more than fifty planning- related skill-shares, critical conversations, place-making exercises, and issue-based discussion groups. None of it would have been possible without the commitment of radical and righteous Systems Administrator Meg Backus, or the generosity of Director Corrine Hill, Assistant Director Nate Hill, or Social Media Coordinator Mary Barnett. Finally, thanks to all of the dedicated librarians working in the Local History department who connected me with incredible archival resources, and who never complained when I asked for yet *another* newspaper clippings file!

Of course, my deepest gratitude is extended to the editorial staff at the University of North Carolina Press, especially Lucas Church, Joe Parsons, Becki Reibman, Mary Caviness, Andrew Winters, and Dino Battista. Thanks, finally and especially, to my intellectual and academic mentors, John Forester, Carole Boyce Davies, and Dr. Fouad Makki, and my wife Rebecca, for their good humor, patience, and unyielding support for this project.

Constructing the Dynamo of Dixie

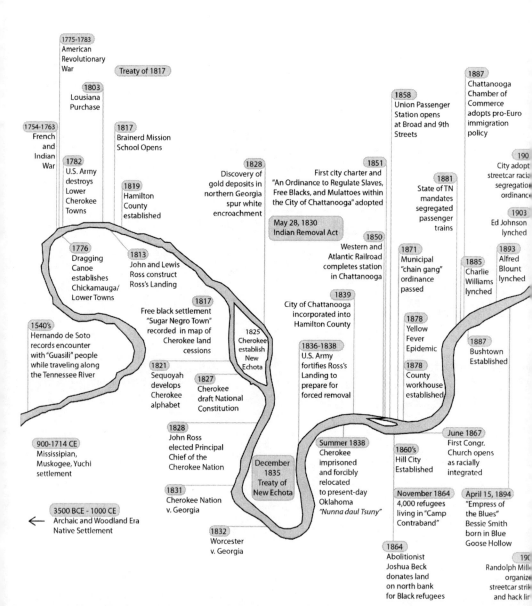

1750's–1865
Enslaved African Americans
imported into Chattanooga area

1775-1783
American
Revolutionary
War

Treaty of 1817

1887
Chattanooga
Chamber of
Commerce
adopts pro-Euro
immigration
policy

1803
Lousiana
Purchase

1858
Union Passenger
Station opens
at Broad and 9th
Streets

1754-1763
French
and
Indian
War

1817
Brainerd Mission
School Opens

1828
Discovery of
gold deposits in
northern Georgia
spur white
encroachment

1851
First city charter and
"An Ordinance to Regulate Slaves,
Free Blacks, and Mulattoes within
the City of Chattanooga" adopted

1881
State of TN
mandates
segregated
passenger
trains

190
City adopt
streetcar racia
segregation
ordinance

1782
U.S. Army
destroys
Lower
Cherokee
Towns

1819
Hamilton
County
established

May 28, 1830
Indian Removal Act

1903
Ed Johnson
lynched

1776
Dragging
Canoe
establishes
Chickamauga/
Lower Towns

1813
John and Lewis
Ross construct
Ross's Landing

1850
Western and
Atlantic Railroad
completes station
in Chattanooga

1871
Municipal
"chain gang"
ordinance
passed

1885
Charlie
Williams
lynched

1893
Alfred
Blount
lynched

1817
Free black settlement
"Sugar Negro Town"
recorded in map of
Cherokee land
cessions

1839
City of Chattanooga
incorporated into
Hamilton County

1540's
Hernando de Soto
records encounter
with "Guasili" people
while traveling along
the Tennessee River

1825
Cherokee
establish
New
Echota

1836-1838
U.S. Army
fortifies Ross's
Landing to
prepare for
forced removal

1878
Yellow
Fever
Epidemic

1887
Bushtown
Established

1821
Sequoyah
develops
Cherokee
alphabet

1827
Cherokee
draft National
Constitution

1878
County
workhouse
established

900-1714 CE
Mississipian,
Muskogee, Yuchi
settlement

1828
John Ross
elected Principal
Chief of the
Cherokee Nation

Summer 1838
Cherokee
imprisoned
and forcibly
relocated
to present-day
Oklahoma
"Nunna daul Tsuny"

1860's
Hill City
Established

June 1867
First Congr.
Church opens
as racially
integrated

**December
1835**
Treaty of
New Echota

3500 BCE - 1000 CE
Archaic and Woodland Era
Native Settlement

1831
Cherokee Nation
v. Georgia

November 1864
4,000 refugees
living in "Camp
Contraband"

April 15, 1894
"Empress of
the Blues"
Bessie Smith
born in Blue
Goose Hollow

1832
Worcester
v. Georgia

1864
Abolitionist
Joshua Beck
donates land
on north bank
for Black refugees

190
Randolph Mill
organize
streetcar strik
and hack lin

Diasporic placemaking in Chattanooga's urban core: 1540s–present.

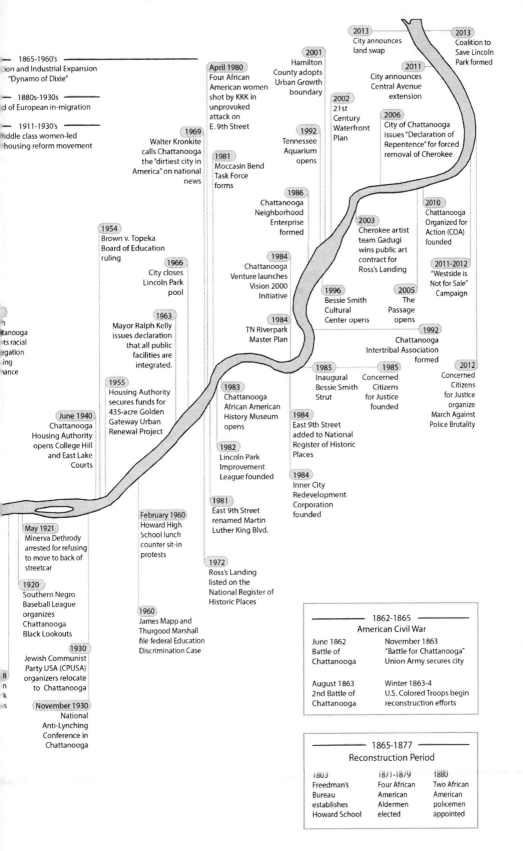

1865-1960's
tion and Industrial Expansion "Dynamo of Dixie"

1880s-1930s
d of European in-migration

1911-1930's
Middle class women-led housing reform movement

1954
Brown v. Topeka Board of Education ruling

1969
Walter Kronkite calls Chattanooga the "dirtiest city in America" on national news

April 1980
Four African American women shot by KKK in unprovoked attack on E. 9th Street

1981
Moccasin Bend Task Force forms

2001
Hamilton County adopts Urban Growth boundary

1992
Tennessee Aquarium opens

2002
21st Century Waterfront Plan

2013
City announces land swap

2011
City announces Central Avenue extension

2006
City of Chattanooga issues "Declaration of Repentence" for forced removal of Cherokee

2013
Coalition to Save Lincoln Park formed

1966
City closes Lincoln Park pool

1963
Mayor Ralph Kelly issues declaration that all public facilities are integrated.

1986
Chattanooga Neighborhood Enterprise formed

1984
Chattanooga Venture launches Vision 2000 Initiative

1984
TN Riverpark Master Plan

2003
Cherokee artist team Gadugi wins public art contract for Ross's Landing

2005
The Passage opens

2010
Chattanooga Organized for Action (COA) founded

2011-2012
"Westside is Not for Sale" Campaign

1955
Housing Authority secures funds for 435-acre Golden Gateway Urban Renewal Project

1983
Chattanooga African American History Museum opens

1996
Bessie Smith Cultural Center opens

1992
Chattanooga Intertribal Association formed

n
tanooga
ts racial
egation
ing
nance

June 1940
Chattanooga Housing Authority opens College Hill and East Lake Courts

1982
Lincoln Park Improvement League founded

1985
Inaugural Bessie Smith Strut

1984
East 9th Street added to National Register of Historic Places

1985
Concerned Citizens for Justice founded

2012
Concerned Citizens for Justice organize March Against Police Brutality

1984
Inner City Redevelopment Corporation founded

May 1921
Minerva Dethrody arrested for refusing to move to back of streetcar

February 1960
Howard High School lunch counter sit-in protests

1981
East 9th Street renamed Martin Luther King Blvd.

1920
Southern Negro Baseball League organizes Chattanooga Black Lookouts

1972
Ross's Landing listed on the National Register of Historic Places

1930
Jewish Communist Party USA (CPUSA) organizers relocate to Chattanooga

1960
James Mapp and Thurgood Marshall file federal Education Discrimination Case

8
n
k
s

November 1930
National Anti-Lynching Conference in Chattanooga

1862-1865		
American Civil War		
June 1862	November 1863	
Battle of Chattanooga	"Battle for Chattanooga" Union Army secures city	
August 1863	Winter 1863-4	
2nd Battle of Chattanooga	U.S. Colored Troops begin reconstruction efforts	

1865-1877		
Reconstruction Period		
1863	1871-1879	1880
Freedman's Bureau establishes Howard School	Four African American Aldermen elected	Two African American policemen appointed

Introduction

Diasporic Placemaking in the Renaissance City of the South

What does it mean to say that a city's evolution is the result of centuries of multiple and overlapping instances of *diasporic placemaking?* And why ask this question in the context of Chattanooga, a small and relatively unknown city nestled between the Tennessee River and Lookout Mountain in the southeastern corner of Tennessee? At its core, *diaspora* connotes the movement of people: uprooting, dislocation, migration, resettling; movement which may be forced, induced, or voluntary. *Placemaking*, on the other hand, suggests homemaking, and the deliberate carving and cultivating of unique socio-spatial identities into new and unfamiliar terrains. In the spheres of community planning and urban design, the fields in which this book is principally, though not exclusively, located, placemaking has become closely associated with a distinct set of quality of life interventions: the reorientation of downtowns away from cars and toward the pedestrian; the infusion of public spaces with urban amenities such as seating, trees and shade devices, identity markers, water features, and wayfaring devices; and the reactivation of underutilized public areas through destination planning and social programming, including community events, farmers markets, cultural development, and the arts.

In its status quo understanding, placemaking has obvious connections to urban *cosmopolitanism*: through the techniques described above, cities improve their images, enhance quality of life, and expand cultural opportunities for their residents and visitors. Placemaking in this sense combines a toolbox of spatial improvements with vigorous place-marketing, in order to enhance the perception, if not the reality, of cities as places rich in culture, innovation, and diverse perspectives.

But, in the context of this book, I mean to treat diasporic placemaking in a more critical, and yet more ordinary, sense of the latter word. The history of diasporic placemaking in Chattanooga, Tennessee, goes beyond New Urbanist facelifts, and goes well beyond the marketing of cities as inviting, cultured, or multicultural communities. In my treatment of the term, *diasporic placemaking* refers to the everyday practices, the collaborations and conflicts, through which historically uprooted and migratory populations—Native Americans, African Americans, whites, Jewish immigrants, Latinos, and others—forge new communities of security and belonging out of unfamiliar, and oftentimes stratified and unequal, yet shared local environments.

Sinister Roots

Though much of this community building and development has been extra-institutional, the city's political-economic structure, with local planners (first military, then urban) at its evolving nexus, has enacted policies and procedures that have deeply influenced, and are increasingly influenced by, everyday diasporic placemaking in the city. Though this phenomenon is not unique to Chattanooga, the city affords fertile grounds to examine it vis-à-vis its historical and contemporary spatial development. Chattanooga's story offers a case for better understanding the politics of race, urban planning, and cosmopolitanism politics in American cities because, since before its official founding, the city has been a diverse but highly segregated place, evolving according to strict—and yet permeable—de jure and de facto codes of racialized ordering and conduct. Due to this history, at its root, life in contemporary Chattanooga is characterized by highly unequal access to land, capital, and opportunity structures.

Though perhaps best known as the subject of the lighthearted 1941 Glenn Miller Orchestra hit "Chattanooga Choo Choo," the modern settlement of the city has much more sinister roots. The town initially was known as "Ross's Landing," serving as a ferry crossing and commercial storage facility on the literal border between U.S. territory and the sovereign Cherokee nation to the south of the Tennessee River. The Landing then became the primary site of military fortification during the forced round-up and removal of the Cherokee between 1837 and 1838—a dispossession commonly known as the "Trail of Tears." Furthermore, African American slave and convict laborers were central to early city-building and industrialization efforts—economic strategies that local boosters proudly endorsed—and in the years that followed the U.S. Civil War (1861–65), Jim Crow planning and policy making drove spatial development and social ordering for nearly a century, leaving behind legacies that, though no longer legally sanctioned, persist and continue to produce repercussions today.

Subverting and Defying Racialized Oppression

Chattanooga is also instructive to the lessons of diasporic placemaking because, despite its slavery and Jim Crow histories, downtown Chattanooga evolved into a prominent center of African American social, cultural, and economic production in the decades following the American Civil War. Among other distinctions, the city was home to dozens of black-owned mutual aid and benevolent societies, boasted an entertainment and cultural district along East Ninth Street ("the Big Nine") that rivaled Memphis's Beale Street, and attracted thousands of families who flocked to Lincoln Park every summer for picnics, dancing, and family activities, and to swim in what was one of only two "colored" public pools in the state during the Tennessee Jim Crow period. Finally, the city has a rich history of antiracism activism and multi- or interracial community building that has subverted and outright defied and rejected de jure and de facto segregation. For all of these reasons, Chattanooga can help us better understand processes of resistance and alternative world building that counteract legacies of racialized state- and market-driven violence, subjugation, and exploitation.

Rebranding the Postindustrial City

Chattanooga can also help us better understand how race and racism influence public participation and citizen-driven planning in purportedly postindustrial, creative, and cosmopolitan urban centers. Once a leader in the New South industrial movement, known internationally as "the Dynamo of Dixie," Chattanooga began experiencing massive deindustrialization and population loss in the decades following World War II. Unsurprisingly, black poor and working-class residents experienced disproportionate unemployment and quality of life burdens during this decades-long period of economic and spatial restructuring and disinvestment. These damages were compounded by the city's Golden Gateway urban renewal program—a housing authority–managed initiative that bulldozed 435 acres of working-class black homes and businesses on the city's Westside—the fourth-largest urban renewal project nationwide in terms of scale and the twelfth-largest in terms of total development costs at the time.

But, unlike many of their Rust Belt counterparts whose population and industry losses produced urban decline through the final years of the twentieth century, committed Chattanoogans got to work early. Motivated to change its public image after being referred to as "the dirtiest city in America" by Walter Cronkite on the CBS national evening news, city boosters formed alliances with civic, philanthropic, and resident leaders to launch the revitalization of the city's historic riverfront and downtown neighborhoods. Beginning with the Moccasin Bend Task Force in 1983 and followed by the Venture 2000 initiative and *21st Century Waterfront Plan* in 2002, Chattanooga has gained a national reputation as a city where a series of connected, citizen-driven local planning and development initiatives effectively brought the city back from the brink of its postindustrial economic and environmental graves.

A key player in these revitalization efforts has been the River City Company, a private nonprofit organization dedicated to coordinating private and philanthropic investments across the urban core. Incorporated in 1986, the organization initially targeted neighborhoods along the historic riverfront for planning and capital investment programs. Over the past twenty-five years, however, the geographic scope of the organization's efforts has expanded. Today, its revitalization work extends into five key areas of downtown Chattanooga: the North Shore, the Riverfront, City Center, the Martin Luther King Boulevard/University district, and the Southside.

In collaboration with city government, key nonprofits, and prominent local philanthropic organizations, River City has leveraged billions of dollars in private and public reinvestment over the past three decades. Its efforts have catalyzed a growing multigenerational Back to the City movement and have radically expanded the city's tourism and high-tech creative economies. These trends are reflected in building and development data for the city. Between 2000 and 2009, 6,943 residential building permits were issued by the City of Chattanooga.[1] In September 2012, the *Times Free Press* reported that the city "[defied] trends" when it came to new housing construction and market rate/luxury housing development in particular, having added 2,539 new rental units to the local housing stock during the Great Recession of 2007 to 2009.[2] Although some of this development occurred outside of the formal urban core, the majority of new development occurred within the districts prioritized by the River City Company and its allies.

Importantly, Chattanooga's renaissance has not been limited to housing production. Employing a combination of aggressive marketing, public subsidies, and quality of life improvements, the city has also reclaimed its industrial heritage by attracting high-tech manufacturing firms and creative class entrepreneurs to the city. In 2011, Volkswagen opened its first U.S. manufacturing plant in Chattanooga, having been lured to the city two years earlier by a robust public incentive package valued at $577.4 million. Today, the $1 billion plant employs 2,415 workers in a variety of high tech manufacturing positions, and economists at the University of Tennessee's Center for Business and Economic Research estimate an additional ten thousand indirect positions generated by the plant, as well as $643.1 million in annual income, $31.2 million in annual state tax revenues, and $22.3 million in annual local tax revenues.[3]

Moreover, Chattanooga earned the nickname "Gig City" in 2010 after investing in the "fastest digital Internet infrastructure in the Western Hemisphere" (1 gigabyte/second) through a partnership with Google, a public investment totaling $300 million (a $220 million bond plus $111.5 million in Federal Stimulus funds). Today, actors driving the city's urban renaissance use this unprecedented Internet speed and capacity to attract web programmers, video game developers, and other high-tech creative professionals to the city. As a result of these advances, sections of the downtown are rapidly transforming into a "playground for pioneers" and entrepreneurs in high-tech, creative industries.[4] The "GeekMove" program, co-sponsored by the Lyndhurst Foundation and Chattanooga Neighborhood Enterprise, the city's premier nonprofit housing developer, promoted a contest to offer $11,250 in mortgage forgiveness and relocation costs to ten high-tech professionals willing to relocate to the city. The program limits the neighborhoods where homes can be purchased to urban core areas either already undergoing or on the verge of experiencing massive gentrification, including the historically African American, working-class neighborhood of Bushtown, and the ethnically and economically diverse neighborhoods of Orchard Knob and Highland Park.

Reinscribing Multicultural Narratives of Place

Importantly, several of the downtown revitalization initiatives described in this chapter have centered Native American and African American history and culture in efforts to reignite the city's tourist and cultural economies while at the same time honoring the historic contributions of local communities of color. Public art and space planning has been used to reinscribe Cherokee and African American narratives of place into the historic riverfront, while a Mayor and City Council-backed "Declaration of Repentance" for the Trail of Tears established a local policy framework to guide the preservation and support of Native American culture and history in the city. These place-making measures have produced unique urban landscapes that are instructive to other cities willing to confront their colonial pasts and engage in the work of cultural recognition and political reconciliation.

Complicating Narratives of Interracial Harmony and Progress

Without question, certain segments of Chattanooga's residents have benefited greatly from the city's revitalization agenda. For this population, urban regeneration has led to better quality, higher paying jobs, a range of social and cultural opportunities, the preservation of historic and architecturally significant neighborhoods, and access to new luxury housing and urban amenities along the riverfront. But while the mainstream story of urban change in downtown Chattanooga is unabashedly progressive and optimistic, other, more critical interpretations have evolved alongside it. These critics observe with irony that though mainstream place-making initiatives center on Native and African American history and culture, those same institution-backed revitalization efforts have had the effect of exacerbating the marginalization and exclusion of people of color from new reinvestment and opportunity structures.

Specifically, the redevelopment of the Riverfront and historic inner urban core neighborhoods has been prioritized to the exclusion of traditionally "less desirable" working-class black and Latino neighborhoods across the city. Personal testimonies from poor and working-class residents, as well as local social justice activists in the areas of housing, workforce development, and transportation, point not to widespread citizen engagement, but instead to complex legacies of unequal access to planning and development decision-making circles and resource pools. The result of this selective engagement and reinvestment is a highly uneven and inequitable urban landscape where most struggle, many lose, and only a few manage to win. The gravity of this double standard is underscored by sources which cited that Chattanooga had the second fastest rising poverty rate nationwide between 2007 and 2009, and two of the top fifteen most racially gentrified zip codes in the United States between 2000 and 2010.[5]

For the majority of Chattanoogans living in the urban core, then, who cannot afford to access the privileged economic and social spaces produced by cosmopolitanism-driven gentrification, the experiences of the city's renaissance are anything but progressive. To the contrary, they are characterized by increasing housing costs that outpace income growth, persistent cultural marginalization and selective co-optation, and the unabated stripping of community assets and infrastructure. According to this narrative of urban change, Chattanooga's renaissance has been, at best, marginally beneficial, and at worst, a scourge, as relentless gentrification produces a local economic climate where fewer and fewer working-class residents of color can continue to afford to call the city their home.

Demographic Impacts

These trends are underscored by changes in the racial composition of Chattanooga's urban core between 1950 and 2010. Historically, most residents living in downtown Chattanooga have identified as either white or black, though the relative proportions of each population have changed dramatically since the middle of the twentieth century. In 1950, white residents comprised more than two-thirds of urban core dwellers (68.6 percent), while African Americans comprised just under one third (31.4 percent). Over the next forty years, the white population decreased by nearly three-quarters, dropping from 86,145 in 1950 to 22,260 in 1990. The local African American population, in contrast, remained more or less constant through the 1970's. In 1950, there were 39,460 black residents living in the urban core; thirty years later the number had decreased slightly to 38,523. Between 1980 and 1990, however, the African American population decreased by more than six thousand residents.

Although white population loss stabilized by 1990 and numbers have increased steadily since then, the local African American population has continued to shrink. By 2010, the total black population living in downtown Chattanooga was at a century's low, having dropped nearly one-third from 38,523 residents in 1980 to 26,102 in 2010. Although African American residents still comprised a slight majority of urban core residents in 2010, this proportion is shrinking steadily and recent American Community Survey estimates suggest that working-class black families are getting priced out of the historic urban core as Back to the City enthusiasts move in.

Importantly, populations from other racial and ethnic categories (including multiracial and self-ascribed "other" categories) have increased more than six-fold over the past twenty years. The local Hispanic or Latino population living in the urban core has also increased dramatically: between 1980 and 2010, it grew by more than five hundred percent, with nonprofit organizations working on the frontlines of Latino community building

Rates of population change for black and white residents in Chattanooga and Hamilton County, 1950–2010

	Total Population				Percentage Change			
	1950	1970	1990	2010	1950–1970	1970–1990	1990–2010	1950–2010
Black Population								
Inner Urban Core	35,676	14,274	12,472	7,089	−59.99	−12.62	−43.16	−80.13
Urban Core	39,460	38,738	31,885	25,982	−1.83	−17.69	−18.51	−34.16
City	40,317	42,547	51,338	58,507	5.53	20.66	13.96	45.12
County	42,556	46,160	54,477	67,900	8.47	18.02	24.64	59.55
White Population								
Inner Urban Core	38,326	15,259	9,727	10,507	−60.19	−36.25	8.02	−72.59
Urban Core	86,145	39,389	26,260	19,935	−54.28	−33.33	−24.09	−76.86
City	123,912	77,179	99,057	97,202	−37.71	28.35	−1.87	−21.56
County	165,699	208,596	227,413	248,716	25.89	9.02	9.37	50.10
Total Inner Urban Core (all races)	74,002	29,533	22,199	17,596	−60.09	−24.83	−20.74	−76.22
Total Urban Core	125,605	78,127	58,145	45,917	−37.80	−25.58	−21.03	−63.44
Total City	164,229	119,726	150,395	155,709	−27.10	25.62	3.53	−5.19
Total County	208,255	254,756	281,890	316,616	22.33	10.65	12.32	52.03

Source: U.S. Census Bureau, "Population by Race, 1950–2010," prepared by Social Explorer, accessed December 22, 2016, http://www.socialexplorer.com/6f4cdab7a0/explore.

arguing that the U.S. Census may be underestimating this local population by as many as fifteen thousand people.

Mapping these demographic changes alongside local housing growth statistics reveals that most new housing development is downtown. Over the past twenty-five years, the city has focused on attracting middle class, predominantly white residents who can afford market rate and luxury housing units. In 2000, the majority of whites living in Chattanooga resided outside of the urban core—although sections of Bluffview/University of Tennessee–Chattanooga (UTC), North Chattanooga, and Orchard Knob in East Chattanooga had begun to transition from predominantly black to more racially mixed communities. Ten years later, white residents comprised the vast majority of residents in new housing located along the riverfront, city center, and the Main Street area of the Southside neighborhood. In the blocks immediately surrounding the aquarium and Bluffview Arts district, more than 90 percent of the total population identified as "white alone" in the 2010 U.S. Census. Similarly, blocks on the Southside that were almost exclusively African American in 2000 had become predominantly white by 2010. Other neighborhoods undergoing significant racial changes include the East Martin Luther King Boulevard/UTC area, St. Elmo in South Chattanooga, Hill City and North Chattanooga (rechristened "the North Shore" by housing and economic development planners), and Highland Park in East Chattanooga.

The racial composition of neighborhoods across Chattanooga's urban core has not been the only demographic shift in the city. Although, for all races combined, average and median household income grew slightly, a disaggregated view allows for a more nuanced understanding: white-headed households saw their average incomes grow by 140 percent during this period, while the average household income among blacks increased by 81.5 percent (with several populations seeing little, if not negative, growth); between 2000 and 2014, median household income among whites grew by 41.8 percent but it only increased 7.1 percent among blacks. The American Community Survey's most recent five-year population estimates (2010–2014) suggest that income gaps among core-dwelling households in Chattanooga continue to widen. Almost 54 percent of households earn less than the median household income, yet the number of households earning more than $100,000 comprises nearly 6 percent of all households. The vast majority of these high-earning households reside within the three inner core census tracts. While some of the changes in income growth and distribution can be attributed to increased social mobility, assessing the figures in

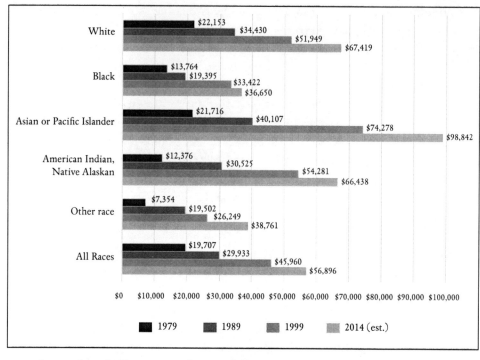

White — $22,153 / $34,430 / $51,949 / $67,419

Black — $13,764 / $19,395 / $33,422 / $36,650

Asian or Pacific Islander — $21,716 / $40,107 / $74,278 / $98,842

American Indian, Native Alaskan — $12,376 / $30,525 / $54,281 / $66,438

Other race — $7,354 / $19,502 / $26,249 / $38,761

All Races — $19,707 / $29,933 / $45,960 / $56,896

$0 $10,000 $20,000 $30,000 $40,000 $50,000 $60,000 $70,000 $80,000 $90,000 $100,000

■ 1979   ■ 1989   ■ 1999   ▨ 2014 (est.)

Average household income in the city of Chattanooga by race, 1979–2014.
Source: U.S. Census Bureau. *Median Household Income by Race, 1980–2014 (5 year estimates).* Accessed December 28, 2016. http://www.socialexplorer.com/6f4cdab7a0 /explore.

light of the changes in median household income by race suggests that most changes are the result of working-class households being priced out of the urban core while middle- and upper-income households migrate in.

Low-Income Asset Stripping in the Renaissance City

While market and luxury rate housing development and coordinated efforts to attract higher-income residents into the city exacerbate Chattanooga's growing housing affordability crisis, uneven geographic development is not fueled entirely by private and nonprofit developers. Chattanooga's housing crisis is also the result of public policies and plans that actively remove public and subsidized housing opportunities from across the urban core with virtually no means or mechanisms to replace them.

Six public housing sites have been demolished in Chattanooga over the past fifteen years. Prior to 2000, the Chattanooga Housing Authority (CHA) owned and managed 3,692 public housing units. As of October 2012, the CHA's public housing portfolio had decreased by 20 percent (N=-750 or -20.3 percent) to 2,942 units. Most recently (in 2012), CHA closed the Harriet Tubman public housing site in East Chattanooga (440 units) due to a lack of maintenance funds, removing approximately three hundred families from the site.[6]

The severe undersupply of public housing is reflected in the CHA's closed waiting list. In 2012, the agency reported that "the waiting list for public housing is equal to 81 percent of the current occupied number of units."[7] Furthermore, the local subsidized housing crisis is not limited to public housing owned and managed directly by the CHA. It also extends to the Section 8 voucher market. More than five thousand individuals sit on a waiting list for Section 8 vouchers. Wait times sometimes take years, and fewer landlords are willing to take vouchers.[8]

Considering the current trends in uneven geographic development, the forecast seems dim: downtown Chattanooga is rapidly transforming into a cosmopolitan playground for the economically privileged—and a place with virtually no safeguards to prevent the displacement of low-income residents from their homes and neighborhoods. Except in communities of color undergoing white-driven gentrification, most of the urban core and first ring suburban neighborhoods remain highly racially segregated; economic, social, and most cultural opportunities are not equally resourced, accessed, or distributed.

As a consequence, historically rooted communities of color are getting priced out of their historic neighborhoods. A city built on the backs of the economically and racially oppressed—and which openly acknowledges Cherokee removal and African American enslavement as parts of its complex, multicultural heritage and writes those stories into its tourism agenda—is completing the historic dispossession of working-class communities of color by inducing the city builders' descendants to peripheral, disinvested spaces, disconnected from families, jobs, urban services, public amenities, and historic connections to place. As unmitigated gentrification mounts around the urban core, then, the continued displacement of working-class people of color from their historic communities seems probable if not imminent.

Alternative World Building

Despite rising inequality across the city and region, there appears to be reason for hope. Several grassroots organizations work diligently to flip the script of urban revitalization in Chattanooga by illuminating the uneven terrain of reinvestment across the urban core while simultaneously demanding a more equitably developed city. Volunteer-based groups such as Chattanooga Organized for Action (COA), the Westside Community Association (WCA), Concerned Citizens for Justice (CCJ), Occupy Chattanooga, Wide Open Floor, Idle No More Chattanooga, Mercy Junction, and the Grove Street Settlement House are complicating Chattanooga's storybook tale of urban progress through a range of creative, place-based public activities and initiatives, including marches, history tours, protests, street theater, justice schools, skill sharing, storytelling workshops, spoken word, free stores, discussions with community elders, and solidarity fundraisers.

At the heart of their organizing strategies has been a push to forge deeper relationships and socioeconomic connections between various uprooted and marginalized residents. Fortunately, these actors have a long local history of solidarity and multiracial placemaking to point to as a foundation for their efforts. At its core, Chattanooga has always been a city comprised of multiple, overlapping diasporic communities. Native Americans, African Americans, whites, Eastern European Jews, Latinos, and other uprooted and migratory populations have labored—in some instances together and in many instances oppositionally—to create places of material security and cultural belonging from shared and often contested environments.

These complex histories of multidiasporic collaboration and conflict are the focus of this book. In it, I define *diasporic placemaking* as socio-spatial practices through which migratory and uprooted people plant new cultural and material roots, and argue that diasporic placemaking offers a practical, yet potentially transformative, conceptual framework to help urban planners and other spatial scientists and practitioners better understand how Chattanooga and cities like it have evolved and will continue to evolve in the future.

Significantly, Chattanooga's evolution has been deeply informed by *cosmopolitanism* narratives which at once obscure and provide inspiration for social and political progress. The *Oxford English Dictionary* defines *cosmopolitan* as "familiar with and at ease in many different countries and cultures; including people from many different countries; having an exciting and glamorous character associated with travel and a mixture of cultures" (Waite, *OED* 2013). This book traces the historical development of Chattanooga—both its physical development and popular identities as a cosmopolitan city in the South—to more deeply understand the politics of cultural recognition and racial reconciliation happening vis-à-vis the arts, cultural planning, and economic development in the city today. In doing so, I demonstrate how competing cosmopolitanism narratives and spatial structures have been central to both mainstream planning and development agendas *and* diasporic communities' efforts to demand a more just and equitable city.

Though local social justice activists frequently call attention to these contradictions, their critical narratives of development and change are overpowered by city boosters, who self-referentially point to the measures described above as evidence of the city's commitment to a cosmopolitan and liberal multicultural future. For this very reason, Chattanooga's history of race, planning, and popular protest can help us understand how diasporic placemaking interfaces with broader political and social movements to advance racial reconciliation and reparations agendas in twenty-first-century American cities. These stories suggest that racial reconciliation and reparations work in the United States is far from complete. On the contrary, in cities where local populations are comprised of multiple, overlapping diasporic communities, the work of social and spatial healing has just begun.

Deep Reckoning

In the spirit of critical and antiracist urban planning scholarship, this book argues that to better support and enable multidiasporic placemaking, we (specifically, urban planners—but also everyday citizens in an increasingly diverse and complex world) must be willing to confront and critically deconstruct the urban progress narratives that we tell ourselves about the communities we know, plan in, and inhabit. It assesses the limits of mainstream urban planning and place-making practice to understand how diverse places with multiple, overlapping diasporic communities work to create places that supported common understanding and mutuality across social difference. It suggests that reframing urban development and change as processes of diasporic placemaking can provide some wayfaring in this regard. Taken together, the histories of multiethnic placemaking in Chattanooga illuminate how collaborations and conflicts between historically uprooted populations can and do generate local social and spatial orders. Evaluating other cities through this analytical frame may help planners and other urban actors discover ways to integrate antiracism and equity agendas into their daily professional practices in more sensitive and transformative ways.

Overview of the Chapters

Chapter 1 charts the historical relationship between Native dispossession and early city planning and development in downtown Chattanooga as a way to understand more deeply the complex relationship that many contemporary Chattanoogans have to the legacies of Cherokee removal that took place within their hometown's borders. In particular, it pays attention to the construction of historical narratives of people and place during the pre-Removal and Removal periods and argues that a paternalistic, yet quasi-reverent and nostalgic popular framing of Native culture and removal has profoundly impacted how many people today relate to and represent Chattanooga's early history. By tracing the genealogy of race, property, and Native removal in the context of early city building, I prepare the ground for a discussion of contemporary Native American place-making activities along the Tennessee Riverfront in later chapters.

Chapter 2 explores the rooting of Chattanooga's black communities through the late nineteenth century. Chapter 3 continues this discussion through the Jim Crow and civil rights eras. African American labor and creative placemaking have been central to urbanization and economic expansion in Chattanooga since before the modern arrival of white settlers. Despite their substantial contributions, African Americans' city building has never been treated with the same level of admiration as exhibited toward the Cherokee. Nor have the centuries-long legacies of exploitation and cultural marginalization been treated with the same levels of remorse or repentance. By showing how mainstream discourses of urban progress have been racially coded and organized such that black urban placemaking and community development have been cast as antithetical to progressive urban cosmopolitanism, chapter 3 also reveals a critical double standard at play in city planning and cultural development. I contend that the antithetical conceptualization of black culture and community development was reinforced so that whites might continue to justify the subjugation and exploitation of African American labor across all areas of the Dynamo of Dixie's rapidly expanding local economy.

Chapter 4 takes a narrower view, examining the stereotype-defying histories of multiethnic placemaking along East Ninth/Martin Luther King Boulevard (the "Big Nine")—a corridor which for more than a century served as a premier destination for African American commerce, social life, and artistic/creative production. Taken together, these four chapters suggest that we—urban planners, geographers, and community activists—take a longer, more critical view of urban planning and development in communities: one that locates the roots of the modern profession not in the urban advocacy movements of the late nineteenth century, but much earlier, in the ongoing interplays between exploitative projects of city, state, and nation building and antiracist community building.

Chapters 5–7 focus on interplays between formal, institution-backed, and grassroots place-making initiatives, demonstrating how creative and cultural development have been central to both Chattanooga's mainstream revitalization agenda and grassroots communities' efforts to demand a more just and equitable city. Chapter 5 assesses the historic rise, so-called decline, and ongoing revival of the East Ninth Street/MLK Boulevard corridor and neighborhood, arguing that public and institutional actors involved with the ongoing revitalization of the MLK Boulevard area stand to miss crucial opportunities for realizing the equitable redevelopment of the district. This loss is particularly acute given the neighborhood's long history of creative, cooperative African American (and, as this chapter will demonstrate, multiracial) placemaking. Chapter 6 explores the politics of public participation in the context of Chattanooga's citizen-driven return to the Tennessee Riverfront.

Chapter 7 extends this conversation by examining the politics of racial recognition and reconciliation happening vis-à-vis public space, art, and cultural tourism planning within the revitalized urban core today. It explores planning and place-making elements of the Tennessee Riverfront's revival to show how public and civic leaders have used urban planning and placemaking to acknowledge and, arguably, reconcile, the city's exploitative colonial past. Focusing on the Riverfront makes sense given its history and current importance to the city's revitalization agenda. The Tennessee Riverfront and areas immediately surrounding Ross's Landing are historical sites of multiracial diasporic placemaking—spaces where overlapping cultural groups have worked with and against one another to carve out communities of material security and cultural belonging. While these diasporic placemaking efforts have occasionally produced new collaborations and deeper affinities, oftentimes they have also resulted in conflict and contestation over physical space and cultural place in the city. Ross's Landing and the Tennessee Riverfront more generally are compelling examples of the complex, oftentimes contradictory, nature of socio-spatial production, having been both crucial ports of entry and critical sites of deportation/removal over the past two centuries.

Chapters 8 and 9 discuss the action research component of this research project to illustrate how an experimental collaboration between urban planners, grassroots organizers, social workers, and public librarians helped enable and expand the politics of multiethnic diasporic placemaking in Chattanooga. Chapter 8 describes the evolution of Chattanooga Organized for Action, the social justice community organizing nonprofit that I partnered with on this project, as they transitioned from a popular protest group into a 501(c)(3) nonprofit that "initiates, supports, and connects" place-based social justice movements across downtown Chattanooga. This chapter also discusses two components of a participatory action research initiative: the Sustaining People and Reclaiming Communities (SPARC) Initiative, an effort that combined urban planning, community organizing, and social work to help residents in historically marginalized neighborhoods to exercise community self-determination and interdependence; and the Planning Free School of Chattanooga, an experimental alternative to mainstream citizen engagement and capacity building in the city. Chapter 9 discusses the politics of public space and neighborhood planning in the historically black, working-class neighborhood of Lincoln Park. Lincoln Park is a demonstrative case for thinking through contemporary struggles over space and place because it is one of the oldest and most historically significant black neighborhoods in Chattanooga (described as the black community's "backyard"). Although the park planning and decision making was controlled by the city and county, the neighborhood that surrounds it is an evolving product of more than a century of cooperative African American placemaking and community building in the city.

To conclude, I synthesize the major lessons learned through my participation in this multifaceted project into three broad areas as diasporic placemaking teaches us about: (1) how cities and regions evolve socio-spatially; (2) how urban planners, planning educators, and others interested in these issues can advance or inhibit diasporic placemaking in complex urban environments; and (3) what we might learn about participatory action research as a set of dynamic methods with the potential for catalyzing social change. And for readers who may be interested in learning more about the unique action research-based methodology or conceptual framework guiding this book, short summaries of both are offered as appendices.

CHAPTER ONE

Settling Chattanooga

Race, Property, and Cherokee Dispossession

For several thousand years, the banks of the Tennessee River where Lookout Mountain faces Stringer's Ridge has been a cradle for human civilization. Its unique geography and rich natural resources have made it highly desirable for settlement: Native artifacts discovered in sites across present-day downtown Chattanooga date back to at least 0–499 ACE,[1] though archaeologists estimate that the downtown Chattanooga area has been continually inhabited since approximately 3500 BCE, first by people categorized in Archaic and Woodland Eras, and later by a series of Mississippian, Muskogee, and Yuchi settlements (900–1714 ACE).

A *Chattanooga City Guide* published by the Tennessee chapter of the Tennessee Writers' Project described artifacts discovered at several local sites to paint a picture of pre-Cherokee social life in the Lookout Mountain/ Tennessee River valley region:

> Long before the white pioneers planted corn in the Tennessee Valley, long before the hostile Cherokee built their stockade village along the Chickamauga Creek, prehistoric Indians were planting corn and building towns in the vicinity of present-day Chattanooga. Their village sites, featured by earthen mounds, by heaps of decaying mussel shells, by ashes and hidden pits, by pottery fragments and by implements of stone and bone, were located all along the winding Tennessee. Moccasin Bend was the site of teeming villages, surrounded by extensive maize fields, "Ball Play" grounds and "Chunky" yards, where the game of Chunky was played with stone disks. Williams Island was well populated in prehistoric times. The great Citico Mound . . . supported a huge ceremonial or town house, large enough to hold several hundred people. In this huge clay-wattled structure the chiefs held councils, the priests performed religious ceremonies, and the warriors and the women danced on the hard-packed earthen floor to the music of drums and rattles.[2]

Though clearly editorialized, this description sheds some light on the socio-spatial structure of the Mississippian-era inhabitants of Chattanooga and its environs. Notably, it also reveals some of the moral and cultural values of civic boosters during the height of the city's economic and physical ascension to "Dynamo of Dixie" status. In contrast to the "hostile Cherokee" who fortified the region during the eighteenth and nineteenth centuries, Chattanooga's pre-modern riverfront was typically described in early promotional materials for the city as a peaceful and thriving seat of prehistoric culture and social life.

Cherokee Arrival and Early Resistance

The modern settlement of the Tennessee River valley is attributed to the Cherokee (GWY/*Tsalagi* or DhB℗ↃT/*Aniyunwiya*/"Principal People"), who established permanent settlements and towns along the Tennessee River in the Chattanooga vicinity as early as the thirteenth century ACE.[3] Traditionally, Cherokee society was matrilineal, and organized into a set of seven clans that were more or less geographically determined. Cherokee towns were managed by a system of decentralized chiefs and community elders; Cherokee men typically migrated as they hunted, while Cherokee women, who were often skilled farmers, planted permanent agricultural settlements throughout the Ohio, Tennessee, and Chattahoochee River valleys. A firmly settled Cherokee presence was recorded in the sixteenth-century travel logs of Spanish conquistador Hernando de Soto who, in 1540, discussed encountering "*Guasili*" people while traversing the southeastern interior along the Tennessee River in search of gold.[4] By the dawn of the American Revolution, white colonial settlers had been encroaching on Cherokee hunting and farming territories on an ad hoc basis for over a century.

Half a century earlier, Cherokee leaders had formally aligned themselves with the British Crown, whose Royal Army swore to respect Native sovereignty and land claims in exchange for political and military solidarity. Although their alignment dissolved in battle during the French and Indian War (1754–63) precisely because British settlers had ignored the moratorium on encroachment,[5] their historic and perceived alliance created a deep distrust between the Cherokee and colonial powers.

Some Native American leaders encouraged white settlement in the region, while others resigned themselves to its inevitability. Still others chose to resist and fight back. Tsiyu Gansini (ᏥᏳ ᎦᏅᏏᏂ or "Dragging Canoe") (1738–92) was an Overhill Cherokee warrior and outspoken critic of white encroachment during the early period of southeastern frontier expansion.[6]

The son of Great Island Town Chief Attakullakulla ("Little Carpenter"), Dragging Canoe rose to prominence as an anti-encroachment activist during the Anglo-Cherokee War (1758–61). During a skirmish between British and colonial soldiers, Dragging Canoe had led assaults against the colonists—an action that resulted in militia troops retaliating through the systematic destruction of several Cherokee Middle (Hill), Valley, and Lower Towns, including the Cherokee capital of Chota.

Although his father Attakullakulla and fellow Overhill Chief Oconostota wanted to sue the revolutionary government for peace, Dragging Canoe rejected the assimilationist stances of his elders. He justified his skepticism and resistance in a now-famous public speech to his father and other regional chiefs: "The white man makes treaties only to break them. He is not satisfied with the land beyond the mountains, or the land beside the Watauga, or the land along the Nolichucky. Now he wants still more. And what we do not give him, he will take anyway until our whole Nation is gone from this earth. Old men make paper talks; young men fight for what is theirs. I will not lose these lands without a fight."[7]

Despite his son's plea, Attakullakulla, along with most Cherokee chiefs, signed the Treaty of De Witt's Corner (1776) with the revolutionary government. In protest, Dragging Canoe broke from his father's Overhill community, and in 1777 led a group of separatist allies south to establish a set of eleven new towns ("Lower Cherokee Towns") along the Chickamauga Creek in the vicinity of present-day Chattanooga. Over the next fifteen years, Dragging Canoe led a series of armed struggles against white encroachers. In 1782, revolutionary soldiers pillaged and burned the Lower Cherokee Towns, including Dragging Canoe's military headquarters at Old Chickamauga Town. Dragging Canoe and his allies moved farther away, establishing five towns several miles further south on the Tennessee River, in the shadow of Lookout Mountain.[8]

Racialized Paternalism in Urban Policy and Planning: A Longer View

The earliest effort to develop modern urban infrastructure in present-day downtown Chattanooga is attributed to Cherokee-Scottish brothers John and Lewis Ross. Fifteen years before he was elected as Principal Chief of the Cherokee Nation (1828–66), John Ross and his brother established a boat landing and ferry crossing on the south bank of the Tennessee River at the foot of what is today Broad Street. His brother Lewis also constructed a commercial warehouse at the site. Known first colloquially and later officially as Ross's Landing, the brothers strategically located their facilities at the administrative border between Hamilton County, Tennessee, located on the north side of the river, and the last remaining portion of sovereign Cherokee territory to its south.

By this time, white settlers had been defying Cherokee sovereignty claims and settling in Cherokee areas for more than two centuries. Their efforts had been largely uncoordinated, individual pursuits, with many white frontiersmen marrying Cherokee women and assuming typical Cherokee lifestyles and cultural mores. The dominant trend of white assimilation into Native American society began to change dramatically after 1810, when the American Board of Commissioners for Foreign Missions (ABCFM) was established by a group of Williams College graduates in western Massachusetts with the goal of spreading Christianity around the "uncivilized" world.

Incorporated by an act of the Commonwealth of Massachusetts in 1812 and charged with "propagating the Gospel in heathen lands" (Commonwealth of Massachusetts 1812), the ABCFM immediately set about assigning missionaries to foreign territories, including sovereign tribal territories within the southeastern United States.[9]

In 1816, a group of ABCFM missionaries identified a site on the south side of Chickamauga Creek as a potential center for social and cultural transformation. The site included a sizable farm and proximity to a gristmill and was located across the creek from Dragging Canoe's Old Chickamauga Town, which had been rebuilt and grown into a small village. A letter written by Reverend Cyrus Kingsbury, a southeastern tribal missionary scout, is instructive. Dated November 25, 1816, Kingsbury addressed Dr. Samuel Worcester, secretary of the American Board of Commissioners for Foreign Missions.

> With reference to such a plan, I sought a place. In doing which, I found a plantation which had been occupied several years by an old Scotch gentleman, who had married into the Nation. As he wishes to remove to another place, he offered me his buildings and improvements, which included about twenty-five acres of cleared land, for five hundred dollars. There are all the necessary buildings to commence, except a school house, and perhaps a dwelling house. I did not hesitate to bargain for the place, as it is situated in a neighborhood where I can immediately commence preaching to a small congregation; convenient to a mill and water course, for obtaining supplies from the settlements. If the Society will furnish the means,

I hope with the leave of Providence to begin the school in February. If the plan should not meet the approbation of the Society, it will be occasion for great regret.[10]

Over the next several months, a small group of missionaries relocated to the old McDonald farm and established a school and mission house on the site. With its strategic location and desirable educational facilities, the Brainerd Mission almost immediately lived up to Kingsbury's promise to Worcester. A daily journal recorded by ABCFM missionaries residing at Brainerd reveals that religious services and literacy training began almost immediately.[11]

In an entry dated March 9, 1817, just one month after arriving by boat to the property, a mission worker recorded that Brother Kingsbury had preached to a congregation of more than forty Cherokee and black disciples.[12] Notably, the missionaries focused on educating and Christianizing Cherokee youth alongside their adult family members and African American (mostly enslaved) neighbors. A Sabbath entry dated April 20 confirmed this imperative, stating "about sixty persons attended Brother K's preaching. Nine blacks and three others attended our Sunday school. We hope these poor ignorant souls may be benefitted by our instruction."[13]

Unlike many at late nineteenth- and early twentieth-century mission schools who used religious education and acculturation as strategies for robbing Native Americans of their land and political sovereignty, the Brainerd missionaries believed that training "poor ignorant souls" to establish Western political and cultural institutions would help them secure and maintain territorial sovereignty and political self-determination in the face of expanding white encroachment. This sentiment is evident from the earliest *Brainerd Journal* entries, and became loudly vocalized following the Treaties of 1817 and 1819. Ross's Landing had become a political and economic focal point for the United States following the Treaty of 1817, which ceded most of the remaining Cherokee landholdings located to the north of the Tennessee River to the United States in exchange for territory to the west of the Mississippi River.

After only three years of instruction and indoctrination at Brainerd, the Cherokee seemed to the missionaries to be making great strides in their progress. The Brainerd missionaries considered their work to be not only in the service of God, but also in the service of an increasingly threatened and marginalized people. "It has been said and thought by many that it is not in our power to instruct them," proclaimed one entry penned on January 25, 1820. "This is now demonstrated to be incorrect. They are willing to be taught—they ask for instruction—and if we do not teach them, their blood may justly be required at our hands."[14]

Another entry proudly discussed the Cherokees' adoption of Western political and legal institutions, which the missionaries considered essential to their sovereignty claims: "They have . . . divided their country into eight districts or counties, laid a tax on the people to build a courthouse in each of the counties and appointed four circuit judges. The Cherokees are rapidly adopting the laws and manners of whites. They appear to advance in civilization just in proportion to their knowledge of the gospel. It therefore becomes all who desire the civilization of the Indians to do what they can to send the gospel among them."[15]

Despite the liberal and altruistic rhetoric of the Brainerd missionaries, the means by which these educators achieved their ends reveal less tolerant projects of acculturation. Kingsbury advocated for a "great missionary family" that would supplant the traditional, matrilineal Cherokee social structure and transform younger generations of Native Americans into planters, industrialists, and political diplomats. The ABCFM administrators insisted that for the Cherokee to become "useful citizens and pious Christians," the missionaries must build a residential school facility in order for "the children . . . [to] be removed as much as possible from the society of the natives, and placed where they would have the influence of example, as well as precept."[16]

While the Brainerd missionaries saw their work as critical to the self-determination of the Cherokee during the period of southeastern frontier expansion, these sentiments were undergirded by a racialized and deeply paternalistic view of Native and African American cultural production. Native and African Americans were not understood to be people possessing a priori humanity. Rather, they were malleable objects; social experiments with the potential to develop humanity—assuming proper indoctrination and religious conversion took place. "These dear Cherokee and African converts, you will not, you cannot forget," professed one missionary writing during the winter of 1821. "They are your treasure. They will be your crown of rejoicing in the day of the Lord Jesus."[17]

Contesting the Means and Ends of Cherokee Sovereignty

Having battled against and lost thousands of people and millions of acres of land to colonial powers between the late seventeenth and early nineteenth centuries, many Cherokee leaders, especially the wealthier, Western-educated ones, agreed that Christian education and the adoption of formal political institutions would be key to Native resistance against white encroachment. On the one hand, the Brainerd missionaries viewed themselves as helping to enable Cherokee self-determination. After the silversmith Sequoyah (ᏍᏏᏉᏯ *Ssiquoya*) developed the Cherokee alphabet and syllabary in 1821, for example, Brainerd Mission leader Reverend Samuel Worcester had the alphabet typecast to facilitate the printing of Cherokee language documents.

But the frameworks for autonomy and self-determination promulgated by the missionaries and their converts were steeped with a deeply racialized and paternalistic view of Cherokee culture. The realization of an autonomous, modern Cherokee state required the forfeiture of traditional Cherokee social, political, and economic arrangements in exchange for westernized ones. Among the hundreds of Cherokee graduates of the school were included Elias Boudinot, who went on to found the first Native American, bilingual newspaper *The Cherokee Phoenix* (ᏣᎳᎩ ᏧᎴᎯᏌᏅᎯ, *Tsalagi Tsulehisanvhi*, 1828–1834), and John Ridge, the son of a wealthy Cherokee plantation and slave owner.[18] These men and their colleagues were formative in transforming the Cherokee socio-spatial structure from a traditional matrilineal, collectivist order into one managed and led by men, and based on the principles of republicanism and individual property rights.[19]

As more youth graduated from the Brainerd Mission School and assumed leadership ranks within the rapidly transforming Cherokee society, their sentiments became louder. This elite group of Brainerd alumni eagerly negotiated with white leaders on behalf of the Cherokee people despite being self-appointed in their authority and lacking the support of the Cherokee people at large. In contrast to this outspoken minority, the vast majority of Cherokee continued to practice traditional lifestyles and were vehemently opposed to land secession and the adoption of white political and economic institutions.[20]

By 1819, the Cherokee had begun holding national council meetings at New Town, near present-day Calhoun, Georgia. Despite their best efforts to exercise national self-determination by adopting "civilized" Western institutions, white frontiersmen and public policy makers persistently ignored and delegitimized Cherokee sovereignty claims. These trends prompted the National Committee and Council of the Cherokee Nation to pass a series of laws meant to seriously limit whites' access to and settlement on lands located within the rapidly diminishing sovereign territory. On October 25, 1820, the National Council adopted a law requiring permits for "single white men" who wished to work as clerks in Native-owned stores and businesses. The law outlined severe financial and physical penalties for Cherokee citizens who ignored the regulation. The law stated that "it is also resolved, that any person or persons, whatsoever, who shall bring into the Cherokee Nation, without permission from the National Committee and Council, a white family, and rent lands to the same, and proofs being authenticated before any of the judges in the district Councils, for such offences they shall forfeit and pay the sum of five hundred dollars, and one hundred stripes on the bare back."[21]

One year later, the National Committee and Council passed even stricter legislation, prohibiting Cherokee citizens from allowing white ferrymen to occupy or lease land within the Cherokee national boundaries.

By 1825, New Town had been renamed New Echota and was established as the political and administrative capital of the Cherokee Nation. Two years later, the Council adopted a national constitution that laid out executive, legislative, and judicial branches modeled on its American neighbor's. The constitution profoundly and permanently altered the traditional social structure of Cherokee society. Historically, family lineages had been matrilineal, with women holding leadership positions and inheriting property. Traditionally, black slaves owned by Cherokee farmers could also own and inherit land and property. After the adoption of the constitution, Cherokee men became the exclusive political leaders and holders of Cherokee assets.[22]

The Georgia Gold Rush (1828–1829) and Gold Lottery of 1832

While the presence of gold within interior Cherokee lands had been rumored among colonial explorers since the sixteenth century, the discovery of two large gold deposits in 1828—in the foothills of what is today northern Georgia near the Tennessee border—accelerated the rate at which white settlers entered Cherokee territory and willfully violated the laws established by the National Committee and Council intended to preserve autonomy and political sovereignty.

Though the Cherokee population had adopted many Western cultural values and practices, their unwillingness to cede additional land frustrated settlers, speculators, and government officials who desired access to the Nation's fertile farmland and newly discovered gold deposits. The Treaty of 1817 had delineated the Tennessee River as the formal boundary between Cherokee landholdings and the state of Tennessee. With the discovery of gold in the northern Georgia hills, white land grabbers lined up eagerly at Ross's Landing, waiting for their opportunity to seize Cherokee homesteads and plantations. These speculators began to lobby the state of Georgia and the federal Congress vigorously, demanding that policy makers devise a permanent solution to the problem of Cherokee sovereignty, which was limiting their access to gold and fertile farmland in this region.

A popular folk song from the time captures the significance of the Chattanooga region to the settlers' socio-spatial imagination:

All I want in this creation
Is a pretty little girl
And a big plantation
'Way up yonder in the Cherokee nation.[23]

While the lyrics describe settlers' longing for the productive, resource-rich lands held by the Cherokee during this period of early frontier expansion, they also speak to the specific processes of physical uprooting and dispossession underway. Contrary to the stereotype of Natives as wandering, nomadic people prone to wasting otherwise productive land, the song describes a modernized, permanent agricultural economy and political structure.

Eager to expand their landholdings and economic assets, frontier speculators found a willing ally in newly elected president Andrew Jackson, a former army general and Tennessee frontiersman who had led American troops to victory against the Creek Indians and British during the Battle of Horseshoe Bend (1814) and Battle of New Orleans (1815).

Pro-squatter advocacy culminated in President Jackson's authorization of the Indian Removal Act on May 28, 1830. The act "extinguished Indian claims" to the lands held by the Five Civilized Tribes (Cherokee, Chickasaw, Creek, Choctaw, and Seminole) to the east of the Mississippi River, and gave the president of the United States power to parcel out unincorporated lands located to the west of the Mississippi River while demanding that members of the relocated tribes accept these allotments as just compensation for their ancestral territories across the Southeast. The act also proclaimed that the president would assume "superintendence" over the tribes following their relocation, granting the federal government the power to assume legal control over any western Indian territories in the case of Native "abandonment" or "extinction."

President Jackson emphasized the Louisiana Purchase (1803) as his rationale for relocating tribal communities west of the Mississippi River. The Louisiana Purchase Treaty had established that legal property titles could be conferred through the physical improvement of wasted (i.e., undeveloped and/or underutilized) land. To this end, supporters of Native American relocation argued that removal would benefit the United States in two ways. First, it would open up previously inaccessible natural resources in the Southeast. It would also facilitate economic development in the vast western territories secured through the Louisiana Purchase.

These paternalistic sentiments were clearly expressed by Jackson during his Second Annual Message to Congress on December 6, 1830. During his speech, the president insisted that the removal of the southeastern tribes was in the best interests of both white and Native communities. To quote his speech at length:

> What good man would prefer a country covered with forests, and ranged by a few thousand savages, to our extensive republic, studded with cities, towns, and prosperous farms, embellished with all the improvements which art can devise, or industry execute; occupied by more than twelve millions of happy people, and filled with all the blessings of liberty, civilization, and religion!
>
> The present policy of the Government is but a continuation of the same progressive change, by a milder process. The tribes which occupied the countries now constituting the Eastern States were annihilated, or have melted away, to make room for the whites. The waves of population and civilization are rolling to the Westward; and we now propose to acquire the countries occupied by the red men of the South and West, by a fair exchange, and, at the expense of the United States, to send them to a land where their existence may be prolonged, and perhaps be made perpetual . . .
>
> And is it supposed that the wandering savage has a stronger attachment to his home than the settled, civilized Christian? Is it more afflicting to him to leave the graves of his fathers than it is to our brothers and children? Rightly considered, the policy of the General Government toward the red man is not only liberal, but generous. He is unwilling to submit to the laws of the States and mingle with their population. To save him from this alternative, or perhaps utter annihilation, the General Government kindly offers him a new home, and proposes to pay the whole expense of his removal and settlement.[24]

Cloaked in the language of mutual respect and the common good, Jackson's remarks reflected his unwillingness to acknowledge or accept as legitimate any alternative to a worldview based on private property and speculative economic development. He positioned this epistemological frame as morally and politically superior to the Cherokees' unenlightened practices of collective, subsistence-based living.

The Cherokee national constitution had clearly defined private property laws; hence, the Cherokee became the first Native nation to test their legal sovereignty in the modern U.S. judicial system. Invoking the Supremacy Clause (Article VI), tribal representatives filed suit against the State of Georgia as representatives from a foreign nation.

The case made it to the U.S. Supreme Court, at which time Chief Justice John Marshall set a paradoxical precedent for determining Native sovereignty. On the one hand, Chief Justice Marshall granted the Cherokee Nation effective autonomy, declaring that the federation was capable to "manage its own affairs and govern itself" (30 U.S. [5 Pet.] 1 [1831]). On the other, he concluded that the nation related to the United States as "domestic dependent nations" do, existing "in a state of pupilage. Their relation to the United States resembles that of a ward to his guardian."

The ruling mandated that Native communities defer to the United States in legal and economic decision-making matters, and negated the Cherokee's power to assert land claims against federal and state governments. Chief Justice Marshall drew a clear distinction between occupancy rights and fee simple, absolute rights to land, declaring that Native Americans' land claims "occupy a territory to which we assert a title independence of their will." With his ruling, the Cherokee people were rendered squatters not only in their ancestral homelands, but also in the new territories reserved for them to the west of the Mississippi River.

Notably, the precedent established by this ruling was complicated a year later by *Worcester v. Georgia* (1832), where Chief Justice Marshall also ruled that the State of Georgia could not impose laws in Cherokee territory, since only the federal government had authority in Indian affairs. In his majority opinion, Chief Justice Marshall declared that the Indian nations were "distinct, independent political communities retaining their original natural rights" (31 U.S. [6 Pet.] 515 [1832]).

Ultimately, Judge Marshall's contradictory rulings reflect the complex paternalistic affect that many white Americans felt toward Native Americans during the first century of U.S. independence from Britain.[25] On the one hand, the Cherokee were considered powerful, independent, and civilized; on the other, their autonomy and capacity for enlightened self-rule was understood as dependent on white Christian sacrifice and intervention—sentiments that arguably carry forward into the present day.

Native Dispossession and *Nunna daul Isunyi* (The Trail Where They Cried)

By 1830, Ross's Landing had become the epicenter of a small but bustling commercial center oriented around the banks of the Tennessee River. John Ross had been elected as Principal Chief of the Cherokee Nation in 1828 (a position he retained until his death in 1866). Ross's anti-removal stance had made him popular among the Cherokee people, who viewed the small faction of pro-removal Cherokees as traitors to the "principal people" and their ancestral homeland. Although he was only one-eighth Cherokee, John Ross became a tireless advocate against removal in the years leading up to the Indian Removal Act, as well as the several years between its passage and the military roundup of his people in 1838.

For the first few years following the passage of the Indian Removal Act, removal was slow moving, partially because the Cherokee were contesting the law in the courts, but largely because there was a strong will among traditionalists to remain in their ancestral homeland despite having had their rights to the land "extinguished" by the American government. During this time, the U.S. government focused on the removal of the four other "Civilized Tribes," including the Choctaw (1831), Seminole (1832), and Creek (1834).[26]

This changed on December 29, 1835, when five self-appointed pro-removal delegates negotiated a treaty with the State of Georgia to concede the complete relocation of the Cherokee Nation to the newly opened western frontier. Dubbed the Treaty of New Echota, the agreement was perceived as illegitimate by the majority of Cherokee citizens and leaders. Nevertheless, despite protests from the Cherokee National Council and the fact that the treaty lacked the signature of Principal Chief Ross, the United States Senate adopted and ratified the contract in March 1836.

In protest against the Treaty of New Echota, Chief Ross wrote a letter to the U.S. Congress. He used his statement as the basis for a citizen's petition that was endorsed by more than fifteen thousand Cherokee citizens. Ross laid out the legal, political, and moral arguments against the Treaty of New Echota, arguing that it had been illegitimately conceived and authorized and was enforceable only through military coercion. Ross claimed that the treaty stripped the Cherokee of their property, livelihoods, and very humanity:

By the stipulations of this instrument, we are despoiled of our private possessions, the indefeasible property of individuals. We are stripped of every attribute of freedom and eligibility for legal self-defense. Our property may be plundered before our eyes; violence may be committed on our persons; even our lives may be taken away, and there is none to regard our complaints. We are denationalized; we are disfranchised. We are deprived of membership in the human family! We have neither land nor home, nor resting place that can be called our own. . . . We are overwhelmed! Our hearts are sickened, our utterance paralyzed, when we reflect on the condition in which we are placed, by the audacious practices of unprincipled men . . . in the face of our earnest, solemn, and reiterated protestations.[27]

With letter and signatures in hand, Ross traveled to Washington, D.C. to personally deliver his petition to the U.S. Congress. Despite his campaign, Ross's plea was rejected and the federal government responded by ramping up its efforts to forcibly remove the Cherokee from their territorial stronghold in the northern Georgia hills.

Just as the geography of Ross's Landing had been significant to the Gold Rush, it was similarly of import once removal organizers began to seriously plan for the roundup and deportation of the Cherokee people. Ross's Landing was a centrally located port town and had both water and land access routes to the western frontier. In 1835, the landing was chosen by the United States Army as one of four locations across the region where internment camps would be constructed. Over the next two years (1836–38), the army fortified the town in anticipation of removal.

Chattanooga native Henry Wiltse's unpublished manuscript, *History of Chattanooga*, has one of the only sets of first hand descriptions of removal planning and implementation at Ross's Landing, as told to Wiltse by retired soldiers who had participated in the military exercise. Several veterans recalled that the soldiers' camp had been constructed on farm property owned by the affluent, slaveholding Gardenhire family, whose homestead was located approximately two miles further up the river from the landing: "There, after clearing the land they built a fort made of split trees, sharpened and set into the ground, picket fashion," recalled army veteran William Jones. "At about the space of every third picket was a porthole, from which a gun could be projected and given wide sweep."[28]

The troops remained in this camp through the winter of 1836–37, during which time they responded to reports of Native disturbances and constructed the crude stockades described above that would be used to warehouse Cherokees prior to their deportation. After fortifying the town, troops began their campaign to uproot the Cherokee from their homesteads and farms across southeast Tennessee and northern Georgia. These efforts were preceded by a public address to the Cherokee Nation by commanding General Winfield Scott, who, on May 10, 1838, recommended that the Cherokee people avoid military imprisonment by voluntarily assembling at Ross's Landing or one of the other three deportation sites constructed by the army.

Promising fair treatment, General Scott declared: "Do not, I invite you, even wait for the close approach of the troops; but make such preparations for emigration as you can and hasten to this place, to Ross's Landing or to Gunter's Landing, where you all will be received in kindness by officers selected for the purpose. You will find food for all and clothing for the destitute at either of those places, and thence at your ease and in comfort be transported to your new homes, according to the terms of the treaty. This is the address of a warrior to warriors. May his entreaties be kindly received and may the God of both prosper the Americans and Cherokees and preserve them long in peace and friendship with each other!"[29]

Despite his promises of fair treatment, virtually no Cherokee citizens willingly abandoned their homes to assemble at the landing. In response, troops were ordered to root them out, capture them, and march them to the holding pen located just north of Ross's Landing. Recalling his own participation in the efforts, removal veteran Moses Wells told Wiltse: "[We] found Indians hidden in treetops, in bushes, in hollow logs and all sorts of places."[30] In sum, approximately 2,200 federal troops and 740 militiamen from Georgia, Tennessee, North Carolina, and Alabama were involved in the Cherokee roundup at Ross's Landing. In total, 3,636 prisoners from the middle military district were transported to the landing between May 30 and June 9, 1838; more than one thousand (N=1,079) arrived on June 6 alone.

Three detachments were deployed from the landing by flatboat between June 6 and 16, 1838. A witness to these events described the violent scene to a journalist with the *Niles Register*, who published the anecdote on August 18: "Then came the whipping off to the west. The agent endeavored to induce them to go into the boats voluntarily; but none would agree to go. The agent then struck a line through the camp; the soldiers rushed in and drove the devoted victims into the boats, regardless of the cries and agonies of the poor helpless sufferers. In this cruel work, the most painful separation of families occurred—children were sent off and parents left, and so of other relations."[31]

The June 6 detachment successfully navigated a water route and arrived in Oklahoma after two weeks with no reported deaths. The detachments deployed on June 12 and 16, however, were both forced to abandon their boats due to low water levels, and complete their journeys by foot. These two groups took significantly longer to arrive and suffered more than two hundred combined casualties. Though the Indian Removal Act had designated funds to assist with relocation, it did not explicitly state how those monies should be distributed or managed, which resulted in widespread corruption and fraud from army subcontractors. Among those who survived roundup and internment, more than sixteen thousand Native and black Cherokees, along with a handful of white missionary allies, were forced to march from southeastern Tennessee to "Indian Territory" in what is today northeastern Oklahoma. In addition to the hundreds who died from illness and malnutrition while held in the stockades, more than four thousand individuals, approximately one-quarter of the Cherokee population at that time, perished over the course of their arduous march west. The nearly 700-mile journey came to be known in the Cherokee language as "*nu na da ul tsun yi*" or The Trail Where They Cried.

Ross's Landing: From Crossing to Crossroads

At the time of removal, Ross's Landing had been transformed into a military camp, with hungry land grabbers moving in to claim property in the wake of Cherokee dispossession.

George W. Fetherstonaugh, an English traveler and geographer, recounted his initial impression of the ramshackle community at Ross's Landing during a visit to the town in 1837.

Fetherstonaugh came ashore at a "beach where there was no appearance of a settlement," and quickly discovered "a small village hastily built, without regard to order or streets, everyone selecting his own site and relying upon the legislature of Tennessee to pass a law for the permanent arrangement of their occupations."[32]

Immediately following the forced removal of the Cherokee during the summer of 1838, Ross's Landing was incorporated into the state of Tennessee. After a lengthy debate between the town's founding fathers, the name "Chattanooga" was chosen because of its linguistic uniqueness and cultural connection to Native American history. In the context of early arts and cultural development in the city, the ironic naming of Chattanooga matters for two reasons.

First, despite not actually knowing what the word meant, the settlers' focus on the distinctiveness of the term signaled perhaps the first coordinated attempt among local leaders to brand Chattanooga as an exceptional and cosmopolitan place. Furthermore, choosing a Native American term for the town's name illustrated a quasi-nostalgia for the unspoiled, natural world and a quasi-reverence for the plight of the dispossessed Natives—two themes that arguably persist to this day.

A famous quote from one of the town's early boosters further illustrates the construction of these exceptionalist narratives in the months following Cherokee removal. Noted for boasting about the city, Benjamin "Rush" Montgomery allegedly made the following claim about the importance of pre–Civil War Chattanooga: "The buffalo worked out the line; the Indian followed it; the white man followed the Indian; the wagon road and railroad take up the same route; the mountains shut in here; the valleys stop here; Tennessee River must pass through here; fact is, don't you see, this is the funnel of the world."[33]

Montgomery's words foretold the city's continued geographic significance in the decades leading up to and during the Civil War. Known as the local market where "cotton meets corn," the opening of the Western and Atlantic Railroad during the spring of 1850 catalyzed a major population boom. Between 1840 and 1860, white settlers, enslaved blacks, and, to a much lesser extent, free blacks, migrated to the town and surrounding county en masse. One year after the forced deportation of the Cherokee, Hamilton County had a total population of 8,175, including 7,498 whites, 93 free blacks, and 584 slaves. Twenty years later, just before the dawn of the American Civil War, the total population had increased to 13,252 (11,641 whites, 192 free blacks, and 1,419 enslaved people).[34]

Louis Parham was an entrepreneur whose family owned the local slave market near the intersection of Market and Ninth Streets.[35] In his 1876 historical survey of Chattanooga and Hamilton County, Parham described the town's rapid settlement during the months following removal. With a tone reminiscent of the racist paternalism that had driven Native encroachment and dispossession over the past century, Parham recalled how white families arrived at Ross's Landing on wooden flatboats, which they disassembled and used as lumber to construct homes once arriving at the landing. Within weeks of removal,

The town was laid off into lots [and sold off] . . . About 250 acres constituted the limits of the new town, which was built near the river, owing to the trade there. In 1841, the name "Chattanooga" was given to the place. . . . The whites began coming in quite freely this year, and the red man was induced to move on toward the setting of the sun.

Now, were it possible for those who in the earlier days of Chattanooga left, ne'er to return, unless in the spirit, to stand upon some eminence and look down upon the scenes presented to the view, what a magic change would they note! The wooded wilds of their native heath has become, lo! a busy, industrious city, with beautiful, wide streets, handsome residences, and substantial business houses; its quiet is disturbed by the hum of business. The tall oaks and pines have been felled, and converted into uses of agriculture and manufacture. A town has risen up, as if by enchantment, presenting to their view the evidences of wealth, of commerce, of learning, and the arts.[36]

Parham's representation of Chattanooga's early settlement underscores the racial and cultural superiority that whites cultivated to justify forced removal. To these early city boosters, the Cherokee removal hardly amounted to cultural extermination or genocide. To the contrary, they believed relocation was necessary to transform the wasted region from "wooded wilds of native heath" into a budding cosmopolitan center of "commerce, learning, and the arts." His account also exemplifies the romanticized mischaracterization of Native Americans as the keepers of an unspoiled natural world. Arguably, these racialized mythologies deeply influence how non-Natives, and Chattanoogans in particular, understand and relate to some of the bloodiest and most brutal periods of their early social history.

CHAPTER TWO

Rooting a Black Diaspora in Downtown Chattanooga

1540–1890

While Chattanooga was a point of departure for the Cherokee and south-eastern Native diaspora, it was also a point of arrival for members of the African diaspora, whose presence in the Chattanooga area dates back to Hernando De Soto's exploration up the Tennessee River in 1541. Between the sixteenth and early nineteenth centuries, encounters between European explorers, their slaves, and Native communities across the Southeast were increasingly frequent.[1]

By the early nineteenth century, four of the largest southeastern Native tribes—the Cherokee, Choctaw, Chickasaw, and Creek—had adopted mainstream western customs and sociopolitical institutions in efforts to secure political sovereignty and ward off encroaching white settlers. Referred to by whites as four of the "Five Civilized Tribes," these nations also adopted the so-called civilizing institution of black forced slavery.

Tiya Miles (2005) argued that, although some examples of Cherokee slaveholding were based on a large-scale, colonial plantation model, traditional Cherokee interpretations of community, kinship, and property created fundamentally different relationships between master and slave on southeastern Cherokee homesteads. Intermarriage and family building between Native Americans and African Americans, for example, were common.[2]

Prior to the adoption of the Cherokee Constitution in 1827, both free blacks (known as "tribal Freedmen") and slaves living within the boundaries of the Cherokee Nation could inherit and own land. Additionally, historical records documented Cherokees hiding and protecting slaves who had escaped captivity and fled into sovereign Cherokee territory. African Americans were also recorded protecting Native Americans who attempted to avoid western relocation following the passage of President Jackson's Indian Removal Act. In some cases, African Americans were taught to read and write by missionary instructors, including those stationed at the Brainerd Mission in present-day Chattanooga. Historical maps and treaties charting the pre-removal territory even depict a free black settlement in the vicinity of downtown Chattanooga (labeled "Sugar Negro Camp" and located at the base of Walden's Ridge) at the time of the passage of the Treaty of 1817.[3]

On October 25, 1819, Hamilton County was established by an executive action from the State of Tennessee. A census conducted the next year reported sixteen free blacks and thirty-nine slaves living within the county's newly incorporated boundaries. To be certain, these numbers underestimate the African American presence in the vicinity, as the census did not include dozens if not hundreds of blacks living in territories held by the Cherokee on the southern banks of the Tennessee River.

Drawing the Color Line

Over the next several decades, Hamilton County and the town of Chattanooga were rapidly settled by white farmers and industrialists—many of whom, as discussed in the previous chapter, brought African Americans with them as slave laborers. In the first ten years after Hamilton County's incorporation, the local population had nearly tripled to 2,136 whites, 25 free blacks, and 115 slaves living in the county.

The first substantial in-migration of African Americans occurred immediately after the forced removal of the Cherokee in 1838. Within one year of removal, the city of Chattanooga was incorporated. During the early years of the town's development, slave labor was used for most large-scale infrastructure projects, including road building, brick masonry and building construction. Slaves were also the primary source of labor supplying rail companies when they began to lay tracks in Chattanooga in 1840. By 1840, Hamilton County's population had more than tripled again to 7,498 whites, 584 slaves, and 93 free blacks.

Although few early promotional place guides outwardly acknowledge the presence of slavery in the Tennessee River valley, Henry Wiltse's unpublished *History of Chattanooga* (written in approximately 1920) illustrated the prevalence of slave labor in mid-nineteenth-century city-building activities. Thomas Crutchfield, for example, was a prominent citizen in Chattanooga during the decades between Cherokee removal and the U.S. Civil War. Crutchfield owned the first local brickyard, which manufactured most of the bricks for the town's earliest modern structures. The Crutchfields also owned a large hotel at West Ninth and Market Streets, across the street from the passenger train depot.

According to the 1860 Slave Schedule for Hamilton County, the Crutchfields owned thirty-nine slaves—many of whom worked at their hotel and

Total population in Hamilton County by race and slavery status, 1820–1860

Year	Total Population	Whites	Free Blacks	Slaves
1820	821	766	16	39
1830	2,276	2,136	25	115
1840	8,175	7,498	93	584
1850	10,075	9,216	187	672
1860	13,252	11,641	192	1,419

Source: U.S. Census Bureau, "Population by Race, 1820–1860, Slave Schedule 1820–1860," prepared by Social Explorer, accessed December 21, 2016, http://www.socialexplorer.com /6f4cdab7a0/explore.

brickyard.[4] During an interview for Wiltse's project, a longtime resident recalled how "the brickyard was down on the river between Market Street and River Transportation Warehouse. The foremen of the yard were Yellow Bill and Mills Crutchfield, negroes [sic]. Mills was the champion moulder."[5]

Michelle R. Scott (2008) argued that, unlike other areas of the Deep South that were rural and based on plantation-scale agriculture, Chattanooga's early economy was organized around subsistence farming and industrial development. In several nearby counties, African Americans greatly outnumbered whites. In nearby Madison County, Alabama, for example, slaves comprised more than half of the total population (N=14,573 or 55 percent); in Franklin County, Tennessee, they comprised more than one-quarter of the total population (N=3,551 or 26.6 percent).

In Chattanooga, slaves comprised just ten percent (N=1,419 or 10.7 percent) of the total population at the eve of the Civil War. More than one-quarter (N=78 or 27.2 percent) of the 287 slaveholding households in Hamilton County in 1860 owned one slave, and nearly three-quarters (N=202 or 70.4 percent) owned five or fewer. At the other end of the spectrum, ten households (2.9 percent) owned twenty or more slaves, and only one family owned more slaves than the Crutchfields. It is important to note that although these numbers are relatively low, several local historians have argued that they do not accurately reflect the prevalence of slavery in antebellum Chattanooga.

The 1860 Slave Schedule offers a total count for only slaves owned by households residing in Hamilton County, but does not factor in slaves who were frequently leased from property owners in the surrounding rural counties to be exploited in industrial work and urban infrastructure expansion.[6] Michelle Scott argued that, with no clear divide between "house" and "field" slave, African Americans living in antebellum Chattanooga were afforded certain benefits and rights not typically granted in other parts of the South. Literacy rates, for instance, were higher among enslaved Chattanoogans than among people confined to rural plantations in other parts of Tennessee and across the border in Georgia.[7]

These liberties, though crucial, were relative at best. Black individuals were systematically subjected to strict regulations, which monitored their movement and mobility across the city, and they were routinely exploited by local businessmen for industrial and development-based profits. These practices were codified in the earliest founding documents for the city.

Chattanooga's inaugural City Charter, for example, was granted by the Tennessee legislature on November 5, 1851. In his unpublished historical account of the city, John Wiltse recorded that the "first ordinance of general character passed in pursuance of this charter" was a law entitled "An Ordinance to Regulate Slaves, Free Blacks, and Mulattoes within the City of Chattanooga." The ordinance mandated that all free persons of color and mixed race present documentation proving their legal freedom within three months of the law's enactment. Additionally, any free persons of color migrating into the city had one month to provide sufficient evidence of their freedom. "If such persons were found in the city without proper evidence of freedom," Wiltse continued, "they were deemed to be slaves and dealt with as such."[8]

The ordinance established sundown laws which forbade slaves not residing in the city from remaining inside it "after sunset, weekdays, and not at all Sundays without permission from owners or employers." African Americans found in violation of these rules would be charged five dollars per day in fines. Furthermore, the ordinance prevented the congregation of African Americans in public spaces and severely restricted cultural and community-building activities. Wiltse recalled that "any collection of slaves within the city for dancing, or any other purpose except public worship, was proscribed." The City Watch and Patrol was required to disburse all collections of slaves and to inflict punishment of not less than five and no more than ten lashes. Worship was also made subject to regulation by the council.[9]

Thus, while the relatively small slave population living in Hamilton County was distinct from its rural plantation-dominated neighbors in so far that African Americans comprised a minority, and mostly urban, population, local policy makers were hardly the racially tolerant liberals that they considered themselves to be—and marketed themselves to northern investors as. To the contrary, white leaders were quick to enact laws meant to control African American physical and social mobility and enforce their subordination at the bottom of the local social hierarchy.

African Americans in Chattanooga during the U.S. Civil War

Three major Civil War battles took place in Chattanooga from June 1862 through November 1863. Over the course of three battles and but only six days of fighting, the Union and Confederate armies suffered 12,591 casualties—combined—in their struggle to control Chattanooga. Unsurprisingly, African Americans were central to all aspects of Confederate military fortification in the city, their labor being exploited to clear forests for lumber and firewood, dig ditches, and construct earthworks in the months leading up to the Union siege on the city.[10]

Black labor was also central to city-building efforts in the months that followed the Union army's November 1863 victory over the Confederacy in the Battles for Chattanooga. The Sixteenth Regiment of the United States Colored Troops (USCT) was assembled in Nashville and deployed to Chattanooga to fortify the city and prepare it to become the major supply depot for an expected invasion into Georgia the following spring. During the winter of 1863–64, Chattanooga was transformed into the center for Union military activity across the western frontier. Many affluent white residents had fled the city earlier that summer, abandoning their slaves and property as they sought refuge from impending federal troops.[11]

Over the next several months, Chattanooga's free black and former slave populations were joined by hundreds of formerly enslaved refugees from rural counties in Tennessee, Alabama, and Georgia. A prominent Quaker abolitionist farmer named Joshua Beck owned most of the property on the north side of the Tennessee River in what is today North Chattanooga/Hill City, and he allowed these refugees to set up a camp on his farm. His property had been an important stop on the Underground Railroad during the antebellum period.

Following the defeat of General Bragg at the Second Battle of Chattanooga, Beck formally donated a portion of his farm to refugees who migrated into the city to seek political asylum from the Confederate government. These refugees were referred to as "contraband" by federal troops; hence, the site where they resided came to be known as "Camp

Contraband." Although it lacked basic infrastructure improvements and its residents lived in tents and makeshift houses that barely protected them from the natural elements, visitors to the site noted the pride that its residents exhibited when describing the settlement. By November 26, 1864, more than 3,893 refugees lived in the camp, while "hundreds more poured in each day."[12]

Immediately after seizing the city, Union officers began enlisting Camp Contraband dwellers into the United States Colored Troops. Colonel Thomas J. Morgan led the Fourteenth U.S. Colored Infantry Regiment into Chattanooga on February 24, 1864. The regiment constructed a camp ("Camp Whipple") on the eastern slope of Cameron Hill overlooking downtown Chattanooga.

Colonel Morgan argued that the Fourteenth USCT troops played a formative role in shaping public opinions about the value of African American soldiers. The regiment's seriousness and integrity were on constant public display from their base at Camp Whipple. Colonel Morgan recalled:

Our camp was laid out with great regularity; our quarters were substantial, comfortable and well kept. The regiment numbered a thousand men, with a full complement of field, staff, line, and noncommissioned officers. We had a good drum corps, and a band provided with a set of expensive silver instruments. We were also fully equipped; the men were armed with rifled muskets, and well clothed. They were well drilled in the manual of arms, and took great pride in appearing on parade with arms burnished, belts polished, shoes blackened, clothes brushed, in full regulation uniform, including white gloves.

On every pleasant day our parades were witnessed by officers, soldiers, and citizens from the North, and it was not uncommon to have two thousand spectators. Some came to make sport, some from curiosity, some because it was the fashion, and others from a genuine desire to see for themselves what sort of looking soldiers Negroes would make. . . . Our evening parades converted thousands to a belief in colored troops. It was almost a daily experience to hear the remark from visitors, "Men who can handle their arms as these do, will fight." General [George Henry] Thomas paid the regiment the compliment of saying that he "never saw a regiment go through the manual as well as this one." We remained in "Camp Whipple" from February 1864 until August 1865, a period of eighteen months, and during the large part of that time the regiment was on object lesson to the army, and helped to revolutionize public opinion on the subject of colored soldiers.[13]

Over the course of their eighteen-month stay in Chattanooga, members of the Fourteenth Regiment USCT de-fortified and restored the city in the aftermath of the Battles for Chattanooga. Typically, these troops performed the hardest, least desirable manual labor. They disassembled stockades, filled ditches, collected unused explosives, repaired roads and railway tracks, and collected and buried the dead. When Major General George Henry Thomas ordered the construction of the Chattanooga National Cemetery to inter Union soldiers fallen in combat, USCT troops prepared the 75-acre site, dug the graves, and buried the fallen soldiers. By 1870, more than 12,000 bodies had been interred. Many nearby battlefield burials were also reinterred in Chattanooga, including nearly 1,500 burials from the Battle of Chickamauga just over the Georgia state line.[14]

Competing Cosmopolitanisms:
Race and Place in the Dynamo of Dixie

As previously stated, slavery in Chattanooga had not followed all of the same social norms as in the surrounding rural regions. Many slaves living in town had labored in industrial positions, and the black-to-white ratio was much lower in the city than in the surrounding plantations. Chattanooga-based historian Raymond Evans (2003) argued that early white policy makers and entrepreneurs used these social differences to construct a narrative about racial tolerance in Chattanooga in order to stymy concerns about slave labor posed by northern capitalists whose investments they wanted to secure.

Following the victory of the Union army over the Confederacy in May 1865, Chattanooga entrepreneurs were quick to extend their hands to northern industrialists and carpetbaggers. An advertisement placed in northern newspapers during this period captures their sentiment:

> *Wanted Immediately Any Number of Carpet-Baggers to Come*
> *to Chattanooga and Settle*

> The people of Chattanooga, no longer wishing to stay in the background, and feeling the necessity of immediately developing the vast mineral resources surrounding them, by which they can place themselves on the highroad to wealth, prosperity, and power, extend a GENERAL INVITATION to all CARPET-BAGGERS to leave the

bleak winds of the North and come to CHATTANOOGA.... Those who wish to come can be assured they will NOT BE REQUIRED TO RENOUNCE THEIR POLITICAL AND RELIGIOUS TE-NETS, as the jurisdiction of the Ku Klux [Klan] and other vermin do not extend over these parts. Persons wishing to immigrate will be furnished with details concerning any business by addressing Box 123 Chattanooga, Tennessee.

VOX POPULI

PS—Those having capital, brains, and muscle preferred.[15]

Importantly, the narrative of interracial harmony came back into play as Chattanooga was pitched to northern businessmen as a connected, cosmopolitan city with plentiful natural resources and inexhaustible cheap labor.

Attempts to lure outside capital investments were wildly successful. In 1850, $13,100 was spent on manufacturing-related capital investments in Hamilton County, while existing establishments produced $12,975 worth of manufactured goods. Ten years later, the county boasted twenty-two manufacturing establishments, which together employed 214 workers. The total annual investment in manufacturing had grown to $209,300, while the annual output of manufacturing products was valued at $395,380.[16]

Following the Civil War, Chattanooga quickly rose to prominence as a leader of the New South urban industrial movement. The city's prolific and diverse manufacturing-based economy was reflected in increases in number of establishments, workers employed in manufacturing, and total capital expenditures and output values for Hamilton County during the decades of southern Reconstruction. By 1890, Hamilton County's manufacturing base had grown to 336 establishments, employing a total of 6,368 workers. The total capital investments and output values in manufacturing increased between 1870 and 1890 by 1,612 percent and 1,013 percent, respectively.

African American place-making and city-building efforts before and during the Civil War set a precedent for black activism and community engagement during the postwar Reconstruction period. In her historical account of community building in New South Chattanooga, Scott (2008) noted that businessman and former mayor John T. Wilder had described the city as "the freest town on the map."[17] For decades, the city had had a reputation as a liberal bastion where African Americans could access certain economic and social opportunities not afforded elsewhere in the Deep South.

This perception of freedom, coupled with the massive expansion of black settlements across the city during the mid-1860s, made Chattanooga a highly desirable destination for African Americans seeking urban alternatives to sharecropping in the aftermath of the war. A period of massive industrial expansion began in the 1880s, and by 1890 more than six thousand workers (N=6,368) were employed at one of the county's 336 manufacturing businesses, a sector whose investments had increased to $8,133,499 (+3,786 percent), and output values had increased $11,264,969 (+2,749 percent) during the thirty-year period.[18]

Diasporic Placemaking in New South Chattanooga

Although African Americans historically comprised less than one-third of the county's population, they were the majority population living in the urban core. Thousands of families moved to the city looking for work in its rapidly industrializing west and south sides. In the thirty-year period between 1860 and 1890, Hamilton County's black community grew by nearly 1,000 percent to 17,717 individuals.

Almost immediately, black Chattanoogans established churches, schools, banks, health care practices, and other social services to serve their community. In 1865, when E. O. Tade of the Freedmen's Bureau established the Howard School—a public high school and the first free public school in Chattanooga—it was one of the first public education institutions for blacks in the postwar South. Initially, the school inhabited a former Confederate hospital building on Broad Street, but it was soon relocated to the burgeoning black cultural center on East Ninth Street. By 1877, Chattanooga's public school system had 1,538 white and 883 "colored" pupils attending classes.[19]

Although policy makers and businessmen drew what they considered to be firm lines between white and black sections of town, de jure and de facto segregation did not stop everyday residents from reaching across the color line in attempts to forge more welcoming and equitable neighborhoods and communities. An excellent example of multidiasporic placemaking is Chattanooga's First Congregational Church, founded at the corner of East Ninth and A (now Lindsay) Streets in the years immediately following the Civil War.

Tade, an African American evangelical minister, had moved to Chattanooga from Memphis to serve the rapidly growing freedmen population. He was initially met with opposition when he tried to organize black soldiers enlisted by the Army of the Cumberland to de-fortify the city in the

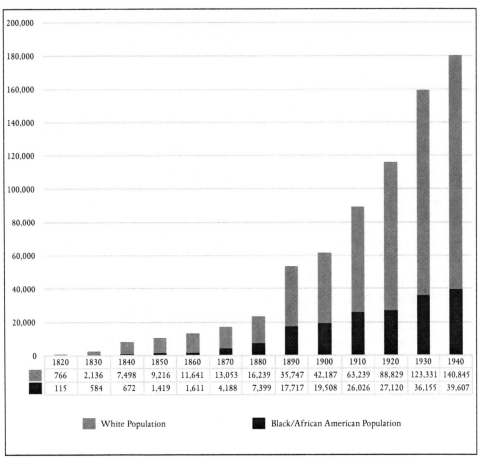

	1820	1830	1840	1850	1860	1870	1880	1890	1900	1910	1920	1930	1940
White Population	766	2,136	7,498	9,216	11,641	13,053	16,239	35,747	42,187	63,239	88,829	123,331	140,845
Black/African American Population	115	584	672	1,419	1,611	4,188	7,399	17,717	19,508	26,026	27,120	36,155	39,607

Total population in Hamilton County by race, 1820–1940.
Source: U.S. Census Bureau. *Population by Race, 1820–1940.* Accessed December 22, 2016. http://www.socialexplorer.com/6f4cdab7a0/explore.

wake of the Civil War, and drew attention for defying strict laws that relegated blacks to the north side of the Tennessee River (Camp Contraband, later Hill City).

However, Tade convinced local leaders to grant him land for the construction of a church on East Ninth Street. Originally meant to be nondenominational, it opened its doors as the First Congregational Church on June 9, 1867, and, in doing so, became the first racially integrated house of worship in the postbellum South.[20]

Tade believed that access to education and safe, secure housing were paramount to the project of black Reconstruction, and so at the same time that he was securing land for the congregational church and working as a cashier at the National Freedman's Savings and Trust Company, he solicited funds from the New York chapter of the American Missionary Association (AMA) to purchase land for the settlement of between fifty and one hundred freedmen and their families. In a letter to the AMA, Tade argued that offering land would "do [the freedmen] good physically, mentally, and spiritually," and promised that "with a little ready money, I can help them to homes—a very important thing in this great work of reconstruction."[21] His plea was successful, and the AMA granted Tade funds to purchase land surrounding the earthen war fortifications in the northeastern section (now Fort Wood) of the city.

A newspaper article from the late 1860s captured the enthusiasm with which the growing black community saved money and carved out places of material security across postwar Chattanooga, contending that the black community was "thriving" and would inevitably share in the comforts of middle-class life:

> One of the surest tests of the thrift and unthrift of a class of men is had by observing their use or non-use of the Savings Bank. This test it is very easy to apply to the colored people lately made free to manage their own concerns. Here, in Chattanooga, a branch of the National Freedman's Savings and Trust Company was established about thirteen months ago. The freedmen themselves knew nothing of such things, and all the whites that despise or that hate the blacks made themselves very active in creating distrust of the bank and its manager. But in spite of all this, the business of the Chattanooga branch has grown, and is now growing faster than ever before. Last week the Cashier went down the Alabama and Chattanooga Railway, among the colored laborers below Gadsden, and in three days' time received on deposit from them very near $5,000. If there are any white laborers and mechanics near Chattanooga that are putting away as much cash as these freedmen, we should be glad to make it known. The short of it is, the Freedmen are earning and saving and are investing a great deal of money; and the time is not very far ahead when they will be an extremely comfortable and well-to-do class.[22]

Black business and civic leaders were also eager to gain positions as elected officials and public sector employees, which they understood to be crucial to the fair representation of black communities in city and county politics. A total of five African American men were elected as aldermen in the city during the Reconstruction period: George Sewell (1871–72), Robert Marsh (1873–74), D. Medlow (1875–76), W. C. Hodge (1878–79), and W. B. Kennedy (1878–79).[23] Additionally, two African Americans were appointed to replace white officers on the Chattanooga Police Commission in October 1880: W. A. Henderson, who represented the Second Ward, and A. F. Thompson, who represented the Second and Fourth Wards, respectively.[24]

Dismantling Reconstruction

Unfortunately, the institutionalized political gains won during the Reconstruction period faced immediate backlash, and ultimately, were short lived. White Republican leaders interpreted growing black political power as a threat to their own relatively privileged social status, and began actively conspiring against black citizens. Faced with the reality that black residents could move freely about the city, and lacking the legal right to expropriate their labor for manual city-building activities, Chattanooga's Board of Aldermen passed laws establishing a municipal "chain gang" (1871)[25] and a county workhouse (1878), charging that "work-house convicts, when not confined in the city prison, shall be under the control and management of the boss of the street force, who shall work the same under the direction of the City Engineer and Street Committee, upon the streets, alleys, etc., of the city."[26]

Although these forced labor regulations did not specifically apply to African Americans, local historians agree that black residents, especially working-age black men, were targeted and disproportionately arrested on vagrancy charges and other nonviolent misdemeanors as a way to fill the chain gang. Unsurprisingly, healthy black men comprised the majority of prisoners confined to the chain gang and county workhouse.[27]

A *Chattanooga Times* editorial published one week after the appointments of W. A. Henderson and A. F. Thompson to the Police Commission in 1880 illuminated the racist paternalism undergirding white Republicans' so-called tolerance of blacks during this critical period of social transition. "We have no objection to the negro [sic] in any station that he is fit to fill," they wrote. "Not one in five hundred of them is at all capable of discharging the delicate and onerous duties of a peace officer. Very few of them have the judgment and discretion required for such a place. A good officer must be a man of superior coolness, courage, independence, and honesty. Of the few white men obtainable for such service, more than half fill the bill."[28]

The authors cloaked their prejudice in a thinly veiled discourse of political and civic rationality, claiming that it was not the appointment of African Americans to public office in and of itself that was the problem, but rather that affirmative action policies replaced qualified candidates, the majority of whom happened to be white, with unskilled laymen ill-prepared for the "delicate and onerous duties of a peace officer."

At the same time that white Republicans were mobilizing against black political gains in the local municipal structure, a series of antimiscegenation campaigns were setting the grounds for the rise of Jim Crow segregation laws regulating private space (e.g., housing) across the city. The City had for decades enforced sundown laws which severely restricted the ability of African Americans to congregate in and move freely around the city. Although formal housing segregation laws would not develop until the first decade of the twentieth century, informal campaigns against the commingling of whites and blacks were in practice on the eve of the Reconstruction period.

A *Chattanooga Times* article published on February 21, 1885, called public attention to Tadetown, the freedman settlement established by E. O. Tade:

> The arrest of James and Nancy Robinson on the charge of miscegenation has developed a most startling sensation, and one which is now receiving the attention of the authorities. For some months rumors have been afloat that a colored minister named Susine was openly advocating intermarriage of whites and blacks from the pulpit, and was sowing seeds which soon begun to bear fruit. He argued that there was no reason why a negro [sic] should be prohibited from marrying a white person, and that the law was a relic of barbarism, and a heritage of slavery. . . . His church had a very large congregation, and when his ideas became known a degraded class of whites and blacks flocked to his church and seemed greatly gratified over his views.
>
> It is stated that a low class of both races and all sexes have been living indiscriminately in the vicinity of Tadetown, and soon plucked up enough courage, backed by the arguments of the preacher, to join their fortunes in marriage. In procuring their marriage license, of course, the color of the contracting parties was not truthfully given. Armed with the license, the preacher made short work of the ceremony. It is reported that this practice has been in progress among the denizens of that locality for some months, until now there are a

score or more of whites and blacks who live together as man and wife. The officers of the law have the matter in hand and the mine will be sprung in a day or two.[29]

A newspaper article published five months later described the arrest of another interracial couple in downtown Chattanooga. The author mocked Frank and Mary Peacock's skin tones as well as her inability to determine her racial heritage. "The woman is to all appearance a full-blooded white," the reporter gossiped. "She knows nothing of her parents, except her mother was very dark, but is unable to say whether she was a mulatto or white woman. Frank Peacock, her husband, is as black as tar. The couple has one child."[30]

Downplaying Local Racism

Chattanooga capitalists and policy makers relied heavily on low-paid African American labor to expand urban infrastructure and financial profits as the city evolved into the postwar "Dynamo of Dixie." Importantly, a narrative of interracial harmony came back into play as local boosters pitched the city to northern businessmen as a connected, cosmopolitan city.

The *Chattanooga City Guide* was published in 1900 as a marketing device to attract northern industrial investors into the city. Its authors boasted that "Chattanooga is one of the least southern of the South's great cities. Before, during, and for a long time after the War Between the States, the straggling community and region round were of definite Union inclinations. There, people are from every section of the country, and the city is remarkably cosmopolitan. The sectionalism that was found in many parts of the South never existed in Chattanooga. The speech is neither northern nor southern, but a definite blending of the two. The Republican Party has been the dominant political force and until recent years polled a sizeable and occasionally conclusive vote."[31]

On one level, these positions opened up new economic opportunities for African Americans, providing labor and lifestyle alternatives to rural sharecropping. But the depictions of Chattanooga as a tolerant place, free from racial antipathy, did not accurately describe daily life for most black residents living and working in downtown Chattanooga. Most of the black community lived in substandard rental housing; three African American men were brutally lynched by police-backed white mobs between 1885 and 1906; and the Klan, though perhaps not as active as they were in some Deep South cities, had an irrefutable presence across Chattanooga and Hamilton County.[32]

Furthermore, industrial labor opportunities were not offered because business owners felt morally obligated to blacks or remorseful toward the local history of black enslavement and exploitation. To the contrary, as more African Americans migrated into Chattanooga searching for honest work, business owners took them on primarily as unskilled laborers; in other words, they were the most cost-efficient laboring class.

Concurrently, the newly formed Chamber of Commerce coordinated a strategy to further consolidate political and economic power into the hands of property-owning white residents. In December 1887, the Chattanooga Chamber of Commerce adopted its first set of bylaws. The Chamber charged themselves with "promoting and fostering the commercial, mineral, manufacturing, and other material interests of, and the architectural and other improvements of the City of Chattanooga and its vicinity . . . also to encourage immigration."[33] The immigration agenda articulated by the Chamber was a direct response to demands from the local African American community to have elected representation in municipal and county affairs. Rather than acknowledge past racial injustices and attempt to build more equitable economic and social structures moving forward, local leaders opted to further dilute local African American political and social power by attracting large numbers of low-wage, European immigrants to the city, hoping to render black labor and votes obsolete.

What is most interesting about these late nineteenth- and early twentieth-century promotional materials is how the constructions of urban citizenship and cosmopolitanism were positioned in direct contrast to the community-building and place-making activities of African Americans. Local leaders preferred the southward migration of white northerners and foreign-born immigrants to the region over the influx of newly emancipated African Americans, many of whom had been connected to Chattanooga for generations.

In a utopian vision of a post-black Chattanooga, one prominent citizen published a *Historical Guide to Chattanooga and Lookout Mountain* (1889), wherein he assured visitors and potential investors that Chattanooga's intelligent citizens would solve the "negro [sic] problem" by encouraging European immigration in order to edge African Americans out of employment opportunities:

> The negro problem is creating some anxiety among thoughtful
> citizens, but the influx of Americans from the North, and of foreign-
> ers from Germany and Ireland, will solve that problem. The writer

will not live to see the pressing southward of that unfortunate race by this invasion from the north and from beyond seas. But the negro has been pressed southward from New England, and his destiny is as assuredly southward as was the Indian's destiny westward. . . . Within fifty years the Negro will be as infrequent in the valleys of Chattanooga and Lookout as he now is in the valley of the Genuessee [sic] in New York. Chattanooga is thoroughly cosmopolitan. All good people who desire to make an honest living are sought after. The gates of the city swing inward to welcome all such, for the commingling of the blood of northerner and southerner will produce the most vigorous race known to the annals of humanity. Such a race will have but one Law, one Union, one God.[34]

In Connor's view, the "commingling of blood" between white ethnic groups guaranteed the evolution of the most vigorous and cosmopolitan society in human history, whereas African Americans, in contrast, were depicted as lacking culture and the antithesis of all "good people who desire to make an honest living."

The desire to replace African American labor with European immigrant labor extended to both factory and private residence, where the majority of working black women were employed by the eve of the twentieth century. The 1890 annual report of the Chattanooga Chamber of Commerce, for example, proclaimed that European immigrant recruitment policies would be a boon to the city:

Chattanooga is a good field for the introduction of efficient house servants. Good white gardeners would be demanded also, and this would grow if there was any supply. The man or company who should settle a colony of Germans, Swedes, Irish, on some of the cheap and fertile lands within easy reach of Chattanooga will be a benefactor of the immigrants and confer a signal benefit on the people at large. An infusion of this kind would stimulate our home workers to closer attention in their contracts, and work much improvement in the present methods of small farming, trucking, fruit raising, and give those who are able and willing to pay liberally for the best domestic service a chance to protect themselves from the unreliability and efficiency of the average negro [sic] house servant.[35]

The substantial in-migration of African Americans during Chattanooga's rise as a New South industrial city was considered both a blessing and a curse to the local white population. For capitalists and industrial business-men, emigrating blacks were perceived as a major laboring class who could be paid unskilled workers' wages. But to white laborers, particularly those lacking advanced manufacturing skills, an African American presence on work sites was perceived as a threat to white economic gains.

Local capitalists took advantage of this tension to further divide and conquer their labor pools. The *Chattanooga Times* reported on February 28, 1885, that the Chattanooga Stove Works had forced between 75 and 80 white laborers to train their African American replacements prior to being laid off from their positions.[36] Two years later, the "color line [was] drawn" when thirty white women and girls working in a canning factory were fired and replaced with African American workers after they went on strike to pro-test the hiring of black women to assist with peeling and canning a large tomato shipment.[37] On April 30, 1889, the *Chattanooga Times* reported that the Lookout Iron Mill dismissed an "entire force of 150 [white, unionized] hands" and replaced them with nonunionized, African American workers imported from Richmond, Virginia. The newspaper concluded that "a small squad of police were detailed to guard the Johnson boarding house, where the new Negro workmen are stopping. . . . It was suspected that some of the ex-mill hands might make a night raid."[38] Although no violent raid occurred against the Richmond iron workers, the perceived threat against white labor was met with the same racist violence and murder characteristic of other Southern cities in the post-Reconstruction period.

Despite these threats to person and property, leaders in Chattanooga's African American community organized relentlessly to secure elected po-sitions in the city. A *Chattanooga Times* article published on May 8, 1886, details one of these efforts. To quote at length:

> Sixty-seven colored men, denominated as the kickers, met in the circuit court room of the Court House last night to bear the report of a committee of fifteen appointed at a previous meeting to select which of the county offices they would demand of the white Republicans. . . . W. A. Manning . . . denounced the white Republicans for their treatment of the colored men and said if the "niggers" did not scramble for themselves they would never receive office. . . . W. C. Hodge took the floor and spoke in favor of adopting the [manifesto] report. He thought it was time for the colored men to assert them-selves. He was tired of voting for white men and heaping honors on them and receiving nothing in return for the colored race. The

colored men composed a majority of the Republican Party in Hamilton County and were going to have an office and some of the "boodle." If the white Republicans did not like the steps being taken by the colored man, they would have to eat crow. H. N. Hutchins denounced the white Republicans for their treachery and said the colored people would have to help themselves or get left.[39]

Unsurprisingly, local black leaders' efforts to demand civil rights and practice self-determination were often met with mocking ridicule from the press and other local white institutions, who misrepresented their campaigns in order to reinforce stereotypes about African Americans as ungrateful, unruly, and prone to interracial violence. These stereotypes reinforced the sense of moral and cultural superiority that most whites felt toward African Americans, and made them feel justified in their actions to exploit black labor for the sake of personal gains via urban development and industrial expansion.

Communal Separatism in the Eastern Flats

Though their efforts were routinely met with white resistance, black families persisted in settling autonomous neighborhoods organized around the principles of cooperation and mutual support. Though a growing autonomous black community called Hill City was evolving on the north bank of the Tennessee River at the site of Camp Contraband, the lack of a bridge connecting the north and south shores made it difficult for Hill City residents to interact with their African American neighbors in the historic urban core.

Faced with ongoing physical and emotional violence as well as physical dislocation, a group of black residents from the south shore decided to form their own autonomous municipality in the unincorporated flats that comprise present-day East Chattanooga. A *Chattanooga Times* article published on December 5, 1887, reported that Hamilton County was going to become home to the first independent "negro [*sic*] city on American soil." Named "Bushtown" by its founders, the settlement's description in the article confirmed that:

Hamilton County has an anomaly in the form of a town composed entirely of negroes. Some months ago the advance in real estate in the city forced a large number of negroes from the valuable hill tops, and they decided to locate on a strip of ground . . . in a natural grove.

They were soon joined by others of the race, and a building boom ensued. Houses followed in rapid succession, and at one time thirty were in course of erection at the same time. There are now about 110 houses in the settlement, and the population numbers about 800. Streets have been laid out and the Belt railroad comes within a short distance of the town. A church and school house have been erected, also four stores and a number of two-story dwellings have been built. . . . The best class of colored people are moving there, the class who own their own homes and are regularly employed. Of the 800 persons now residing there, all are colored except one family and they live at the outskirts of the town. . . . Steps will be taken in the spring to incorporate the town and it will be the first negro city on American soil. Of course, the mayor and all the city functionaries, teachers, ministers, store keepers will be of the colored race. The progress of the community will be watched with great interest, as it will demonstrate the fact whether or not negroes can successfully administer the affairs of a large community without the assistance of the whites.[40]

Despite ridicule, paternalism, and occasionally violence from whites living in Chattanooga, the story of Bushtown's settlement illustrates how black residents persisted in carving out spaces of material security and cultural belonging from the evolving physical and social landscapes of the city. Though white leaders emphasized urban cosmopolitanism and racial tolerance as qualities of Chattanooga, news and institutional records reveal practices and intentions that mark this boosterism for what it was: a public relations strategy meant to conceal or at least distract outside investors from much more sinister racial attitudes and practices fundamentally designed to keep black residents in their place. Thus, by emphasizing interracial harmony, city boosters distracted public attention away from the persistently racialized and unequal economic, political, and social opportunity structures undergirding urban planning and development in the city.

CHAPTER THREE

Cosmopolitanism as Concealment
The Dynamo of Dixie during Jim Crow, 1890–1968

By the turn of the twentieth century, city boosters had refined their inter-racial harmony pitch to investors. The *City Guide* published in 1900 meant to attract capital into the "Dynamo of Dixie" by similarly stressing the economic, social, and cultural opportunities available for African Americans. The authors bragged, "Chattanooga Negroes are on every economic level. Some are on relief, many work in factories or foundries, and others monopolize domestic service. Chattanooga has been and remains nearly free from racial maladjustment. The politicians have found a place for Negroes in the political machines, a procedure simplified by the highly reasonable attitude taken by leaders of both, operating through an inter-racial committee. Most picturesque are the all-day-and-night dances on the southwest side, the rummage sales at Five Points, and the policy marts of Ninth Street. There are colored lodges of the Masons and Knights of Pythias, a local chapter of the Alpha Phi Alpha fraternity, local YMCA and YWCA, and numerous churches of many denominations."[1]

Powerful institutions like the Chamber of Commerce often appropriated black economic gains and social progress, claiming they were indicative of a sophisticated urban center "nearly free from racial maladjustment." Although the successes highlighted above are indeed impressive, one must consider that the gains forged by black residents living and working in downtown Chattanooga during the New South period were entirely of their own making. Often, their successes were earned despite coordinated efforts by self-professed liberal whites to keep black residents in their place.

Marketing documents like the *Chattanooga City Guide* (1900) had the effect of naturalizing uneven geographic development and socio-spatial inequality in discourse and in place. As was the case with Bushtown described in the previous chapter, African American residents, regardless of their economic class, were regularly dislocated from the lands they occupied as real estate and land redevelopment pressures mounted across the city. Poor and working-class communities of color in particular were vulnerable to these forced and induced evictions, as the majority of households were renters or land squatters who resided near the industrial plants and factories where they worked. Instead of acknowledging how low-income communities had been forced into unsafe districts, urban boosters juxtaposed their over-crowded, polluted living conditions against the "stable . . . above average conditions" of more affluent black neighborhoods:

> Nearly one-third of Chattanooga's population is made up of Negroes, who tend to live close to their work—either domestic service or industrial. They usually occupy the depressions and bases of higher elevations, and sometimes the entire areas, where smoke and dirt are bad. There is a racial gradient, especially noticeable on Cameron Hill, Bluff View, and Fort Wood Hill, where Negroes live in the hollows and on the low banks of hills, while the white residents occupy the upper slopes and crests. . . . The main Negro residential areas are Churchville, College Hill, Tannery Flats, Bushtown, and Fort Choatham. Houses range from well-kept homes, seen in some sections of College Hill and on East 8th Street, to the barest possible shelters of South Chattanooga and Tannery Flats. In Churchville, regarded as the most stable Negro community, living conditions are above the average. The residents occupy neat single, duplex, and small tenement houses. The contrast is the situation in the College Hill area where the industrial menace of smoke and smell has driven out previous dwellers, and where there are seven or eight Negro families to the house.[2]

Such uncritical optimism from city boosters was often contradicted by African American citizens' narratives of personally experiencing discrimination and exclusion from emerging economic and social opportunity structures on the basis of their skin tones. The *Biography and Achievements of the Colored Citizens of Chattanooga* (1904) described a hopelessness felt by the majority of local African American citizens residing in the city. Many had migrated to Chattanooga under the impression that it was a southern city of uncommon liberalism and relative racial tolerance.

These families had arrived eager to work hard and expecting to find legitimate economic opportunities in return. Instead, many black Chattanoogans encountered racist stereotypes and low-wage, hard labor jobs. The authors of the 1904 volume described the discrimination encountered in Chattanooga as thus:

> Of those who, in a climate where nigh all the labor they are called upon to perform, is so arduous as to keep those who most readily

make this charge, at a distance. It is said with much reason however, that as a worker he is careless, irresponsible, and therefore unskillful. While we ourselves have seen no convincing evidence that the negro [sic] is below others here, we should be much surprised if conditions such as confront him, fail to produce the above named characteristics. We believe too little has been said when considering this charge, of the correlation of good wages and good work. But aside from wages there is another and even greater incentive to good work, of which the negro is generally deprived. The laborer, who would be most worthy of his hire, is the one that has ever before him a reasonable hope of advancement. But the negro knows such hope, for at every turn in the great field of labor he is met with the energy crushing "Thus far shalt thou go." The men who would bring Southern labor to par in skill with that of other sections must first enlarge the field of opportunity.[3]

To whites, who viewed development and economic expansion in zero-sum terms, enlarging the field of opportunity was akin to forfeiting one's own fair share of the wealth. Racial integration was a direct threat to the structures of white property and privilege. Eager to prevent the com-mingling of white and black families and workers in the rapidly expanding city, local policy makers began implementing Jim Crow laws. Public schools had been segregated since before the Civil War, but the State of Tennessee is credited for having enacted the first postwar Jim Crow law when it mandated racial segregation on passenger trains in 1881.[4]

The earliest Jim Crow ordinances applied in the city of Chattanooga involved the separation of whites and blacks on streetcars (1905), followed by a housing segregation law passed in North Chattanooga (1915), an almost exclusively white, affluent community that bordered the historically black township of Hill City. Worried that integrated blocks would depreciate the values of their newly improved real estate, white residents persuaded the Commission to adopt "progressive" separate but equal housing legislation to outlaw both blacks and whites from moving into homes on streets that were populated primarily by members of the opposite race.

A journalist with the *Chattanooga Daily Times* reported with enthusiasm, "The ordinance was carefully written, based on similar ordinances in other cities, but with all the objectionable or unconstitutional features eliminated. It places restriction on one race as much as it does the other, the one that happens to be in the majority receiving the chief benefit. Mayor Voigt has received many compliments on his segregation ordinance. The North Chattanoogans seem to feel proud of the fact they not only are to soon have a complete sewerage system, but they are also the only exclusively white city of its size in the state."[5]

These regulations were rooted in the same racist paternalism that had characterized local urban policy making since before Cherokee removal. Proponents of the ordinance claimed the law avoided the racist tropes characteristic of Jim Crow housing laws in other Southern cities because it similarly restricted whites *and* blacks from residing beside one another. In this sense, the ordinance did not unduly target one race and was perceived as being adopted in the best interest of all citizens.

The formal adoption of Jim Crow policies in Chattanooga was met with ongoing resistance from African American residents, who saw through the "separate but equal" rationales used to racially segregate the city. Randolph Miller was an ex-slave who had moved to the city during the Union occupation, and worked as a pressman for several white-owned newspapers before launching his own paper to serve Chattanooga's black community, *The Chattanooga Blade.*

In addition to being a journalist and human rights champion, Miller was a labor organizer. Miller famously worked with a group of prominent African American businessmen to launch a streetcar strike in July 1905. Outraged that local policy makers were relegating African Americans to substandard transit accommodations despite their ability to pay for first-class services, the group proposed a black-owned and managed transit company so that local African Americans could "be transported with dignity and respect" around the city.[6]

Between July and early October, Miller and his collaborators organized and ran a three-route, horse-drawn streetcar "hack line" system that connected outlying African American communities to employment centers and the central business district. The service began on July 16, 1905 and, at five cents per ride, quickly reached ridership capacity.

Immediately, influential white leaders called for an end to the hack lines, arguing that they promoted a "spirit of resentment" between the races. Despite these protests, Miller's horse-powered, three-train streetcar program serviced Chattanooga's black community for the next four months, until it was ultimately shut down by municipal officials.

Miller turned the misfortune into an opportunity to speak out publicly against de facto and de jure racism in the city. In an October 1905 issue of *The Chattanooga Blade*, Miller published the following outcry against racial and spatial injustice in the city: "They have taken our part of the library; they have moved our school to the frog pond; they have passed the 'Jim Crow' law; they have knocked us out of the jury box; they have played the devil generally, and what in thunder more will they do no one knows."[7]

Although Miller's streetcar system was dismantled, the 1905 streetcar boycotts inspired many individual acts of protest in the subsequent decades. Their work inspired the development of underground jitney taxi companies which have served Chattanooga's black communities since 1921.[8] In one instance of civil disobedience that predated the famous 1955 Montgomery Bus Boycott by more than three decades, Minerva Dethrody "violated the 'Jim Crow' law—she got on the North Chattanooga streetcar, seated herself in a section 'across the line,' and refused to move. The car was held up five minutes until the police could arrive and then she got a 'free ride' to headquarters."[9]

Sweeping Out "No Jim Crow" Zones

By 1910, Hamilton County's population had soared to 89,267 people. Nearly all 26,026 black residents resided within the historic urban core of the city. As industrial development expanded across the west and south sides of town, poor and working-class residents of both races resided in housing that lacked basic infrastructure such as running water or sewage connections.

In response to these deplorable conditions, a civic group called "The Women's Club" set out to diagnose and improve the city's urban ills. The women described themselves as "patriotic, energetic, practical, and self-denying ladies, inspired by an impulse to do those things for the city which politicians and ordinary men have left undone." Reflecting on one particularly abhorrent section of town known as "Cocaine Alley," a reporter following the women recalled how

> The little back streetlet, just off from Ninth, where according to tradition, the denizens are wont to apply portions of cocaine to their systems . . . presumably to alleviate pain, but ostensibly . . . to harden their sensibilities against the open-faced vileness of their locality. . . .
> An entire community in this alley depends upon a system of closets that would disgrace the worst environs of the filthiest city in the United States. . . . A distinguished citizen draws rental from these shacks, right in the heart of Chattanooga, and seems to defy the police in their efforts to enforce regulations for the protection of public

health. In one section of this block are a series of huts built in the shape of an upper deck of a steamer, and known among the Negroes as "The Boat." If any filthier scene can be imagined than the men of the party witnessed there, it would be a revelation indeed. A prominent real estate man who has the rental of "The Boat" will be seen with reference to the sanitation of the craft, and if something is not done there will be some scuttling.[10]

Clearly, while Chattanooga's urban housekeeping movement emphasized physical and social issues such as sanitation, plumbing, and fire safety, activists were also highly motivated to sweep out personal lifestyles and social activities deemed obscene and inappropriate by upstanding, moral citizens. Activities targeted by the crusaders included living in darkness, alcoholism and substance abuse, gambling, prostitution, and presumed idleness.

Arguably, the greatest threat that slum areas posed to social and moral order were their potential to be havens for miscegenation and neighborhood integration. By 1930, black Chattanoogans had been subject to Jim Crow laws for decades. In the sociocultural and political context of Jim Crow-era Chattanooga, racial integration, whether intentional or the unintended consequence of concentrated, racialized poverty, stood in direct defiance of municipal and state laws.

During an inspection of an abandoned school located two blocks from City Hall, officials discovered with horror that "No Jim Crow" zones could be found in a place called Hoboes' Paradise. "Men not only sleep there," the reporter marveled. "A few live there. Whites and Negroes together." The story went on to describe how some of the squatters were employed in local industries, most were desiring work, many were not actually engaged in illicit activities but had nowhere else to sleep, and public officials had been contributing directly to the problem: "The flop quarters of the city and county jails have been cleaned out," one squatter told the inspection team, "and men who ask for a place to sleep now are directed to the school house." Municipal and county officials exacerbated the illegal living conditions found in Hoboes' Paradise by treating the building as a de facto flophouse. Essentially, they fueled a social situation (i.e., racial intermingling and integration) that they also criminalized, and ultimately used the misbehavior to justify slum removal.[11]

Early housing improvement and clean-up campaigns in Chattanooga and industrial cities across urban America were rooted in the City Beautiful movement, a philosophical and architectural tradition that emphasized infrastructure improvements alongside civic engagement, public space development, cultural development, and urban beautification.

In March of 1936, the women of Wesley Community Center, a service group associated with the missionary department of the Southern Methodist Church, launched an initiative to rechristen a notorious section of town known as Hell's Half Acre as "Sunshine Drive." Determined to spearhead a "physical as well as moral clean-up" of the area, the Wesley group declared their intent to sweep out houses, clear refuse, improve vacant lots, and plant a rose bush in the yards of each of the one hundred properties that comprised the Acre.

Cloaked in altruistic rhetoric, the group was explicit about the exact boundaries of the "Sunshine Drive" area. Although they acknowledged that there were "to begin with, three 'Hell's Half Acres' in Chattanooga," the missionary group focused exclusively on "a section of squalid shacks inhabited by white persons." The other two hellish areas, located in the African American sections of Tannery Flats and Moses Street (South Chattanooga), respectively, were disqualified.[12]

Several years later, another group described scenes of interracial cohabitation that read as "sordid fiction." A reporter who accompanied the group described the offense to her readers in an exposé article about the tour: "Mr. and Mrs. Average Chattanoogan, who live in a clean house, raise clean children and eat decent food, would recoil in horror if they were to enter any one of the four houses at 1716, 1800, 1802, and 1804 Citico Avenue. In the heart of a Negro section, these houses, owned by one of the city's largest holders of slum property, are occupied by white families."[13]

These examples of racialized exclusion illuminate the sociocultural, legal, and administrative contexts of low-income housing politics and development in Chattanooga at the height of the Jim Crow period. Though many white sections were similarly overrun with "bootlegging, assault, drunkenness, and other petty crimes," whites were considered capable of moral and social improvement, and faith-based urban reform associations like the Wesley group considered it their spiritual duty to help poor whites improve their conditions in order to participate fully in the modern cosmopolitan city.

Black Chattanoogans, in contrast, endured ongoing dehumanization and paternalism, and were systematically excluded from City Beautiful improvement programs on the grounds that financial investments in black neighborhoods would fail to produce significant social or moral returns. Though volunteers and public officials readily acknowledged that the unsanitary conditions in many African American sections were the fault of negligent slumlords, African American sections fell outside the scope of civic urban improvement programs. Exploited by white slumlords, and neglected by the city and mainstream civic organizations, working-class African American neighborhoods were left to deteriorate further without recourse. Through these processes, black poverty was further naturalized and pathologized in mainstream local discourse, and codified through urban planning and policy-making strategies that privileged and centered on white communities.

Jim Crow Enters Public Housing

Slum clearance efforts in Chattanooga ramped up on October 21, 1938, after the United States Housing Authority (the precursor to the Department of Housing and Urban Development or HUD) approved loans in eleven cities across the country, including Chattanooga, for inner-city slum eradication and low-cost housing development in a program that effectively launched the U.S. public housing movement.[14]

The Chattanooga Housing Authority (CHA) was approved for a $2.262 million loan to cover 90 percent of redevelopment costs. The CHA was charged with clearing slums and providing low-rent "dwellings for Negroes in the area bounded by Main Street to the south, Grove Street on the west, West Twelfth Street on the north, and Poplar Street on the east."[15] In a letter written to citizens residing within the redevelopment area, CHA chairman P. H. Wood confirmed that "the Chattanooga Housing Authority expects to pay reasonable, fair prices for all the property needed." However, he clearly distinguished that all options and compensation would be negotiated directly with property owners. Low-income renters, who were the primary population living on the Westside, would not be eligible for compensation.[16]

Shortly thereafter, the CHA announced a second award of federal funds to construct a public housing project for white households three miles across town in East Chattanooga. The white project was named East Lake Courts, and constructed on undeveloped farmland. The project was designed to house 437 families, with rents ranging from $3.10 per week for a one-bedroom apartment to $3.45 per week for a three-bedroom home. By June 1940, both College Hill Courts (97 units) and East Lake Courts (437 units) had been built, and several apartments were open for demonstration tours. These state-of-the-art garden-style buildings were constructed with firewalls, had full plumbing and sanitation systems as well as fenced-in yards with space for kitchen gardens, and they contained novel luxuries like electric heaters and hot water heaters. All utility costs were included in weekly rents.

By September, 125 African American families had moved into the Westside development.[17] When College Hill Courts reached full capacity that December, tenants were self-organizing, and by 1941 published a monthly newsletter to advertise events and activities hosted by the Housing Authority. These associations mark the genesis of a three-quarter-century legacy of tenant organizing on the Westside that continues, in an adapted form, today.

Modernist Urban Transformations

During the twenty-year period between 1950 and 1970, downtown Chattanooga underwent massive structural and social transformations. The anti-blight campaigns launched by urban housekeepers during the first four decades reached their peak in 1955, when the Chattanooga Housing Authority secured a USHUD Urban Renewal grant to plan and redevelop the Westside district of downtown. In a plan that spared only College Hill Courts and the First Presbyterian Church, the 435-acre "Golden Gateway Urban Renewal Area" was the fourth largest Urban Renewal project nationwide, in terms of scale, and the twelfth in terms of total development costs.

As in the slum eradication programs of the 1930s, the Chattanooga Housing Authority negotiated property acquisitions directly with landlords. Although public officials promised the local African American community that no families would be forced out of their homes without first finding a new residence for them, no records were kept to track those commitments. Local officials suggested that all of the dislocated white families would be absorbed by the private housing market, but that very low-income African American households would likely need to have additional public housing projects constructed for them. Over the next decade, more than three thousand households and over one hundred businesses were purchased and demolished by the Chattanooga Housing Authority. By 1960, the Westside district had been fully cleared and development-ready.

As Urban Renewal planners coordinated the demolition and redevelopment of the Westside, local policy makers found themselves in the middle of a racial desegregation battle. On May 17, 1954, the United States Supreme Court issued the *Brown v. Board of Education of Topeka* ruling, which effectively outlawed legal segregation in public schools. As leaders of a highly segregated city with a long history of Jim Crow planning, Chattanooga's elected officials and civic leaders emphasized the sections of the ruling that put the responsibility of integration on local school boards.

Maintaining that liberal and altruistic policy makers had always acted in "good faith" when it came to local race relations, one editorialist issued the following declaration to assure white residents that the integration of Chattanooga's public schools would only happen when the community agreed that it was time to do so: "The Supreme Court placed the responsibility upon the local School Boards. It put no time limit on the integration process but merely asked that the Boards act in good faith. The Chattanooga School Board has proved time and again that it acts in no other way but in good faith. . . . The Board says: 'We can decide whether our community should take a little step or a big one or a series of little steps over a period of years. But once the Court decides we are not acting in good faith, the Court will tell us what to do.' "[18]

A series of skirmishes instigated by white teenagers during the winter of 1956 afforded policy makers further justification to ignore the Supreme Court's ruling and keep Chattanooga's public facilities segregated. The city made national headlines for a race brawl that erupted in Memorial Auditorium on January 31, 1956, after a white spectator tried to force one of performer Roy Hamilton's band employees from a white section of the audience, and a violent fight between patrons ensued.

Following the fight, the auditorium's manager used the event to justify continued segregation of the facilities, going so far as to publicly proclaim: "I will recommend to the board that it bar whites from entering the auditorium while the colored people are having a dance and colored people from entering when a white dance is being held. . . . Every time we have a Negro dance in the auditorium and admit white spectators, those teenage white children, or many of them, will try to get onto the dance floor and dance, not with the Negroes but with themselves. We have a terrible time often, keeping them off the dance floor. Sometimes we have had to put them out of the auditorium. They also try to go backstage and dance back there. It just won't work and I believe the auditorium board will go along on this recommendation."[19]

Embarrassed by the national attention, local boosters issued a statement expressing their disbelief that such a disruption would occur in a city as liberal and racially tolerant at Chattanooga. "It is ironical that the city which has done so much to foster peaceful relations between the races would be the first Southern city to witness a mass racial demonstration," they declared. "That the bitterness shown by leaders and groups on both sides of the segregation question had a bearing on the brawl cannot be doubted."[20]

Although local white leaders stressed interracial tolerance, their actions spoke louder than their words. In response to black activists who, in response to the event, demanded the immediate integration of all public facilities, the Chattanooga Board of Education referred to the civil unrest of the previous months as evidence that successful integration of public schools would not be possible for at least five more years.[21] And when the U.S. Supreme Court outlawed segregation on city buses the following year, white supremacists waged a campaign of violence and terror against members of the Chattanooga branch of the National Association for the Advancement of Colored People (NAACP). The *Chattanooga Times* reported: "The U.S. Supreme Court has ruled segregation on buses is unconstitutional. It was in compliance with that ruling that Southern Coach started without public notice the painting out of the segregation signs. Anderson said that the city's responsibility now involves the quelling of disorder if any should arise. Generally, white persons have continued the practice of sitting toward the front of the buses and Negroes toward the rear. There have been instances of Negroes sitting near the front but these instances have not precipitated any disorderly incidents. Police officers early yesterday removed a dummy hanging from the Walnut Street Bridge. On the dummy was written: 'All NAACP bus-riding niggers.'"[22]

In June 1958, local attorney and black civic leader James Mapp petitioned the school board to have public schools integrated, beginning in the 1958–59 academic year. Once again, the Chattanooga Board of Education unanimously refused. Faced with the reality that local policy makers would not voluntarily or willingly desegregate the city's public facilities, local blacks decided to take matters into their own hands. On February 19, 1960, thirty black students from Howard High School staged Chattanooga's first lunch counter demonstrations at the Woolworth's and McLellan Stores on Market Street. Over the next four months, students organized sit-ins at S. H. Kress, Woolworth's, Miller's and Loveman's department stores. During one demonstration where more than fifty protestors were arrested and charged with loitering and disorderly conduct, white business owners and the Chattanooga Police Department escalated their response to the nonviolent sit-ins. Officers armed with hastily constructed billy clubs formed a line and marched the protestors out of the Central Business District while the fire department used their hoses to force the students back into the black section of East Ninth Street.[23]

At the same time that high school students were taking over lunch counters on Market Street, James Mapp and NAACP Legal Defense and Educational Fund head Thurgood Marshall filed a lawsuit against the board of education meant to forcibly desegregate Chattanooga's public schools.[24] The downtown disturbances, plus Mapp's lawsuit against the city schools, attracted considerable national media attention. By early June 1960, there were representatives from CBS, NBC, *Newsweek*, *Life* magazine, the *New York Times*, and the United Press covering the events. The national attention given to Chattanooga's desegregation struggle further fueled white resentments. Their antipathy worsened as neighborhood demographics rapidly changed, the result of displacement caused by urban renewal on the Westside.

This aggression culminated in a series of attacks against black families. Between July 16 and August 22, five homes were bombed with Molotov cocktails and homemade explosives. Journalist Springer Gibson, who covered much of Chattanooga's civil rights movement during the 1950s and 1960s, reported that "city officials are becoming firmer in support of the theory that the explosions are the work of an organized group for the purpose of terrorizing Negroes. The bombing cases, officials have said, appear to have some connection in each instance with the shortage of Negro housing in the city, resulting in Negroes moving into sections where white persons reside. This shortage has been created by the urban renewal project on the West Side and by the freeway. The Chattanooga Housing Authority has reported several times in recent months that enough safe, sanitary, and decent Negro housing has not been supplied for Negroes."[25] Unable to ignore racial strife in the city, the Chattanooga Board of Education released a statement in December 1960 declaring it had developed a three-tiered desegregation plan that would begin in 1962. In reality, Chattanooga's public schools were not actually fully integrated until 1969, nearly a decade after this proclamation.

Over the next two years, the civil rights movement escalated in Chattanooga and across the South. Local protestors boycotted movie theaters, buses, and commercial businesses. By the time Mayor Ralph Kelley persuaded the City Commission to adopt a resolution declaring Chattanooga an open city (1963) where citizens had full rights and access to all public facilities regardless of race, color or creed, local boosters' claims that Chattanooga was a racially tolerant city had crumbled down around them.

Conclusion: Stepping Back from the Archives

Throughout Chattanooga's modern history, local boosters have co-opted important wins from within the African American community in order to argue that the city was progressive and racially tolerant. This chapter has shown that this liberal rhetoric often conceals highly conservative policies and practices enacted precisely to control and limit the movement of black bodies in physical and social space. Attempts from individuals and groups to dismantle the local Jim Crow structure and promote racial equity have systematically been met with reservation and bureaucratic stalling from elected officials, hostility from white employers and neighbors, and fear on the part African American elders who had lived through even more violent times than current generations knew firsthand.

These stories can be captured at length outside of the local archives, as well. Interviews with more than forty local placemakers interviewed for this research project captured diverse personal accounts of race and racism in Chattanooga. One participant interviewed was civil rights activist and local council member Moses Freeman, one of the original lunch counter protestors. As a child, Freeman had visited the City Commission with a group of white children to request permission to play baseball together. To quote his memory at length:

> I [cannot] tell you what was going on in the white community, except that in my job as a newspaper boy, I ended up working with all white newspaper boys. I was the only black boy who worked with these white kids. The difference was that, even though I lived in the projects, I felt that I was better off than most of them. They came from *very poor* homes, and they came there to support themselves and their homes, to buy their shoes and clothes—and most of them were dropping out of school. They lived in parts of the Westside but were more toward the river—down on Chestnut Street and Pine Street and over by the university—those were white communities. We had some interminglement. As kids, we played sports, and naturally our neighborhood wanted to play their neighborhoods, and we were able to do that as kids and met some lifelong friends in that environment.

What we did with playing competitive sports was frowned upon by the general population. In a lot of instances, we were forced not to do so. I was part of a group of whites and blacks who went to City Hall to *get permission* to play with each other. We were naïve, I guess, at that time. Of course, the Commissioner told us that *could not happen*. And so, you know, it didn't happen. We were afraid of the police and the enforcement mechanism. There were a lot of mean white people who said mean things to us as kids, so we stayed and shied away from any environment that would put us in confrontation with them. But we maintained some of our friendships through the years.

There were a few of the boys who sold newspapers who I went on to study with, and that's when I first realized that we had different textbooks. They had newer textbooks and we had the older books that came from those same schools. But we competed with each other academically and with studying, with learning the states and geography and history; who could speak the best English language and stuff. A couple of them went on to become teachers, and I became a teacher; so we met as teachers and that sort of thing. Some of the kids we would meet, even growing up downtown, we would have to ignore each other as if we didn't know [one another], because if they let on to their parents particularly, that would be the end of that. They'd get in serious trouble. And if we let our parents know that we had white friends, our parents would become so frightful and afraid. And so they'd discourage the mingling out of fear, more so than out of hatred, which was prevalent in the white section at that time.[26]

Freeman's passage is illuminating for several reasons. First, he cites a "natural" desire to interact and compete with other children, a narrative that fits into a historical legacy of interracial mutuality despite and *in spite of* de facto and de jure forces working to keep whites and blacks apart.

Moreover, it was through these unsanctioned social interactions that Freeman's own sense of racial inequality formed. Given the fragility of the possessive investment in whiteness in Chattanooga, it is unsurprising that many whites living in the city would have felt personal stakes in maintaining a segregated spatial order: allowing youth to interact would have given them opportunities to compare notes about the varying qualities of life (or, in the case of the passage above, qualities of public education) in their communities.[27] As with Freeman comparing his textbooks with those of his fellow newsboys, personal observations of inequality often produced an acute sense of inequity and injustice, and inspired many people to become involved with the civil rights demonstrations ramping up across the Southeast during the early 1960s.

Coming of age in the Jim Crow South required that black residents learned to obey a "second set of rules" for public and private conduct that were both racialized and gendered. Instructed by their elders to act demure, accommodating, and to never talk back to white people, young African Americans living in Jim Crow-era Chattanooga, and women in particular, became targets for all sorts of race-based emotional, physical, and sexual violence. Often this harassment would occur in the workplace, with some of the most egregious violations happening in private homes.[28]

Lincoln Park Neighborhood Council activist Vannice Hughley described how her father protected the women in her family from potential exploitation by forbidding them to work in private homes. She recounted: "My dad wouldn't allow us to work in a private home. As his girls, we weren't allowed to work in a private home. Or baby-sit. He was so mean! We'd be lucky if we had fifty cents, if we got fifty cents or a quarter. Everyone else worked on the weekends and in the summertime. They had money to buy themselves new clothes. And we didn't. I couldn't understand why my dad never wanted us to work in a private home. My mom did; but we didn't. We *couldn't*. . . . He had this little bitty axe, and if anyone ever messed with his girls, well . . . he was always sharpening that axe. We used to laugh at him because of that axe, but now I understand why he never, ever allowed us to work in a private home. Nope! We couldn't do it."[29]

Although the extra income from a private household job would have likely created new economic opportunities for her family, many preferred to live with less money and, in doing so, gain greater physical safety and security against local violence. The next chapter explores the abundant social, cultural, and political life of these protected subaltern spaces, tracing how multidiasporic placemaking and solidarity has always been present to resist and counteract the damages of racist policy making and social discrimination in the city.

CHAPTER FOUR

Defying Racist Stereotypes

The Big Nine and Lincoln Park as
Sites of Diasporic Cosmopolitanism

The 1858 opening of the Union Passenger Station at the intersection of Ninth and Broad Streets had a profound impact on the development of black neighborhoods and commercial districts across downtown Chattanooga. Nowhere was this change more evident than along "the Big Nine," a section of East Ninth Street that evolved into one of the South's premier Blues and black entrepreneurship meccas during the nineteenth and twentieth centuries. In addition to hosting the city's passenger depot, Ninth Street was a thoroughfare connecting the eastern and western districts of downtown.

As discussed in previous chapters, Hamilton County's African American population surged following the American Civil War, rising from 1,611 in 1860 to 19,508 in 1900, with the vast majority of blacks settling in neighborhoods within the inner urban core. Moses Freeman described this phenomenon during an interview for this project, recalling his sense, as a young child, that Chattanooga was a city full of economic, social, and cultural opportunities for African Americans despite the pervasiveness of racial discrimination and segregation: "Chattanooga . . . was a way station. During the migrant years of people going off from the rural areas of Mississippi and Alabama and Georgia, going north they came through Chattanooga, which was at the crossroads for travel. As a result, a lot of people got to Chattanooga and decided that this was a place to be, and stayed here; they settled here. So you had two factors of people living in Chattanooga: you had people who lived here all their lives, who were born and raised here; and then you had the people who came through Chattanooga and found it as a destination. As such, it was just a great mixture of people with different experiences and so forth."[1]

The vast majority of African American laborers and their families settled close to industrial jobs, many of which were located near the western terminus of Ninth Street on the west side.[2] Parham's *First Annual Directory of Chattanooga* (1871) lists African American laborers employed at and living on the grounds of a variety of heavy manufacturing facilities, including

Vulcan Iron Works and the steel rolling mill on the Westside. By the late 1860s, several new African American and multiracial neighborhoods had begun to evolve in the areas to the east of the Union Terminal Station.

Twenty years later, East Ninth Street—and the eight-block-long segment between Houston and Magnolia Streets in particular—was flourishing. Sanborn Insurance maps published in 1889 reveal the following commercial and civic uses located on the blocks along the strip: the Howard Colored Academy, the African Congregational Church, a Sunday school, eleven grocery stores, fifteen lunch shops, four boardinghouses, five cobblers, four barbers, three salvage yards, two feed stores, two tin shops, a drugstore, a wood and coal yard, an undertaker, two offices, a harness shop, a second-hand store, two carpenters, a liquor storage facility, a cigar store, a meat shop, a "Chinese laundry," and a general store.[3]

By 1917, the East Ninth Street corridor had transformed further into an entertainment and cultural center: the street contained the Volunteer State Life Insurance headquarters, three "moving picture" houses, five pool halls, a theater, a lodge hall, a bicycle shop, more than 140 small shops and services, an ice cream factory, coal yards, a stock yard, a meat processing plant, a bakery, and several churches. Thirty years later, with Prohibition long overturned, the commercial and civic mix had expanded to include two hotels—including the fifty-room Martin Hotel that, for a period, was the largest full-service hotel owned by and operated for African Americans in the South. The district was home to the Liberty Theatre, eighty-five small shops, twenty-three restaurants, four filling stations, several beer and liquor warehouses, and more than a dozen additional skilled services, goods warehouses, and manufacturing industries.[4] By 1957, East Ninth Street had 163 registered businesses. Zion College, an institution dedicated to higher education for African Americans, and Walden Hospital, the city's first African American-owned and -operated hospital, were also established in the neighborhood.

African American-Jewish Placemaking on the Big Nine

While East Ninth Street/the Big Nine has long been associated with African American culture and commerce, a lesser known and acknowledged history is that of the complex, multiracial community building and development that occurred on the street and in the surrounding neighborhoods, beginning in the late nineteenth century.

The Big Nine neighborhood was also an important site of diasporic placemaking for a sizable and ethnically diverse Jewish merchant community, as well as a small Chinese population living in the city at the end of the nineteenth century. Several social historians have studied the significance of Jewish merchants and entrepreneurs to the Southern economy since before the Civil War, when they began migrating beyond the eastern port cities to pedal goods and services in more rural areas across the southeastern and western frontiers.[5] During these travels, the merchants certainly would have interacted with and bartered goods and services with African Americans, and some social historians argue that these interactions made Jewish merchants more willing to establish permanent businesses in predominantly black urban neighborhoods in the decades following the war.

While a portion of Chattanooga's late nineteenth-century Jewish population was likely made up of native U.S. citizens who had moved from other parts of the country in the years surrounding the war, massive influxes of eastern European Jewish immigrants into the United States between 1881 and 1924 likely accounts for most of the population growth. Prior to the Civil War, Hamilton County had a negligible foreign-born population, totaling twenty-nine individuals in 1850. By 1860, this population had grown to 331 individuals, or 2.8 percent of the county's total population.

The 1870 Decennial Census was the first survey where detailed origin of birth data was collected, and in Hamilton County these numbers reveal that, although the majority of immigrants living in the county ($N=582$) were from Canada and western Europe, there were growing Germanic ($N=143$ or 24.6 percent) and eastern European populations migrating to the county as well. Over the next several decades, the eastern European and Russian immigrant communities in Hamilton County continued to grow: the German-born population alone nearly tripled in the ten-year period between 1880 and 1890, while the Russian-born population increased from zero in 1880 to 436 in 1910.[6]

The *Chattanooga City Directory* published in 1890 provides further insight into Jewish–African American relations along the Big Nine at the dawn of the twentieth century: interspersed alongside black-owned barbershops and grocery stores were Jewish loan companies, cobblers, jewelers, clothiers, tailors, photographers, and dry goods merchants. The same directory also reveals two Chinese-owned businesses on the street, including Sam Wah's laundry service, which cohabited a commercial building on East Ninth Street with J. G. Higgins, an African American barber.[7]

By 1930, the eastern European immigrant populations in Hamilton County represented nearly a dozen countries, including Russia, Germany, Hungary, Poland, Czechoslovakia, Lithuania, Greece, and Austria. While part of this growth can be attributed to the pro-immigration agendas adopted by the Chattanooga Chamber of Commerce that were intended to dilute the political and economic power of African Americans during the Great Migration, the migration trends must also be put into their global historical context. Though considered "white" by census takers, many of the eastern Europeans and Russians who migrated to the United States between 1881 and 1924 were ethnic Jews fleeing their home countries to avoid religious and cultural persecution in the wake of the Russian imperial expansion.

Scholars who study historic Jewish-black relations debate whether this commingling was the result of shared diasporic experiences, or one of opportunism and ambivalence. In the context of downtown Chattanooga, black-Jewish relations were likely not a case of either-or, but both-and. In the predominantly black sections of town—especially East Ninth Street—small business owners of both races worked and, to a lesser extent, lived side by side as early as the Reconstruction period.[8] But, in the white-owned and -controlled Central Business District along Market Street, African American civil rights demonstrators were met with ambivalence if not outright resistance from the Jewish merchants who owned the large department stores where the sit-ins were staged (for a discussion of the Chattanooga sit-ins, see chapter 3).

The complexity of multidiasporic placemaking along the Big Nine was further complicated by the presence of more radical social actors who sought to build an equitable society outside of the capitalist marketplace. As early as 1876, members of the Socialist Labor Party of America (SLPA) organized industrial workers across downtown Chattanooga. The influx of Jewish radicals ramped up in the months following the stock market crash of October 1929. Earlier that year, several members of the Communist Party of the United States of America's (CPUSA) National Textile Workers Union had moved to the region to stage a massive labor strike at the Loray Textile Mill in nearby Gastonia, North Carolina.

Sixteen organizers with the union were arrested and charged with murder and conspiracy after a policeman was shot and killed during a camp raid on the night of June 7, 1929; the three women (Amy Schecter, Sophie Melvin, and Vera Bush) faced long prison sentences, while the men faced execution by electric chair. In response to the arrests, the CPUSA began a major campaign to free Loray Mill organizers, and following national protests against "Gastonia-style justice," most of the defendants were exonerated and allowed to resume their work.[9]

Less than four months after the Loray Mill strike, the stock market plummeted. Realizing that the crash presented a political opportunity, CPUSA organizers decided to leverage public discontent against big capital in order to expand the party's base. With its expansive and diverse manufacturing base, rapidly growing pool of nonunionized labor, and regional proximity to Birmingham, Atlanta, and Knoxville, Chattanooga quickly became the center for the CPUSA's southern organizing efforts.

According to Chattanoogan historian Chuck Hamilton, "The CPUSA's first inroad into the city of Chattanooga came in 1930 via the Trade Union Unity League (TUUL). The TUUL was the CPUSA's arm for organizing labor at the time, setting up parallel organizations to and within existing trade unions as well as organizing the unorganized. Its headquarters was at 2207 South Broad Street. . . . The local was staffed by Amy Shechter, Fred Totheroe, Red Hendricks, and an 'unnamed Negro.'"[10] Both Schechter and Hendrix had been defendants in the Loray Mill strike trial, while Totheroe worked as a textile worker in Gastonia. Although the African American organizer was never named, he was described by the press as a "Georgia Negro with a Harlem accent."[11]

Though their office building was several blocks across town, at least one of the organizers (Schechter) resided on East Ninth Street.[12] The TUUL quickly set about building their membership base, which, because of widespread racial antipathy among whites, was comprised almost exclusively of African American laborers. During TUUL's inaugural meeting in Chattanooga on February 1, 1930, Schechter appealed to workers on both sides of the color line, proclaiming that their common experiences of economic exploitation united them more than their races divided them. "The Trade Union Unity League is an avenging angel," Schechter warned participants during the meeting, "sent to strike down the bosses and heal the wounds of the working man."[13]

Despite their emphasis on racial unity, local racial tensions and white laborers' resentments toward African Americans threatened to divide and conquer TUUL's membership base. Not only were white laborers unwilling to place themselves in solidarity with blacks, whom they viewed as inferior to themselves, but the workers' solidarity ideal was also rejected by prominent black residents in town who (at least publicly) professed racial "harmony" above racial equity and justice. Following the TUUL meeting,

D. C. Harper, a well-known African American citizen, made the following statement in an interview with the *Chattanooga Times*: "The colored people are against the movement made by the communists in this city. It can do nothing more than stir up strife among the whites and blacks. We want harmony and we are doing everything we can to get it. I know that the better classes of the whites are doing the same thing. Of course, we are not asking for social equality, but we do want, more than anything else, to get along with the white people and this I believe will help us. I am asking every negro [sic] pastor in Chattanooga to instruct his congregation about these communists. . . . I want these pastors to tell the people that it can bring nothing but ill feeling among the whites and blacks if they join the movement."[14]

Harper called on local black ministers to "condemn" and "flay" the communists. Eager to appease the white power structure, fourteen black pastors spoke out publicly against the "reds" organizing on Broad Street, declaring that interracial organizing antagonized preexisting white aggressions.

In response to this threat, and fueled by their moral opposition to the hundreds of African American lynchings that plagued the Southeast, the CPUSA used their newspaper *The Southern Worker* to launch an antiracist and lynching awareness campaign from their headquarters in Chattanooga.[15] The editorial staff published numerous first-person accounts of the unequal and inhumane working and living conditions experienced by many black laborers and their families, in addition to political cartoons and editorials emphasizing the interconnectedness of white and black class liberation.

As part of their antiracism work, TUUL collaborated with the Southern Provisional Organizational Committee of the American Negro Labor Congress to organize a national Anti-Lynching Conference in Chattanooga. The conference was held on November 9, 1930, at the Odd Fellow's Building on East Ninth Street, and attracted fifty-four delegates from three southern states. African American autonomy and self-determination were central themes during the event; both were understood as hinging on the cooperation of white workers, whose potential solidarity could help create a critical mass to overpower the divide-and-rule strategies waged by politicians and businessmen in the Jim Crow-era industrial South. In an editorial advertising the conference, organizers professed:

No step made by the workers of the South towards liberation from wage-slavery and for the immediate improvement of their conditions can be made unless that step is taken by the white and colored workers together. That is the only method by which lasting gains can be made. It is first necessary to destroy the edifice of "white supremacy" and the wall of segregation built so carefully by the ruling class. That color line is being wiped out by unemployment and starvation which draws no line between races—although it is exactly at this time when the white rulers intensify lynch law persecutions in order to prevent an effective fight against unemployment by the workers. White workers are beginning to understand that lynching is a weapon used against them also, not only in the sense that they see militant white workers killed by boss men, but also in the sense that they understand the underlying purposes of the lynching of Negro workers and farmers, that a rope placed around any worker's neck—be he black or white—is strangulation for all.[16]

Blues on the Big Nine

Despite racism and legal segregation, black Chattanoogan artists, civic leaders, and entrepreneurs created a flourishing economic and cultural base in black sections across the city. These creative community-building activities included music, religious and spiritual practice, civic participation, performance and visual arts, and a range of private and cooperative enterprises, and produced a sense of freedom and opportunity that in some ways transcended—or at least distracted from—the physical confines of spatial segregation during the Jim Crow era.

At the center of African American cultural production during this period was a burgeoning popular musical form known colloquially as *the Blues*. Local Chattanoogan and Blues social historian Clark White described turn-of-the-twentieth-century Chattanooga as a city in rapid flux, a place where Mississippi Delta and Southern Appalachian cultural, economic, and social traditions converged, overlapped, adapted, improvised, and reconfigured:

[Blues] was the music of the black rural peasant slowly becoming a new industrial working class. They came from land defined by the soil to land covered with concrete. They no longer had to labor as plantation hands—they now found employment as industrial workers in the emerging foundry industry of the city. The music of these proletarians was the blues. It was rooted in and defined by the laws of black folklore, which included songs, rhymes, stories, sayings, jokes, and sermons that reflected an African American point of view. The blues is not exclusively and primarily a "sad" music as it is so often represented. However, this essentially existentialist worldview encompasses feelings that include affirmation, lamentation, celebration, contemplation, irony, wit, and ambivalence. Blacks in Chattanooga had a lot to sing the blues about.[17]

With its numerous restaurants, theaters, dance halls, and other creative community spaces, East Ninth Street quickly evolved into a center for Southern Blues culture. But while the image of Bessie Smith street performing is the most popular icon of Chattanooga's Blues history, Clyde Woods (1998) argued that the Blues as well as other uniquely diasporic forms of cultural expression go well beyond their popular definitions as black musical genres (for more information, see Appendix A).

Randolph Miller, the former slave turned journalist, newspaper editor, and labor organizer who led the July 1905 streetcar protests discussed in the previous chapter, had his office and printing press in the vicinity of the present-day Bessie Smith Cultural Center at the heart of the Big Nine. Unwilling to endure racist policies in public transportation, Miller not only publicly rejected Jim Crow streetcar laws—he organized an alternative transit system to transport African Americans around the city in dignity and with respect. In Woods's sense, Miller's transportation justice work was a form of the Blues as spatial practice—activities that resisted oppressive white structures and articulated alternative worlds based on the principles of social equity and racial justice.

Black and multiracial placemaking also produced a number of civic, fraternal, and mutual aid organizations; unsurprisingly, many were located on or in the vicinity of the Big Nine. These formal and informal associations provided crucial social services to members of the black community in the absence of economic, political, and technical support from white public and private institutions.

A powerful example of an informal mutual aid association from this period was the Loomis and Hart Manufacturing Company. Located at 719 East Ninth Street, the company employed a multiracial workforce, and these men were known to donate a portion of every paycheck to a fund to support the Steele Home, an orphanage established for the hundreds of African American children orphaned by the Yellow Fever Epidemic of 1878.[18]

The Chattanooga branch of the Supreme Officers of Knights of the Wise Men, a fraternal order associated with the Freemasons, was one of the most prominent cooperative associations to serve Chattanooga's black community at the turn of the twentieth century. Formed in Nashville in 1879, within ten years the Supreme Officers had expanded to 278 lodges across the Southeast; for a time, the Chattanooga lodge had the largest membership in the United States. Headed by J. L. Brown, the Supreme Officers provided fraternal insurance and burial benefits to their members—services that few working-class African Americans could afford. The association was so popular that it nearly bankrupted itself paying out benefits to members following a smallpox epidemic during the winter of 1882–83.

In an advertisement published in the *Biography & Achievements of the Colored Citizens in Chattanooga* (1904), Brown described the organization's commitment to the principles of friendship and mutual aid, defining their work as a form of "disinterested mutual regard" rooted both in the shared experience of economic marginalization and the wisdom of recognizing the fundamental equality of all races:

> In its degrees the necessity of brotherly love is taught, and the importance of the relief of distress, and consoling the afflicted. Some may ask: "Is friendship taught, and what is it?" We would answer: "It is disinterested mutual regard." . . . We fully recognize the fact that we are poor and need no weight upon us, and to make our way successfully through life requires organizations of the masses, without which our future cannot be a bright one. It is only by our good qualities rightly set forth that we are to succeed in the future. First by educating every boy and girl and teaching them from the cradle to the grave honesty, industry, economy of time and means, and the fullest enjoyment of all rights as citizens, and the destruction, death, and burial of the accursed idea that the negro [*sic*] is inferior, simply because he has been in time deprived of life, liberty, and property. Let us all be wise men and women.[19]

Black Cosmopolitanism in Jim Crow Chattanooga

Despite pervasive economic and social inequality between whites and blacks living in the city, many local African Americans today who lived during Chattanooga's Jim Crow period maintain that the tight-knitted-ness and sense of opportunity within the African American community itself made up for the lack of opportunities available to them in the broader white-controlled city and region. Regardless of socioeconomic status, the Big Nine offered African Americans living in and visiting the city a place to create and appreciate art and music; shop, sell, and barter goods and services; participate in black civic and political life; and seek out and build community through churches, social clubs, businesses, and other place-based associations.

For current Chattanooga city councilman and longtime civil rights worker Moses Freeman, who grew up in the College Hill Courts public housing project on the Westside and was a lead organizer of the department store sit-ins of the 1960s, Jim Crow-era Chattanooga was a thoroughly "cosmopolitan" place for African Americans, in large part because of the artistic and cultural opportunities located along the Big Nine and in other black sections of downtown:

> Chattanooga at that time . . . was a cosmopolitan community—both in the white community and the black community. There was lots of entertainment; lots of restaurants and nightclubs—particularly in the [present-day] MLK area—but there were a few in the downtown area, as well. . . . There were a lot of rooftops; a lot of living space above businesses; there were thriving businesses of all types that were there during the day and nightclubs that operated primarily at night. There were a few what we called "juke joints" that operated all day and night long. But, by and large, it was just full of restaurants.
>
> The people who lived above the businesses, all up and down Ninth Street, really were the clients, the primary clients, of the businesses up and down the street. And, of course, we came from all over town to the central area to do business, and so it was *thriving*. Just about anything you could want to do in life could be found there—you know, of any type and variety.[20]

Juke joints and other somewhat underground community spaces were critical sites of diasporic placemaking, wherein African Americans articulated and enacted communities of cultural belonging and material security without fear of hostility or retribution. Avoided by, but not off-limits to whites, these at times underground spaces afforded working-class African Americans reprieve from the interpersonal and structural discrimination that influenced their access to opportunity structures across the burgeoning city.

Although it was predominantly a low-income, renter population, the East Ninth Street area defied negative stereotypes about poor, segregated communities. In 1950, the neighborhood (census tract #15) had 7,184 residents, comprising 3,305 households, and 80.5 percent of residents were black; the remaining 19.5 percent were white. Compared to the urban core as a whole, the Big Nine neighborhood had a lower median household income ($1,246 versus $2,066), lower median school years completed (6.8 versus 8.8), lower median contract rent ($19/month versus $25/month), and a slightly higher unemployment rate (8 percent versus 5.4 percent).

Though in these ways disadvantaged, the East Ninth Street neighborhood was socially tight-knit and economically stable. Of the 1,933 housing units in the district, only 2.4 percent were vacant. More than three quarters of residents had lived in the neighborhood for at least one year, and workers were employed in a diverse range of manufacturing and service-oriented economic sectors.[21]

For Freeman, education and gainful employment were keys to being able to participate fully in the "cosmopolitan" urban social life that Jim Crow-era Chattanooga offered. Oftentimes, children in low-income families like his worked in addition to attending school, in order to contribute to the family's income and economic security, and help build access to some middle-class amenities.

> It was cosmopolitan to the extent that living even—we were poor. My family was poor—we lived in [public housing]—but we never had a sense of being poor, or in poverty, or deprived. You could live whatever life you could afford. I started working, myself, in the third grade, selling newspapers up and down the street, primarily on West Ninth Street. So I was in and out of the businesses selling papers. I got to see the lives that people were living, and I guess you could say it was a pretty picture. I could see what was going on and wanted to live that life myself. And I just enjoyed Chattanooga.
>
> Chattanooga was just a *unique place*. We had [Ku Klux] Klan activity, but it was isolated and infrequent. So it really didn't bother us. In some instances, we ran the Klan off—the adults—and . . . we had guns, too.
>
> So we sort of lived a segregated life and we lived a *good life*, for that matter. During my teenage years, in order to socialize as a teenager, I had to own a tuxedo. I had to have a white dinner jacket for spring and summer, and a black tuxedo for the fall, because we had a lot of events; we were a close-knit community. We *lived* the typical middle-class lifestyle even though we were poor.[22]

Vannice Hughley, a civic leader from East Chattanooga's Lincoln Park neighborhood, was born and raised along the Big Nine. Hughley recalled being a young woman in the 1940s and 1950s, growing up under strict Jim Crow rule. Like Freeman, Hughley grew up working class, but unlike Freeman's impression of cosmopolitanism, she sensed she had somehow been protected from the limitations of her family's socioeconomic status by parents and a community that protected and cared deeply for their families and one another: "I was raised on the corner of University and Ninth Streets. And most of us, if not all of us, were born at home. Black folks didn't trust the hospital. We had doctors who came to our house. And midwives. All of us were born at home. And that was just the norm. Family came; ladies came in and helped; it was so *simple*. . . . We were simple, and it really was a good thing. It was a good thing. You didn't even realize there were rich people and there were white people."[23]

Both Hughley and Freeman acknowledged that, though there were obvious drawbacks to living in a racially segregated city—black students would have to travel far to get to public school, for example, and their schools were always stocked with outdated, secondhand curriculum books from white schools. Despite these inequalities, though, both nostalgically recalled the tight-knitted-ness of the East Ninth Street community. The Big Nine was a place where folks cared for one another; its people worked and played hard, and fought tirelessly to protect younger generations from the racist hostilities they stood to encounter and inherit.

Black Chattanooga's "Collective Backyard"

If the Big Nine was black Chattanooga's adult entertainment and shopping district, Lincoln Park—a public space located a half mile up Central Avenue from the terminus of East Ninth Street—was its "collective backyard." On April 12, 1918, the Chattanooga City Commission announced their plan to construct a public space that would "compare favorably with any colored park in the country." Lincoln Park would be one of only two recreation grounds for African Americans in the state of Tennessee. However, unlike Church's Park and Auditorium in Memphis, Lincoln Park would be the first publicly owned and financed park in the state.[24] The site chosen for the park was a cornfield located adjacent to a large and established black settlement located between Erlanger Hospital and Citico Creek. The city had previously acquired the property to construct a tuberculosis hospital, but later determined that the site had unfavorable conditions for a clinic, and earmarked it for a park instead.[25]

The plan for Lincoln Park was unprecedented in its attention to design details and state-of-the-art recreational amenities. The initial plan featured a children's playground with sandboxes, swings, see-saws, and other playground equipment, a dancing pavilion, a carousel house, a refreshment stand and restrooms, a fountain and lily pond with surrounding gardens, and landscaping throughout. Presumably, the "large negro [sic] community" mentioned in the article went on to become the Lincoln Park neighborhood. Fire insurance maps published in 1901 and 1917 show the presence of two black churches, dozens of residences, and the Steele Orphanage for Colored Children in the immediate vicinity of the proposed park.[26]

Works Progress Administration Era

By the late 1920s, the park had expanded to include baseball fields, a miniature golf course, and an open-air dance pavilion. Articles published during this period reveal that the park had become a regional destination within a decade of its construction. In May 1935, the *Chicago Defender* reported that the James Henry YMCA (located on the Westside of Chattanooga, adjacent to College Hill Courts) used Lincoln Park to hold a week-long interschool sports and civic competition called "Boy's Week." One month later, the *Defender* advertised that renowned African American composer Hershel Banks and his twelve-piece orchestra performed a free concert in the park's open-air pavilion.

Locked in to the north and east by the Southern Railway Company's massive railyard, to the west by Erlanger Hospital, and to the south by Harrison Avenue (now East Third Street), Lincoln Park had a fixed and relatively small geographic area. As the park improved, the surrounding Lincoln Park neighborhood evolved to accommodate the growing black population moving to and visiting the city. By 1929, there were nearly one hundred single-family homes, eighteen duplexes, two large apartment buildings, several shops, and four churches within the small area. Many renters living in the neighborhood were affiliated with the Southern Railway.

The Citico Hotel on Scruggs Street, for example, was constructed as a dormitory for African American men working for the company. Unlike the nearby park, however, the Citico Hotel was not a family-oriented establishment. Characterized by "poker games that . . . could go on for weeks," the Citico, or as it was more commonly called, "the grap" or "the beanery," was, despite these unsavory activities, a critical site for diasporic placemaking and cosmopolitanism. Chattanooga had the largest terminal on the Southern Railway system; railroad laborers from Atlanta, Birmingham, Knoxville, and Cedartown often boarded at the hotel.

Former Southern Railway employee Duane Mintz recalled how important the Citico was for these men from across the Southeast as a place to gather and build community through storytelling: "The main thing I miss most after all those years of labor with the Southern Railway was the camaraderie that existed among the employees I was associated with. . . . My cognizance of the individuals I'm speaking of goes back to the early days of the old Citico Hotel. . . . The long front porch that faced east and afforded us a shady place in the hot afternoons to engage in conversation in regards to the rules, good trips, as well as bad ones, and plain old bull-shooting."[27]

On September 26, 1936, the *Chicago Defender* reported that Works Progress Administration (WPA) district director J. W. Gentry announced he would consider constructing a public pool in Lincoln Park as part of the federal WPA program. Less than one year later, the City Commission voted to approve $36,000 in coupon bonds to fund the city's Department of Parks, Playgrounds, and Utilities. The goal was to use the money to build up to fifteen new play parks around the city. The majority of the funds ($29,000), however, were earmarked for the Lincoln Park pool.[28]

Constructed using the labor of more than one hundred WPA workers, the pool was completed in less than a year's time. When it was finished, it became the first and only Olympic-sized public swimming pool for African Americans in the South. During the groundbreaking ceremony on August 3, 1937, Dr. Spencer J. McCallie, headmaster at Chattanooga's private McCallie School for Boys, called for a "united front" of whites and blacks to help create a more racially equitable city. In McCallie's estimation, the pool's social value went well beyond the temporary jobs that had been generated by its construction: it was a concrete symbol of the city's commitment to the long-term health and well-being of all its citizens, regardless of their race.[29]

An opening ceremony was held in the park on July 1, 1938. It featured guided tours by local Boy Scouts and a performance by the Royal Knights Orchestra. Several members of the citywide interracial committee offered speeches to the more than five thousand, mostly African American spectators in attendance. During his remarks, Reverend L. D. Cartwright, chairman of the Negro Division of the Interracial Committee, urged his fellow citizens and civic leaders not to stop their efforts with the swimming pool.

The black community in Chattanooga, he contended, also needed a library and cultural center. Stressing the interdependence of all citizens and the intersectionality of racialized oppression, Rev. Cartwright proclaimed: "We must have a library for Negroes that will be a cultural center. It has long been the habit and tendency of the South and this community in matters of finance and community improvements to forget the Negro. But this must not be done in the future, for what affects one affects all."[30]

Similar to McCallie, Cartwright saw the ongoing improvement of Lincoln Park as one layer in a multifaceted racial equality agenda, and investments in black public spaces and facilities as a means to make up for two centuries of racist exclusion and neglect. Though not *reparations* in the monetary settlement sense of the term, public investments into state-of-the-art recreation, educational, and cultural facilities in African American sections of town were understood as crucial for leveling the playing fields between white and black communities.

Lincoln Park and the Southern Negro League of Professional Baseball

The demand for expanded facilities was healthy. Two months after the swimming pool opened, Lincoln Park staff hosted a citywide playground pageant featuring youth and nine African American playground workers from recreation department-sponsored summer playgrounds around the city. Later that summer, the city installed floodlights on the baseball field, making Lincoln Park's facilities the only field in the South where black athletes could practice at night and hold nighttime games.

The construction of electrical floodlights profoundly affected the popularity of games at the park. However, even before the installation of the lights, Lincoln Park's facilities were critical to the historical development of African American organized sports. In 1920, just two years after the park opened, the Southern Negro League of professional baseball organized a team in Chattanooga. Although they disbanded after one season (but were reestablished for two seasons in 1926), the Chattanooga Black Lookouts practiced in Lincoln Park for several years preceding the 1930 construction of Engel Stadium.

In the 1940s, Lincoln Park once again became a seat of professional black baseball in the South. Engel Stadium had been built on an East Third Street property, located less than a quarter mile from the playing fields in Lincoln Park. Although the local Southern Negro League team representing

Chattanooga at this time (the Chattanooga Choo-Choo's) were permitted to play their games in the stadium, black players and fans were forced to enter the field through a back entrance and sit in the most undesirable seats of the state-of-the-art facility. The Choo-Choo's were also not permitted to use Engel Stadium for practice games.

For these reasons, the ball fields at Lincoln Park became the preferred venue for African American baseball players and their fans. With bleachers and a lighted field, the black baseball community could enjoy the sport in an environment free from the hostile stares and restrictive policies of white policy makers. Several important players who went on to pave ways for African Americans in national sports made their professional debuts in Lincoln Park. A sixteen-year-old Willie Mays, for example, played his first professional game as a centerfielder for the Chattanooga Choo-Choo's. Although he was underage and could not legally sign a contract, Mays toured extensively with the Choo-Choo's until their manager folded up the team in 1947. Other notable players who frequented Lincoln Park included Satchel Paige and Jackie Robinson.[31]

The 1940s were arguably the park's most popular and thriving period. The Lincoln Park Recreation Center was constructed and opened in late December 1946; it quickly became one of the most heavily used centers in the city. The Center hosted a neighborhood kindergarten school, summer camp, and extensive year-round youth programming.[32] The Howard High School football team played their games in the park, and often the school's famous marching band would march from their school on East Ninth Street to the park along Central Avenue. A 1947 Fourth of July celebration attracted approximately fifteen thousand patrons to the park.

By then, the facilities had been expanded to include several amusement park rides, a roller skating rink, and a miniature zoo area. Lifetime Chattanoogan and Lincoln Park resident Vannice Hughley emphasized the park's significance as a destination for African American families from the city and across the South, recalling:

The park backed up to Wiehl Street. And out there where the nursery is, that was part of the park. It was all part of the park. We had a monkey cage—I don't know how many monkeys we had in there—and a bear cage. Those were the only animals that we had there in the park. But our main draw was that Olympic-sized swimming pool. People came from all over the Southeast to swim in that pool. Every weekend we had buses coming into that park, and it would be *spilling over*. People from out of town, and home people would go. We could go to the park and have a good time when we couldn't go anywhere else. We had picnics in the park every weekend. A lot of black people couldn't have a picnic in the park during the week because we had to work. But on the weekends, it was *it*. It was filled with hometown people and out of town people. They had buses every weekend that would fill up [pointing] that part of the park; they'd go and park over by the Center. Remember when they used to have buses parked over on the other side of the swimming pool?[33]

Conclusion

Asking any native Chattanoogan over the age of fifty about the significance of the Big Nine or Lincoln Park will yield a variation on the same story. To most white residents, these places were the premier commercial and public recreation grounds for black Chattanoogans during the Jim Crow period, and today stand ripe for revitalization. To African Americans who intimately knew these spaces, however, both were, and still are, much more than antiquated Jim Crow-era shopping districts or public spaces. Instead, East MLK Boulevard and Lincoln Park are sites where black and multiracial communities were safely forged, and where cultural diversity and interaction were fostered and protected, in implicit if not outright defiance of legal and socio-spatial marginalization and exclusion.

CHAPTER FIVE

Singing a Big Nine Blues Revolution

As the most heavily industrialized city in the Southeast, Chattanooga suffered dramatically as the city transitioned away from a manufacturing-based economy during the second half of the twentieth century. Chattanooga sustained immense damages following the global economic restructuring of 1973. As international trade barriers were lifted and the world opened itself up to the flows of global capital, economic disinvestment in U.S. urban centers accelerated. This resulted in massive growth of urban unemployment, decreased center city property values, property abandonment, physical neighborhood deterioration, and the exacerbation of racial and socioeconomic polarization.[1]

Unsurprisingly, working-class communities of color were hit hardest by the economic restructuring of this period. Unemployment disproportionately impacted Chattanooga's black communities. In 1970, the unemployment rate in Hamilton County was 2.9 percent. Rates were more or less equally distributed across race (2.6 percent white versus 4.9 percent black) and gender (2.3 percent men versus 3.82 percent women). Ten years later, the countywide unemployment rate had increased to 6.8 percent, with African Americans suffering the greatest employment losses (11.7 percent unemployment versus 5.9 percent among whites).[2]

Although several African American neighborhoods across the urban core suffered even greater physical and economic deterioration than East Ninth Street did, the impacts on the once vibrant commercial and cultural district were also dramatic. The total unemployment rate in the census tract that bounded the Big Nine increased from 2.9 percent to 19.2 percent between 1970 and 1980, with black workers and families enduring virtually all of those losses (rising from 3.1 percent to 17.8 percent). Over the next twenty years, unemployment in the neighborhood steadily increased: by 2000, nearly one-third of black workers were unemployed.

In Chattanooga, inner-city disinvestment and decline were exacerbated by the rampant suburbanization of outlying greenfield areas, as well as the desegregation of housing, which meant that, for the first time, middle-class black households could rent and purchase homes outside of the inner urban core.[3] The East Ninth Street neighborhood's population had peaked in 1950, with 7,184 residents and 1,933 housing units; the majority of the community lived in multifamily dwellings. Over the next ten years, both declined slightly. However, the most dramatic losses occurred between 1960 and 1970, when the neighborhood lost more than half of its population—dropping from 5,934 to 2,612 residents—and more than one-third of its housing stock, losing 625 units.[4] The outward and downward population and economic trends negatively impacted the vitality of East Ninth Street. Some longtime residents theorize that the successful black-owned businesses followed the black middle class to the suburban neighborhoods east of Missionary Ridge, and what remained were the establishments unwilling (or unable) to keep up with the times.[5]

Although many Chattanoogans attribute urban flight during this period to a combination of macroeconomic forces and individual preferences, others interpret the economic decline of the Big Nine as being symptomatic of a systematic neglect of Chattanooga's African American communities by elite political and economic institutions. To this end, the roles of professional planners and elected public officials in coordinating uneven geographic development across the city during the middle twentieth century must also be acknowledged and understood.

In the 1950s, planners involved with the Golden Gateway Urban Renewal Project on the Westside persuaded the City Commission to approve the conversion of East Ninth Street from a two-way street into a one-way outbound street as a way to mitigate traffic congestion between the central business district and eastern suburban neighborhoods. This conversion had the effect of transforming East Ninth Street from a pedestrian-oriented small business district into a car-oriented thoroughfare, unconducive to stopping, parking, or walking. While the reorientation did not ignite economic deterioration along the Big Nine, it did exacerbate and arguably accelerate suburbanization already underway in other districts of the city.[6]

In late 1976, the Chattanooga City Commission proposed to use federal Community Development Block Grant (CDBG) funds to raze the 900 block of Market Street and clear the land for redevelopment. The block was one of the few remaining black business hubs in the post-Golden Gateway Urban Renewal city. Local business owners threatened with displacement pleaded with the city, arguing that the block, which abutted the entrance to East Ninth Street, was a critical center for black commerce and employment.[7]

Business owners suggested the city use the funds to make improvements along East Ninth Street, which had been struggling economically for more than a decade. In response to this pressure, T. D. Hardin, the executive director of the Chattanooga-Hamilton County Regional Planning Commission, stated that the area of East Ninth Street between Market and Central had never been included in any of the proposed downtown redevelopment and revitalization plans, and that this avoidance had been done intentionally as a benevolent gesture to the black business community. "There are no plans for that area," Hardin stated in a public meeting, "and we have shied away from it, because it would not be economically feasible for the businesses in that area to move to other areas and would put many of them out of business."[8]

On April 19, 1980, public attention turned to East Ninth Street after four African American women were ambushed by members of the Ku Klux Klan during an unprovoked drive-by shooting. The shooting sparked three days of civil unrest, where eight policemen were injured and "scores of blacks were arrested for throwing firebombs in housing projects."[9] Although four men were initially arrested, Criminal Court Judge Jo DiRisio later dismissed the charges of assault with intent to commit murder against three of the men. Ultimately, an all-white jury acquitted three, while the ringleader received a reduced punishment involving a $250 fine and a nine-month workhouse sentence.[10]

In response, religious leaders in the African American community convened a meeting with Mayor Charles Rose and issued a list of demands to benefit the city's sixty thousand African American residents. While the list included public safety provisions, such as a ban on Klan cross burnings, leaders also demanded solutions to address structural discrimination and inequality, including "more hiring and job training aimed at . . . black residents, and improved maintenance of recreation facilities at city housing projects." Finally, the group called on the city to rename East Ninth Street "East Martin Luther King Boulevard" to honor King's legacy and his commitments to peace and nonviolence.[11]

Their proposal to rename East Ninth Street was quickly rejected by prominent white developers who felt threatened by the association with black space that the name suggested. For example, T. A. Lupton, a local developer building the Chattanooga Convention Center on a parcel located on West Ninth Street, threatened to pull his project if his address was listed as "Martin Luther King Blvd." The City Commission responded by proposing a name change for only the section of the street located to the east of Market Street—a move that was quickly rejected by the leaders who had brought the proposal to the table.[12]

Outraged by their white neighbors' resistance to renaming the street, black community organizers took matters into their own hands. In May 1981, approximately four hundred African Americans assembled on the street where the women had been shot the previous year. The group marched up the boulevard while singing "We Shall Overcome"; as they moved, they pasted signs reading "Martin Luther King, Jr. Blvd." over the existing street signs along the corridor. Though many demonstrators were filled with frustration and anger, others, including Dr. Virgil Caldwell, saw the event as "a day of joy." In a speech to the crowd, Caldwell commended the "many people [who had] taken it upon themselves to do what we must do to honor Dr. Martin Luther King—what the city fathers chose not to do."[13] Ultimately, the City Commission voted to change the street name only on the east side of the street, despite the community's protests.[14]

A Turning Tide

As will be discussed in the next chapter, the early 1980s marked a turning point for urban planning and redevelopment in Chattanooga. During the winter of 1984, nearly one thousand individuals participated in at least one of the thirty-two sessions held as part of the Vision 2000 process: an initiative established to "determine community priorities relative to the development of and the future of the Chattanooga area."[15] Chattanooga Venture used these input sessions to develop goals and recommendations outlined in a priority workbook.

Rampant neighborhood deterioration was one of the major issues identified by residents. Planners quickly zoomed in on East MLK Boulevard as one of the neighborhoods most in need of attention. Believing that it would catalyze redevelopment along the business corridor, Venture leaders decided that a museum dedicated to "Empress of the Blues" Bessie Smith should be one of the initiative's five "wish list" priority projects. Venture also solicited funds from the Lyndhurst Foundation to sponsor a blues festival on the street as part of the annual Riverbend music festival.

Community-based developers were already rehabilitating housing in the neighborhood at this time. The Inner City Development Corporation formed in 1984 with the goal of stopping the outflow of people and resources from East MLK Boulevard. Over the course of two years, the group rehabilitated seven houses in the MLK neighborhood. Seeing their success, local lenders began to finance their efforts, which had previously been considered too risky to back financially.[16]

While many residents lauded Chattanooga Neighborhood Enterprise (CNE) and other community developers' efforts in the MLK neighborhood, others were skeptical of their long-term impacts on housing affordability in the neighborhood and across the city. An editorial published in the *Chattanooga Times* captured this tension, arguing that any neighborhood revitalization ought to directly benefit those long-term, working-class residents who had endured the hard times: "A hearing on whether the entire M. L. King area should be designated as a redevelopment area . . . may be a good idea, as long as the low-income families now living in M. L. King don't get shunted out of the center city the way the people living in what is now Golden Gateway did a generation ago. If we can keep the decent, struggling M. L. King–area families who refused to be driven out of their homes by the petty thieves and drug pushers, the prostitutes and pickpockets— and draw in dozens or even hundreds of equally committed new inner-city residents—we'll have taken an enormous and long-overdue step toward improving the changes of restoring the M. L. King area itself, and that can do nothing but help the neighboring center city."[17] Ultimately, the neighborhood was designated as a target area, and CNE began identifying properties for rehabilitation and redevelopment. Between 1980 and 1990, the neighborhood lost approximately half of its single-family homes and duplexes. Ten years later, those numbers were once again cut in half: only 115 single-family homes, 62 duplexes, and a fraction of the three-plus multifamily structures remained.

As more units were rehabbed and the neighborhood's worst eyesores targeted for demolition, middle-class residents and university students seeking off-campus housing began to view East MLK as a potential destination. The evidence of this shifting perception is found in some of the physical and demographic changes underway across the neighborhood during this time. It is clear that the majority of housing units targeted for demolition were rental units: the number of renting households living in the neighborhood, for example, decreased by -60.8 percent between 1980 and 2000. The number of owner-occupied units also diminished, though African American homeowners, in particular, held their ground during this period of transition.[18]

Mounting Development Pressures

One of the most celebrated moments for urban planning enthusiasts in Chattanooga came in 2001, when Hamilton County adopted an urban growth boundary. Supported by both urban revivalists and environmental conservationists, the measure incentivized urban infill development while discouraging suburban sprawl and greenfield development. For many local planners and community developers, the growth boundary was considered a boon because it promised to accelerate downtown revitalization. But, for local leaders concerned about economic and social justice issues, the policy was contentious.

Chattanooga Rainbow Coalition chapter president Johnny Holloway expressed deep concern that African Americans would fail to benefit from the economic revitalization associated with neighborhood infill development. Although some merchants with small businesses on East MLK Boulevard. supported the boundary on the grounds that neighborhood gentrification meant the potential for more commercial activity, Holloway feared too much investment too quickly would price out the longtime residents who had "remained there through the lean years."[19]

Holloway's concern stemmed from learning about the gentrification and displacement patterns that emerged after Portland, Oregon adopted its growth boundary. Although his statement reflected a growing awareness of the negative externalities associated with urban revitalization, his opinion was a minority voice in the city at that time. Many local stakeholder groups, including homeowners, small business owners, local developers, municipal and county staff, and university officials, hailed the boundary as a foolproof strategy for wrangling investment capital into the city's historically African American neighborhood.

In May 2003, Chattanooga Neighborhood Enterprises and the Lyndhurst Foundation announced the MLK Tomorrow Initiative. This $28 million public-private investment program committed funds for the renovation and construction of more than one hundred market rate homes in the "classic, cool, and close to downtown" MLK neighborhood over a two-year period.

Organizers hoped to capitalize on the revival already taking root in the neighborhood vis-à-vis the University of Tennessee–Chattanooga's Community Outreach Partnership. Launched in 2000, the partnership revolved around the university's goal to develop more than 1,600 beds of student housing and promote faculty and staff homeownership in the neighborhood by 2005. "People want to live downtown," The president of CNE, Gerald Konohia, announced during the public kick-off event: "Providing incentives for them to buy and renovate homes will help bring them into the neighborhood, therefore raising property values and spurring commercial development." During the same event, a staff person with the Lyndhurst

Foundation promised that the MLK area "is well on its way to being a place where people who have all of the choices would want to come and live. And why not? It is a great place, great houses, wonderful people, and strong schools."[20]

The testimonies of people who took advantage of the early housing incentive programs sponsored by CNE, Lyndhurst, and University of Tennessee–Chattanooga (UTC) are instructive. One UTC employee, a white mother of two children who had recently moved into the neighborhood, was asked whether she and her family had been reluctant to relocate to the historically African American neighborhood given its history and reputation. The woman responded, "We were absolutely not hesitant. I haven't seen any of the crime. I don't know any of the history, but I know it's a nice area now."[21]

Although homebuyer incentive programs clearly benefitted already middle-class people moving into the area, *affordability*, as is always the case, was a highly relative term. The existence of homebuyer incentive programs did not mean that everyone who wanted to buy a house could access them. The focus of the MLK Tomorrow Initiative, according to Donna Williams, a consultant working with the Lyndhurst Foundation at the time, was to develop the new and rehabbed housing units and sell them at market rates. When pressed about the inclusion of below market rate units, the Williams replied that, with all of the additional incentives available to homebuyers, most of the new housing would still be "affordable" to working families.[22]

A longtime administrative staff member at UTC painted a different picture of housing affordability in the revitalizing neighborhood. When she had attempted to access the incentive package and purchase one of the MLK Initiative's new homes herself, she was denied on the basis of her income. "I would hate to see a program like this be lost on workers," the UTC employee told the *Times Free Press*. But the trend seemed inevitable: even with long-term, steady employment, a commitment to the neighborhood, and access to the UTC staff homebuyer subsidy, moderate-income households were already being priced out of what had once been a highly affordable, centrally located community.[23]

Reviving the Commercial Corridor

While the MLK Initiative focused primarily on housing development in the residential neighborhood between East MLK Boulevard and the university, others in the community development field focused on the commercial corridor itself. By the early 1980s, many formerly thriving businesses on the street had relocated or shuttered their doors. Though the Bessie Smith Strut blues festival began in 1985 with the goal of reigniting the social and economic vitality of the corridor, the Strut was an annual event. And while planning for the Bessie Smith Hall and Chattanooga African American Museum also began around this time, it would be another twelve years before the project would be completed and the facility would open. In a 2004 article titled "MLK Ripe for Development," a local real estate professional argued that there was great potential for local African Americans to share in the economic benefits of revitalization along the Big Nine, citing that "70 percent of E. MLK properties [were] owned by African Americans." However, one local property owner interviewed for the article was skeptical: "If we don't become involved, every black person is going to lose his property."[24]

A Twenty-First-Century-Engaged University?

In 2010, the University of Tennessee–Chattanooga convened their Master Plan Steering Committee and hired a team of planners and architects led by consultants from the internationally acclaimed firm Perkins+Will to guide an update to its 2000 Master Plan. Over the next eighteen months, these professionals organized a process related to "[guiding] the critical aspects of campus growth" into the surrounding neighborhoods, including parts of the former commercial district of East MLK Boulevard.[25]

The document stated that the "hallmark of the planning process has been its highly participatory and consensus-building activities," and it pointed to the university's designation by the Carnegie Foundation as an institution holding Community Engagement Classification as one of the primary factors motivating the update of its long-term vision and strategy. The document defined the benefits of university-community engagement as: "UTC's engagement with the surrounding Chattanooga community promotes the partnership of knowledge and resources with the public and private sectors, with a goal to enrich scholarship, research, and creative activity; enhance curriculum, teaching, and learning; prepare educated, engaged citizens; strengthen democratic values and civic responsibility; address critical societal issues; and contribute to the public good."[26]

To achieve this vision, the plan outlined ten ambitious development goals to help guide the university's growth over the subsequent fifteen years.

These strategic goals ranged from improving technology and research infrastructure to reducing ecological footprints and improving university-wide sustainability practices. Unsurprisingly, facilities expansion and university-owned student housing were central features of the plan.

The *2012 Master Plan* was released subsequent to the university's *Comprehensive Housing Master Plan* (2011)—a several-hundred-page document produced by the consulting firm Brailsford & Dunlavey, based on data collected during "focus groups, administrative interviews, a competitive context analysis, an off-campus housing market analysis, a student survey, and a detailed analysis of the Plan's financial feasibility." Consultants projected that UTC's full-time student population would increase by approximately 2.4 percent per year, reaching 13,542 students by 2020–2021. They estimated that total enrollment would grow to fifteen thousand students in the medium-term, and as many as eighteen thousand over the long term.[27]

In reality, the university may reach these enrollment goals even sooner than expected: the full-time student population has surpassed the projected headcounts outlined in the *Housing Master Plan* every year. Citing the university's capacity to serve 28 percent of its student population with university-owned housing, the *Housing Master Plan* identified development goals and defined an implementation path to build and maintain a 35 percent on-campus population for full-time students. The plan recommended the addition of 1,800 new student beds, built in approximately 600-bed increments, to locations adjacent to campus and existing student housing neighborhoods over the next several decades. In the spirit of promoting a vibrant and cosmopolitan urban university, the *2012 Master Plan* also called for increased mixed-use development and "living-learning spaces to create vibrant, 24/7 residential communities," and identified a Master Plan land acquisition and improvement target area along with several "Key Acquisition/Partnership Sites" to steer expansion over the next fifteen years.[28]

The university's Master Plan "Development Opportunities Boundary" extended for several blocks in every direction beyond the existing 123-acre campus footprint. The area included all of the East Ninth Street/MLK Boulevard corridor and adjacent neighborhood, along with Engel Stadium, Fort Wood, and several blocks of commercial and industrial properties extending as far south as East Eleventh Street. It also included a 272-acre historic factory and brownfield property close to the riverfront, known as the Enterprise South site.

Texts and Subtexts of University Expansion

The university's proposed southward expansion is arguably more significant than its growth in other directions, because the East MLK Boulevard corridor has historically served as a physical and psychological marker between the so-called desirable and safe parts of the neighborhood and those areas considered undesirable or dangerous. University students, for example, recall being instructed during their freshman orientations not to walk along or to the south of the corridor.[29] In part because of this institutional neglect, but also because of its proximity to the Chattanooga Community Kitchen, a multiservice homeless outreach ministry, the blocks between MLK Boulevard and East Eleventh Street have remained a popular area for homeless encampments.

The Master Plan's "Development Opportunities Boundary" area clearly encompasses the corridor and its adjacent streets, referring to it as the "MLK Redevelopment Corridor" in maps and planning discussions, and outlining several major campus expansion projects along the street as part of Phase III of the university's Master Plan. The university's long-range development plans for the corridor include three major student housing complexes (totaling 332 beds), student services buildings, a fuel cell research facility, two major "academic research expansion zones," and open space and streetscape improvements.[30]

The plan summarized the university's rationale for expanding to East MLK Boulevard in terms of the mutual stakes and benefits that arise from being a community-engaged, urban university: "Much like the medical center, the MLK corridor represents an opportunity for UTC for future development to become more integrated with the neighborhood and support common goals for the future. Planning activities have been established along the corridor and future UTC housing along MLK Boulevard would be consistent with this vision with retail or office-type uses on the first floor."[31]

The plan goes on to describe the intersection of East MLK Boulevard and Douglas Street as a future "gateway" to the university, stating that "campus gateways and landmarks are primary access points to the University and should create an inviting appearance and begin to define the campus experience."

Critical Omissions

The University of Tennessee–Chattanooga's southward expansion onto East MLK Boulevard and beyond poses both opportunities for and threats to equitable neighborhood redevelopment in the future. On the one hand, new opportunities for long-term community engagement and mutually beneficial urban redevelopment exist between UTC and its neighbors in the areas of education, public health, workforce development and training, affordable housing, and public space. On the other, as history has demonstrated, an expanded target area suggests new frontiers of gentrification and the future displacement for working-class communities of color from their historic urban core neighborhoods.

These demographic transformations have been underway in the residential neighborhoods surrounding East MLK Street since the mid-1980s. In 1980, 91 percent of the population was African American. By 1990, the black population had dropped to just over three-quarters (76.7 percent) of the total population—a rate that persisted through 2000. However, the 2010 Census reveals dramatic changes underway: for the first time in the neighborhood's history, the white population outnumbered black residents. While population growth across all racial groups occurred during this ten-year period, white residents accounted for the majority of this growth, rising from 145 (17.5 percent of total population) to 1,899 residents (62.1 percent).[32]

While some local leaders maintain that the university's expansion southward will be the neighborhood's saving grace, on closer scrutiny, an analysis of the policy and planning recommendations outlined in the 2012 *Master Plan* reveal a failure to think through the broader social and political implications of the university's proposed campus expansion into several historically significant and still racially and socioeconomically diverse neighborhoods. To be sure, university officials have adopted the language of urban institutional embeddedness and community-university engagement. Yet, the recommendations outlined in the *Plan* are firmly rooted in the university's own expansion and redevelopment interests, and thus fail to consider how UTC fits into a rapidly gentrifying urban core as both a public institution of higher education and a socially responsible neighbor.

For example, the 2012 *Master Plan* does not consider the long-term affordability impacts of student- and faculty-driven gentrification on non-university-affiliated community members living in nearby neighborhoods. Nor does it fully evaluate the prospects for black entrepreneurship and cultural development along the historic Big Nine corridor. In the 2012 *Master Plan*, consultants argue that, "given the urban context of the campus, open space should be treated as a sacred space."[33] But, by failing to plan for the equitable redevelopment of the district, the university's expansion threatens to squander the potential of honoring and preserving an historic neighborhood with one of the most vibrant legacies of multiracial diasporic placemaking in the American South.

Placemaking as Creative Resistance against Displacement

There are several community-based arts and cultural organizations celebrating African American history and culture along the Big Nine, actively contesting physical and cultural displacement underway within the neighborhood and beyond. The most well-known institution working to preserve the historical integrity of the MLK Boulevard district is the Bessie Smith Cultural Center. The Cultural Center, which houses the Chattanooga African American Museum, is leading the charge to educate locals and visitors about the long histories of black community building and development in Chattanooga.

Carmen Davis, the director of educational programming at the Cultural Center, described her organization's commitment to realizing its original goal of catalyzing economic and cultural revitalization for the local black community: "We consider ourselves the 'cornerstone' of M. L. King Street—the main vein or artery of M. L. King. So, we really want to promote this street as growing, with a lot of things happening. With the Bessie Smith Heritage Festival, which is an indoor-outdoor festival, we get to highlight the businesses all up and down the street and draw attention to the area. This is one of our major goals: to draw people back onto M. L. King. It's our biggest program and draws the most people for us."[34]

In 2012, the Bessie Smith Cultural Center assumed management over the nearly three-decades-running Bessie Smith Strut. Earlier in the year, then mayor Ron Littlefield suggested discontinuing the wildly popular blues festival because of concerns about public safety and potential financial losses. The local community responded en masse, taking over a City Council meeting and lambasting the mayor for threatening to do away with the "only time [each year] when whites and blacks truly mingle in the heavily segregated city."[35]

In a last-minute attempt to save the Strut, the Bessie Smith Cultural Center offered to oversee management responsibilities from the Friends of the Festival, a nonprofit charged with planning Riverbend. Davis described the Cultural Center's motivations for taking on such a behemoth of a task, arguing that many of the changes in security and admission that resulted were imposed from the top down:

We were kind of thrown into the round to take on the [Bessie Smith] Strut, and, of course, that *really* highlights the entire street. In a very short amount of time, we were able to pull it off—with major changes, which were kind of forced upon us. [The Strut] is an institution in this city. People love it. It [was] the one free night of Riverbend. And we had to make some changes which I really don't think were fair, because if you look at the Strut's twenty-something-year history, there were maybe one or two incidents—and neither of them actually happened on Strut property. So I think there was sort of an unfair . . . . "whatever" . . . attached to the Strut, which really wasn't there, and created this atmosphere that *luckily* the public didn't fall for. The public was like, "I've *never* had any issues, and I've gone for ten, twelve, fifteen, *twenty* years!"

We had to bump up all the security, and it was just—to me—a bunch of unnecessary changes had to be made to accommodate our administration. . . . Last year was the first year we had to charge an admission because we had to pay to block everything off; for fencing and additional security and all these things that normally . . . I mean, the Strut incurs costs, which are handled by Friends of the Festival normally. But since it was sort of thrown in our lap, we had all these extra costs that we had to take care of, and that the City was not willing to give us a break on. So to handle that, we had to charge admission in order to pass some of those costs on.[36]

While the Cultural Center has catalyzed redevelopment along the East MLK corridor through a place-based, historically and culturally rooted framework, the organization increasingly brings its message to residents living in other sections of the city. For Davis, this transition to traveling programming seems inevitable: as more black residents are priced out of the urban core, the Cultural Center and Museum must devise new ways to reach their audiences. Davis described a number of the Museum's current youth engagement programs, illustrating how they use interactive, creative workshops to help young Chattanoogans connect with the gravity and depth of their local histories.

Art Fun Factory is basically visual and performing art lessons, but the kicker is that this year we took it up a notch and connected an historical component to it. So they took African Drumming, but then their African Drumming teacher also played rhythms where the kids recognized that, "Oh, this is the base of a country rhythm, or the base of a rap rhythm; or the base of an R & B rhythm." Then we meshed them together, and they got to see—we had an exhibit at the time that covered African American music—so they got to tour the exhibit. So it's kind of these multiple connections that were made through this one program.

So those are the types of things that we do. We have an exhibit coming up that's called "We Shall Not Be Moved," which is about the civil rights movement in Tennessee, and I have a fifth grade class coming because they're studying the civil rights movement now. So *I love* to make those connections, because when they see the artifacts— for example, if they're studying slavery, I like to take the shackles out and let them hold it; to feel the weight and *understand the weight* and how far these people had to walk *with that weight*. I think that hands-on experience gives them a better understanding of history.[37]

Another organization doing important place-making work in the East MLK neighborhood is Mark Making, a volunteer-based public arts organization dedicated to using art to advance "individual empowerment, beautification of visual landscapes, visual art education, and teaching opportunities."[38] Over the past eight years, Mark Making has spearheaded nine major public art projects in the neighborhood: "We Speak" (2009–2010), "I Have a Dream" (2011), "We Inspire" (2012), "Eight on the Big Nine" (2012), "Principle Colors" (2012), the "M. L. King Street Art" wheat-pasting project (2012), "Big Nine Legends" (2012), "We Shall Not Be Moved" (2013), and "A Dream Built on Faith" (2013).

Mark Making's projects often use creative placemaking to connect historic and contemporary struggles for community empowerment and social justice in the city. The *Big Nine Legends* mural on the side of the Live and Let Live Barbershop—East Ninth Street/MLK Boulevard's longest operating business—was their first project to hone in on the transformative power of art and creative expression to produce complex narratives that connected history and memory to place.

[*Big Nine Legends*] really struck a lot of chords in people's hearts— [especially] in black peoples' hearts. We do these things and we don't know where that energy goes or what it means to other people. We're very careful when we make it. We're not black—but we sat down with the right people and said "OK, you need to make this decision because we're not black and not from here, so you need to make this decision for your neighborhood. We are here to serve and not tell you . . . [right from wrong]." So we got a lot of help. What it means on the back end—and I forget sometimes—we choose these musicians and we're learning all about these musicians and I'm *feeling all this*, but then when you're doing the work, you're not paying attention to all of that. You're thinking, "That texture won't work there; chalk off that edge and stick it over there." *You're doing the work*. So then it's all said and done and the phone rings and this lady says, "I'm Johnny Smith's daughter! I'm so honored that you chose to feature *my father on your wall*."

I'm like, *so shocked*. It's like oh, my God! But then I'm like, well, *yeah*! If I were her I'd be feeling the same way. But it just surprises me that it actually gets that far. Because we do what we do and we do everything the right way, it's just—you do it because it's the right thing to do, not because anybody else thinks it's the right thing to do. You do it because *you* think it's the right thing to do. You just do your best; you don't know where the cards fly. But when they fly and it comes back and it's a good thing you think, "Oh, I guess I did it decently!" It's so surprising.[39]

Conclusion: Toward a Blues Movement in Downtown Chattanooga

This chapter discussed the ongoing revival of the East Ninth Street/MLK Boulevard corridor and neighborhood in order to further illuminate and contextualize the politics of multidiasporic placemaking in downtown Chattanooga. Institutional actors, especially public officials, foundation officers, nonprofit developers, and university planners, have been involved with the ongoing revitalization of the MLK Boulevard corridor and neighborhood over the past thirty years. These actors stand to miss crucial opportunities for realizing the equitable redevelopment of the district—a loss that is particularly acute given the neighborhood's long history of creative, cooperative black and multiethnic placemaking.

The history of multiracial diasporic placemaking in the East Ninth Street/MLK neighborhood explored in chapter 4 suggested a much more complex urban social environment than most people associate with the segregated South—and Chattanooga in particular. Through everyday acts of community building and creative resistance against exploitation, residents living, working, and playing together in the neighborhood have long understood themselves to be economically, politically, and culturally connected.

Historically as well as today, this recognition has taken place through worship, commerce, political organizing, the arts, and more. The emphasis on multiracial placemaking along the Big Nine in no way means to diminish the powerful African American base that evolved in the neighborhood over a century of Jim Crow segregation. It does, however, intend to disrupt mainstream narratives that represent interracial place-making efforts in the segregation-era South as superficial at best and, at worst, wholly antagonistic.

In order to do justice to the dynamic history of multiethnic placemaking along the Big Nine, the revitalization of East MLK Boulevard and the MLK neighborhood into a vibrant twenty-first-century cultural district must continue to go beyond status quo gentrification activities (i.e., façade/ streetscape improvements and promised injections of capital investment from UTC) and support and enable equitable development through a multiethnic diasporic placemaking frame. Given the neighborhood's rich cultural history, special opportunities exist for linking equitable community development to the arts and creative and cultural development.

The successes of the Bessie Smith Cultural Center and Mark Making are powerful testaments to what is possible when a city's marginalized residents are offered space and resources to express themselves creatively and intellectually. By continuing to expand the politics of neighborhood stakeholdership to include the neighborhood's significant homeless and low to moderate income, nonstudent population will do much to help planners and policy makers understand and counteract the negative impacts of gentrification underway across the neighborhood.

While expanding the range of who is included is a crucial aspect of equity planning, commitments to more democratic engagement must also be complemented by commitments to a more equitable distribution of urban opportunities and reinvestment benefits, including affordable housing, education, workforce development and employment opportunities, arts and cultural development funding, public transportation, and environmental amenities. The University of Tennessee–Chattanooga and community institutions like the Bessie Smith Cultural Center, in partnership with place-based neighborhood associations and directly impacted residents, will be central to realizing an arts and culture-based equitable redevelopment agenda moving forward. And noninstitutional, community-based actors such as Mark Making will also be critical to the realization of a fair and equitable neighborhood, where marginalized and historically underrepresented voices are included and valued as integral fibers in the neighborhood's physical and sociocultural fabrics.

Ultimately, by reframing urbanization and community development in the city as processes of multidiasporic placemaking, city and institutional planners might gain fuller perspectives about why it is so crucial to make sure contemporary culture-based revitalization initiatives—especially those meant to boost tourism—directly benefit those marginalized communities whose stories and experiences are being preserved or rewoven into the urban landscapes.

United States Colored Troops (USCT) established an infirmary and rehabilitation center on Citico Mound, 1864 (Paul A. Hiener Collection, Chattanooga Public Library).

Camp Contraband quickly evolved into Hill City, Chattanooga's first autonomous black community in the post–Civil War period (Paul A. Hiener Collection, Chattanooga Public Library).

The Golden Gateway urban renewal project redeveloped more than 400 acres of predominantly black working-class neighborhoods into civic, office, and commercial uses, June 1964 (Paul A. Hiener Collection, Chattanooga Public Library).

A bustling scene at Market and East Ninth Streets, the entrance to the Big Nine (East 9th/Martin Luther King Boulevard), 1890 (Paul A. Hiener Collection, Chattanooga Public Library).

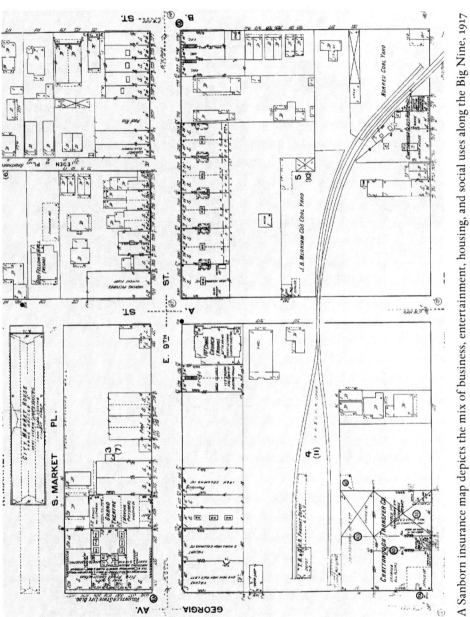

A Sanborn insurance map depicts the mix of business, entertainment, housing, and social uses along the Big Nine, 1917 (Sanborn Library, LLC/Environmental Data Resources).

The Communist Party of the USA organized anti-racism campaigns from its southern headquarters in Chattanooga (Southern Worker/Communist Party of the United States of America).

Workers from the Loomis and Hart Manufacturing Company, a firm known to defy the color line and employ a multiracial workforce, 1897 (Paul A. Hiener Collection, Chattanooga Public Library).

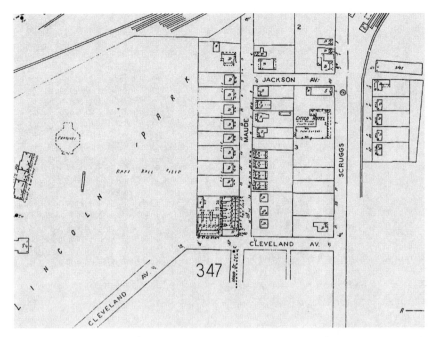

A Sanborn insurance map depicts a variety of recreational amenities in Lincoln Park, 1929 (Sanborn Library, LLC/Environmental Data Resources).

Mark Making's *We Speak* mural project engaged teens from the foster care system in public art and storytelling (author's photo, 2011).

Vacant clubs and businesses along the Big Nine face increasing pressure from university and market rate housing developers (author's photo, 2016).

The Passage, designed by Cherokee artist team Gadugi, tells the story of Cherokee resistance, displacement, resilience, and survival in Chattanooga and beyond (author's photo, 2016).

Andres Hussey's *Ascending Path* (2007) is a tribute to the "weary travelers" who have migrated to, through, and away from Chattanooga (author's photo, 2013).

Luxury apartments stand in contrast to the Walnut Street Bridge, an iconic public space with a dark history of multiple lynchings (author's photo, 2016).

Despite protest from residents, city planners hope to widen Central Avenue and extend it to Riverside Drive, bisecting the historic park space (author's photo, 2016).

Members of the Coalition to Save Lincoln Park brainstorm with their neighbors during a Planning Free School workshop, Chattanooga Public Library (author's photo, 2013).

Chattanooga Organized for Action director Perrin Lance trains graduate social work students in community assessment and planning tools (author's photo, 2013).

Free School participants pretest a neighborhood assessment toolkit developed collaboratively during a previous workshop (author's photo, 2013).

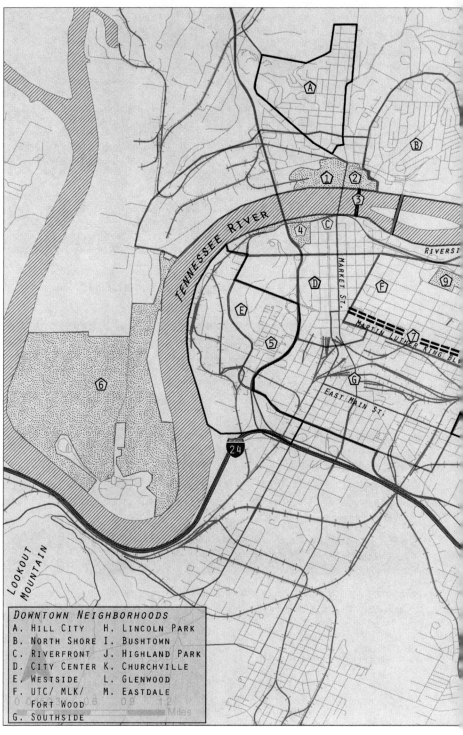

Key sites of diasporic placemaking in Chattanooga's urban core.

CHICKAMAUGA
MOUND 1 MILE

M

CITICO
MOUND SITE

CENTRAL AVE.

H

I

M I S S I O N A R Y   R I D G E

L

K

8

J

BRAINERD MISSION &
CHICKAMAUGA TOWN SITES
3.5 MILES

LANDMARKS & POINTS OF INTEREST
1. CAMP CONTRABAND (CC)/   6. MOCCASIN BEND ARCHAELOGICAL DISTRICT
   RENAISSANCE PARK   7. EAST 9TH STREET/ THE BIG NINE
2. CC/ COOLIDGE PARK   8. CHATTANOOGA NATIONAL CEMETERY
3. WALNUT STREET BRIDGE   9. CHATTANOOGA CONFEDERATE CEMETERY
4. ROSS'S LANDING/
   THE PASSAGE   ├──────────┤
5. COLLEGE HILL COURTS   1 MILE

N

MAP CREATED BY THE AUTHOR, 2016

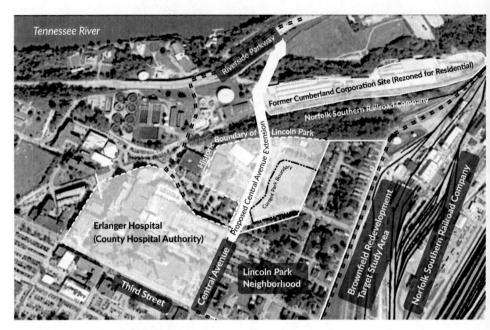

Political and spatial tensions in and around Lincoln Park.

CHAPTER SIX

Chattanooga Homecoming

Citizen-Driven Planning along the Tennessee Riverfront

Following the removal of the Cherokee in 1838, Chattanooga's riverfront industrialized. By the turn of the twentieth century, much of the downtown riverfront was occupied by heavy, water-dependent manufacturing facilities. The properties adjacent to Ross's Landing underwent several transformations over 150 years, serving as locations for: goods, grain, and cotton warehouses; a wagon and cattle yard; a foundry and machine shop; a maritime navigation company; a traveling shovel tramway; a bus repair shop and parking area; a wholesale liquor distributor; a marine hardware manufacturing factory; a scrap iron yard; and a neon sign manufacturing business. Late nineteenth-century-era fire insurance maps of the landing area also reveal the presence of black workers' housing (labeled "negro shanties" by surveyors) on the historic landing site.[1]

In 1972, Ross's Landing was added to the National Register of Historic Places because of its significance as a Cherokee trading post and its central role during the Trail of Tears. Three years later, a 3,100-foot strip of the site was dedicated as a park, and a small plaque was added to highlight the historical significance of the site. Despite these efforts, the cultural meaning of Ross's Landing was lost to many of the people who lived in or visited the city for the majority of the late nineteenth and twentieth centuries.[2]

The Urban Design Studio

Though the full-blown revitalization of Chattanooga's downtown riverfront did not begin until the early twenty-first century, public attention began to focus on the river beginning in the early 1980s. The first group to involve themselves with community planning-related activities along the historic riverfront was the Urban Design Studio, a small collaborative architecture center cosponsored by local philanthropy group the Lyndhurst Foundation and the University of Tennessee–Knoxville (UTK). The Studio was founded and coordinated by Stroud Watson, a professor of architecture at UTK who had taught internationally before moving to

Chattanooga to help launch the Urban Design Studio collaboration. Watson described the original Urban Design center as "a little place with a wood stove on Vine Street"; he recalled how it provided a physical space to convene public meetings and allow residents to drop in and share their concerns about and ideas for the city.[3]

Watson worked with the Architecture Department at UTK to develop undergraduate studio projects so that architects-in-training could practice managing the various stages of community planning and collaborative design—from information gathering and visioning to strategic design development. Out of these studio workshops came some of the earliest visions for Ross's Landing and the twenty-first-century public return to downtown Chattanooga and the Tennessee riverfront.

Around the same time that the Urban Design Studio was gaining local political traction, the Hamilton County Planning Commission honed in on a largely undeveloped area on the north shore of the river, known for centuries as "Moccasin Bend." The 597-acre Bend housed a state mental hospital, golf course, and wastewater treatment center, and was otherwise undisturbed. Watson recalled the serendipity he felt when, at the same time the Urban Design Studio was trying to draw attention to the river, the Planning Commission announced they would fund a study of the land use and development potential of the Bend.

City planners partnered with the recently formed Urban Land Institute to launch a participatory visioning process. The first public meeting was held in November 1981, and attendance was high. This group tapped into the "Chattanooga Spirit" legacy of bipartisan, economics-driven collaboration; planners spearheading this process recalled how the Chattanooga Spirit was in full force during these early workshops.[4]

Planning staff noted that typical planning disagreements arose, such as whether to allocate more funds to open space and public-oriented uses or expand the local tax base through industrial and housing development. While many public comments focused on the Bend itself, several outspoken civic leaders, including Watson, recommended expanding the study area to include the whole length of the city's riverfront in order to maximize the physical, social, and cultural benefits of the historic area:

> There were some developers from the city who wanted to develop over there. . . . So they brought in [the Urban Land Institute] ULI. . . . They interviewed everybody, including me, and heard from people like me that nothing should be done there, when we've got plenty to

take care of in the city. And heard from people who thought what a great open-field development it would be and, boy, would we like to get our hands on it. And then from some historians who started showing up talking about the Indian [settlements]. So they said this is a very important study, and what their real recommendation was that they form a joint county-city task force to look at it.

[I was asked] to be an advisor. We met, and in the very first meetings I spoke out about one thing in particular, . . . I said we're actually asking the wrong question. We shouldn't really be concerned at the beginning with what to do about Moccasin Bend. We should be more concerned about the river, from the Georgia line to the Chickamauga Dam.[5]

Watson documented a handful of publicly accessible spaces along the riverfront, and argued that the physical disconnection had detrimental social, cultural, and economic effects on the city.

Socially, the lack of public space kept individuals and communities apart who would otherwise not interact. Culturally, the lack of riverfront access kept Chattanooga's residents, not to mention potential tourists, from experiencing the historical and cultural heart of the city: the Tennessee River. Economically, the prevalence of underutilized industrially zoned land along the banks of the river, combined with an economically depressed, deindustrialized inner core, kept Chattanooga from realizing its full potential as a twenty-first-century cosmopolis.

The Moccasin Bend Task Force's work complemented another initiative underway in the city: planning a historically themed riverfront tourist park dubbed "River's Bend." The proposal for River's Bend was submitted by Landmarks Chattanooga, the city's primary historic preservation group; it included a section on preserving and renovating the then-defunct Walnut Street Bridge.[6] Ultimately, committee chair and then Lyndhurst Foundation president Rick Montague endorsed Watson's position.

As the larger committee began to get on board with these ideas, Chattanooga's civic return to the river began to crystalize. These early planning visionaries understood that place—which is to say, the local historical, cultural, and geographical context of the city—must form the bedrock of any major revitalization effort to reimagine downtown Chattanooga. In a small, tight-knit city, where many residents had roots that went back several generations, connection to place was a popular and relatable idea. Ultimately, hundreds of residents joined the planning effort.

Bruz Clark, current president of the Lyndhurst Foundation, described how the Task Force's emphasis on Chattanooga's unique environmental and cultural assets produced an engaged civic spirit in the city (dubbed the "Chattanooga Way"), one that continues to motivate community planning and redevelopment initiatives across Chattanooga today. To quote him at length,

> The people, history, culture, environment—all of those elements are a huge part of our identity, and I think one of those ah-ha moments was to capitalize on the assets that were here and authentic, and not to be somebody else. That was really the revelation of the Moccasin Bend Task Force and the initial study of Moccasin Bend. . . . Nobody knew really what should be the outcome there. Maybe develop a historic cultural center or what have you. Then the people that were involved in that, including our former director, took a step back and said, "No, what we really need to do is focus on the entire river, from the dam to the gorge. Use that as a fulcrum for economic development, to attract people back downtown.
>
> That was a very significant milestone in this community's history because people from all walks of life were brought together to develop a vision for this place, and they truly had a voice, I think, in the outcome. It was not artificial. It was sincere. To be able to think about your past, present, and future, collectively, and do something about it was inspiring and led to so many of the things that happened as a result. Forty-two goals, I think it was. . . . As a result of that process, the nickname for that now is the "Chattanooga Way," people coming together, being exposed to data and imagery and all that sort of thing, but having a forum for conversation and sharing of ideas, and I think that has been a good way to accomplish things.[7]

Importantly, the Chattanooga Way was distinct from past participatory planning initiatives—such as the Model Cities program—because, in addition to bringing together large numbers of people from all walks of life, efforts were made to build citizen capacity to understand technical planning data and to make rational, informed decisions about future land uses and developments, rather than relying on visceral or gut reactions to growth and change. The *Chattanooga Way* continues to be a popular term; for three decades it has been used to underscore the exceptionalism and cosmopolitanism of progressive, citizen-driven urban and community development in the city.

The Moccasin Bend Task Force recommended that a comprehensive study be commissioned; the contract for this riverfront planning study was awarded to internationally renowned design firm Carr/Lynch Associates. The efforts coordinated by the Task Force culminated in the *Tennessee Riverpark Master Plan*, a proposal for $750 million in public space and land use upgrades. The document defined "a vision for the future development of the inaccessible or industrial edge of Tennessee River as it passes through Chattanooga," and called for "the sensitive distribution of new development, nature preserves, and public parks" and a continuous trail system along twenty miles of the river.[8]

Chattanooga Venture and Vision 2000

In early 1984, local planners and civic leaders persuaded the Lyndhurst Foundation to provide a seed operating budget for a new planning initiative. The group hoped to capitalize on the civic momentum produced by the Chattanooga Way by launching a new citizen-driven planning initiative. Dubbed "Chattanooga Venture," this "self-organized citizens planning group" initiative kicked off its efforts with Vision 2000: a series of thirty-two public meetings organized to "determine community priorities relative to the development and the future of the Chattanooga area."[9]

Then planner, now former Chattanooga mayor Ron Littlefield served as Chattanooga Venture's executive director for its first three years of operation. Littlefield described his team's motivation for organizing Chattanooga Venture as being rooted in a desire to both illuminate and break down the nepotistic political and economic structures that had controlled planning and development activity in the city for generations.

In total, sixty individuals from "all walks of life" volunteered on the Venture Board, and more than one thousand citizens from across Chattanooga and Hamilton County participated in at least one of the thirty-two sessions held over the course of the Vision 2000 initiative. Littlefield recalled the group's rationale:

> The reason for that was there was always the underlying feeling, the undercurrent that Chattanooga was being controlled by a nefarious group of very wealthy people. . . . Chattanooga was like that at one time, we had a small group of people who had a lot more money than everybody else and they did pretty much decide what was going on. By the 1980s, that had certainly diminished quite a bit and so we

decided that the best way for Chattanooga to get its act together and to carve out a future for itself was to tap into everyone's energies. . . .

We went through a long marathon process of planning and thinking and came out with a small group of projects that we could undertake, some related to the riverfront, those are the ones that get all the press now, but others that were really just more social necessities like a women's violence shelter, places . . . things that we had talked about for a long time but [had] never been able to accomplish. We set about checking out the blocks on that short list of projects and when we got through that we just kept moving.[10]

The concerns, priorities, and goals articulated during these workshops were condensed and compiled into a document entitled the *Chattanooga Venture Commitment Opportunity Workbook*. The Venture Board used the document as the basis for its planning and development agenda across the riverfront and historic urban core. The *Workbook* contained brief sketches of thirty-four goals and objectives. Each contributed in a unique way to the organization's strategic mission "to offer an avenue of citizen participation in community problem solving and decision making and to be an agent for change through projects that require widespread, diverse support."[11]

Shifting Public Perceptions

The need for broad and diverse representation and support were crucial to the success of Vision 2000 as a citizen-driven movement. Venture's coordinators wanted to intentionally organize a board that would include a range of political, social, and economic interests. Littlefield explained their reasoning accordingly:

Chattanooga had a history of being an old industrial union town, [and] in the South unions were considered, like, cancer. There was no compatibility between the Chamber of Commerce and the unions. In Venture we very carefully structured the board so that we had everyone from the captains of industry to the heads of the unions and the teamsters union—which was just considered, that was like bringing some wild, dangerous element into a meeting—but we had them sitting across the table from each other. The charge was, if Chattanooga is going to survive, we've got to all work together—and it worked. They worked together, they found that really there was a lot that they agreed about, and as a result of that we were able to move forward and not get hung up on all of these prejudices that had been developed over the years.[12]

The Vision 2000 initiative was an example of the power of public, private, and nonprofit collaboration to produce dynamic and progressive results. Chattanooga Venture and Vision 2000 became as much about creating a new positive public image—particularly to outsiders, and especially to capital investors—as they were about making physical and social improvements in residents' everyday lives.

During the opening remarks at Visions '86, a Venture-sponsored planning and community development conference that attracted more than three hundred attendees from across the city, state and region, Littlefield contested the stereotype of Chattanooga as a "backward" city, pointing to the Vision 2000 process as proof of the city's progressivism and inevitable comeback. "I still hear comments about Chattanooga describing it as a backward, backwater community," he told conference participants. "And we are dispelling that view of Chattanooga. [The city is] becoming known throughout the state and throughout the South as a city of the future instead of a city of the past."[13]

The connection between place-based social movements and cultural identity was a prominent theme of the Visions '86 conference. Though the Moccasin Bend Task Force had previously stressed the significance of the district to Native history, Vision 2000 marked the first time leaders outside of the local black community had acknowledged the African American roots of city and community building across downtown Chattanooga. In this sense, Venture and Vision 2000 opened up new spaces for exploring the multiple, overlapping roots of diasporic identity and placemaking in the city.

The keynote speech at the Visions '86 Conference was delivered by Alex Haley, a native Tennessean and the Pulitzer Prize–winning author of *Roots: The Saga of an American Family* (1976). Haley discussed his own family's journey from freedom in Gambia, to slavery in antebellum Maryland, and eventual emancipation and relocation to Henning, Tennessee. He drew explicit connections between historic fights for freedom against the "Southern inheritance" of slavery and Jim Crow segregation, and contemporary struggles for community self-determination and neighborhood revitalization, and maintained that self-determination and racial justice were only possible through the cooperation and mutual gain of all races.[14]

In the context of race, planning, and urban cosmopolitanism, Haley's keynote presentation was significant for two reasons. First, it occurred during a popularly attended, mainstream planning function. Haley's emphasis on African American placemaking showed participants the importance of acknowledging and valuing African American contributions to the city and society. Furthermore, his optimistic narrative of racial reconciliation and equality became talking points for city boosters eager to throw off the city's negative image and market and sell Chattanooga as a twenty-first-century progressive cosmopolis.

Though aspects were manipulated by local boosters, the Vision 2000 process should be recognized as one of the most widespread and popular efforts to acknowledge and plan to counteract discrimination and racism in the city. Had the board lacked diverse participation and representation, it is unlikely that antiracism priorities would have evolved during discussions that involved only members of the traditional power structure, who were overwhelmingly male and middle to upper class, and almost exclusively white.

Through the discussions, disparate people and communities related to one another temporarily. Regardless of the long-term outcomes of the visioning initiative, the process of bringing a diverse group of citizen stakeholders together to share ideas and solutions, and engage in processes that supported communicating, relating, and empathizing, produced an end in itself: a sense of deeper shared understanding.

Translating Priorities into Strategies

While most would agree that broader engagement and representation created a more inclusionary process, not everyone in Chattanooga who lent their voice to the Vision 2000 initiative agreed with Littlefield that the means outweighed the ends. When Governor Lamar Alexander announced his plan in early 1986 to award Chattanooga Venture $9 million out of the Homecoming '86 fund to support initiatives outlined in the *Commitment Opportunity Workbook*—he did so assuming the group could reach consensus about which projects should be funded.

The *Venture Commitment Opportunity Workbook* contained thirty-four priorities, ranging from the development of an aquarium along the riverfront to the improvement of the low-income housing stock across the inner core. In response to his offer, Venture submitted a five-project wish list to the governor's office, including an aquarium, a riverside walkway, a museum honoring Chattanooga-born music legend Bessie Smith, a fishing park, and the restoration of the historic Tivoli Theater. While it is clear from local news reports that this list had been developed using participatory means, it is not evident how the Venture Board narrowed their expansive list down to five projects—all of which were concentrated within a very small area in the inner urban core.

During public meetings related to the allocation, Mayor Gene Roberts reminded state lawmakers that all Venture projects would be managed and overseen by the Greater Chattanooga Partnership, a private corporation established by government and business leaders to encourage economic development. This announcement soothed skeptics and helped create buy-in among the city's leading development institutions. The Allied Arts of Chattanooga and the Chattanooga Area Chamber of Commerce quickly endorsed Venture's wish list, arguing that the organization had to "start somewhere," and the key to widespread urban revitalization lay in first returning the city to the Tennessee River.

But the priorities established by the wish list frustrated many others who had hoped to see their own neighborhood priorities represented alongside downtown interests. The wish list quickly became a contested agenda. The disagreement compelled Senator Ray Albright, who was helping administer the Homecoming '86 program, to chide Chattanooga's leaders for being unable to reach consensus. "Now that Governor Lamar Alexander is supporting $9 million in state funding for a state-of-the-art aquarium and four other projects here that just might do the trick, in-fighting among area residents is endangering the city's chances of getting the money."[15] The five projects were ultimately approved by the state, and Chattanooga Venture received Governor Alexander's $9 million award.

Though the money was used to support the five wish list projects, Chattanooga Venture's early efforts were not limited to them. An important proposal to emerge from the Venture initiative was the creation of a fifteen-member Human Rights and Human Relations Commission to "investigate alleged instances of racial, sexual, and other forms of discrimination" in public and civic affairs.[16] Another outcome was the creation of Chattanooga Neighborhoods, Inc. (CNI), a nonprofit organization formed "to serve as a clearinghouse and work with community groups, the city, businesses, churches, and others."[17] The initial $2 million in funding for CNI (later renamed Chattanooga Neighborhood Enterprise, or CNE) was provided by local foundations and an unnamed private business.

Over the course of the year, Chattanooga Venture convened seven public meetings focused on housing, crime, jobs, youth, schools, growth, and city/county governance. During the crime forum, almost seventy residents attended, and participants spoke out about police brutality and the need for improved trust between African American residents and police officers.

Out of this civic discourse came commitments from public officials to provide universal housing in the city, and to explore innovative ways to rehabilitate the local housing stock while supporting individual and community empowerment. "One of the latter commitments we are making in Chattanooga is that none shall be ill-housed or ill-fed," Mayor Gene Roberts told a press conference. "That commitment may take a decade or a lifetime to reach, but we are going to do it."[18] Chattanooga Venture invited premier urban designer James Rouse to the city to assess their efforts to date, and several months later, Rouse's organization, the Enterprise Foundation, released a report that concluded: "This composite commitment, and the spirit of energy that rise out of mutual cooperation and visible success are the keys to making Chattanooga the first city in America to make all housing fit and livable in a decade. The very act of an entire city making this commitment, putting in the initial funding and beginning programming will be a truly significant model to hold up for the rest of the country."[19]

Over the next two years, Chattanooga Venture engaged residents and community leaders in issue-based task forces relative to the commitments outlined in its *Workbook*—though, without question, the main impetus was behind the redevelopment of the riverfront and central business district. These priorities were edified in January 1988, when the organization announced it would hire staff and establish an office in downtown Chattanooga in order to support groups such as the Allied Arts of Greater Chattanooga, River City Company, Chattanooga Neighborhood Enterprise, and the Chamber of Commerce.[20]

Meanwhile, Venture hosted public forums about the state of the city, and racism and inequality continued to be salient topics for concerned members of the black community. On May 16, 1989, the Venture Choices Forum sponsored a public discussion on Race and Economic Development. Held at the Chattanooga-Hamilton County Bicentennial Library, Venture staff facilitating the meeting articulated a long-cited link between racial harmony and economic development, voicing their desire to "take advantage of the racial and ethnic diversity within the community to improve the economic conditions for all."[21]

But some civic leaders from the black community contested this idealism, maintaining that deeper cultural and structural inequalities must be addressed before Chattanooga could rightly call itself a city of equal opportunity. George Key, former local NAACP president, questioned Chattanooga Venture's liberal multiculturalism rhetoric, stating, "I don't think there's as much diversity as we like to say. There are some differences, but we play up too much on the diversity side." Moses Freeman, representing Those Interested in Chattanooga's Economic Progress, called attention to deep-seated forces of racism permeating society and influencing local residents' understandings of citizenship, civic participation, and community. "We are born, we worship, and we are buried segregated," Freeman declared. "Some even still feel we will go to a segregated heaven. It is most difficult to merge two societies that have been segregated for years. We must begin to have a sense of community. This city belongs to us all."[22]

The skepticism of Venture's citizen engagement, planning, and development practices was strongest in the city's poorest neighborhoods, which had struggled for generations to exercise self-determination in the face of paternalistic policy makers and planners. After Venture's annual meeting featured a presentation by Washington, D.C.-based public housing tenant organizer Kimi Gray, the organization proposed a meeting with the City Wide Tenants' Association, a group composed entirely of representatives from public and subsidized housing developments around the city. Venture wanted to discuss the potential for a "resident manager concept," which they understood had had positive effects on tenants' qualities of life in other cities. In response to the invitation, Annie Thomas, vice president of the Chattanooga City Wide Tenants' Association, issued the following statement to the press: "We operate under the auspices of the National Tenant Association and individual tenant associations across the city and we consider any intervention in our association by organizations other than those named above as a deliberate attempt . . . to stifle our independence and a blatant attempt to control our communities by electing white-controlled gatekeepers to leadership positions."[23] Although Venture staff maintained that they were only interested in "exploring" the concept of a resident manager program, the City Wide Tenants' Council's response to the invitation reflected a deep sense of betrayed trust toward centralized, formal processes managed by experts from outside the directly impacted communities.

Ultimately, the success of Chattanooga Venture and the Vision 2000 process as democratic, citizen-led local planning movements was and is contested. Despite the disagreements about means and ends, few would disagree that Chattanooga Venture played a crucial role in coordinating participatory processes that led to substantial reinvestments in the downtown area. Nearly $100 million in private capital alone was leveraged to build the city's aquarium,

Creative Discovery Museum, the IMAX 3D Theater, Miller Plaza, and the River Center visitor's facility during the 1990s. The River City Company estimated that, in the period between the construction of the aquarium in 1992 and the commencement of the 21st Century Waterfront Plan a decade later, five new hotels were constructed, hotel revenues doubled, and overall employment in the downtown area grew by more than eleven thousand jobs.[24]

Public Space, Cultural Development, and Reconciliation Politics in the Renaissance City

On February 12, 2002, the City of Chattanooga announced it had awarded a ninety-day, $250,000 planning contract to Cambridge, Massachusetts-based planning and landscape architecture firm Hargreaves Associates. The contract hired the firm to explore expanded revitalization and public access along the downtown Tennessee riverfront. The cost of the services were split between the City of Chattanooga and River City Company; the geographic scope of the 129-acre planning study area included both sides of the downtown riverfront, from Veteran's Bridge and the Bluffview Arts District to the western terminus of Martin Luther King Street on the backside of Cameron Hill. During their announcement of the study, River City Company president Ken Hayes connected the initiative to the twenty-year-long citizen planning movement that had already transformed targeted sections of the inner urban core: "I want to remind everyone that downtown is everyone's district," Hayes stated during a press conference. "Downtown is everyone's neighborhood."[1]

But while Hayes's rhetoric described a downtown held in common by all Chattanoogans, many actual planning and development priorities, as had been the case throughout Chattanooga's historical development, paid more credence to outsiders' interests than local working-class communities—especially communities of color.

The economic rationale for these priorities seemed apparent to civic leaders, who for more than a decade had favored tourism as an antidote to the city's deindustrialization and economic decline. In an editorial published in the *Chattanooga Times Free Press*, a supporter of the contract argued, "The creation of the proposed Moccasin Bend National Park, with a unique Trail of Tears interpretive center on the park's north shore riverfront, would present an unprecedented opportunity to showcase the city and attract visitors and broader economic development. Properly executed, the potential exists for the city to capture a substantial portion of the visitorship which, at 10 million a year, makes the Great Smoky Mountains National Park the most visited park in the nation."[2]

Over the next month, project managers from Hargreaves worked with the River City Company to facilitate three public input meetings. These forums attracted hundreds of participants. One participant published an editorial in the *Times Free Press* detailing the discussions and commending the organizers for hosting a lively, visionary event: "the broad sense of the discussions, and the compelling range of ideas that emerged in the lively work groups where participants envisioned their hopes for the riverfront, intuitively fixed on central themes: an expanded riverfront; enhanced connectivity and recreational opportunities; festival venues; and respectful residential, retail, and marina development."[3]

These values and priorities translated directly into the planning and development recommendations articulated in the planning study. In May 2002, Hargreaves released the culmination of their research and engagement efforts in the *21st Century Chattanooga Waterfront Plan*. Major elements of the *Plan* included: recommendations for substantial public space and riverfront improvements, including the addition of more than 30 acres of new parkland; the construction of a pier and over 2,000 linear feet of docking for recreational boats; the expansion and rehabilitation of several museums and the local aquarium; the design and construction of a pedestrian walkway network; and $1.2 million in public arts funding. Hargreaves estimated the total development cost at $120 million, and recommended combining $69 million in public and $51 million in private funds to ensure its realization.[4]

One week after the *Plan*'s release, then mayor Bob Corker delivered his first-ever "State of the City" address, publicly announcing the major tenets of the plan and describing how the city would leverage a recently instated local hotel-motel tax to finance the public portion of the $120 million price tag.[5] In a public challenge to his own administration and the rest of the local development community, Corker proclaimed he would see to it that most of the *21st Century Waterfront Plan* was realized during the remaining thirty-six months of his mayoral tenure, and challenged local private and nonprofit developers to construct at least 750 new units of housing in downtown Chattanooga during the same time period.

To Corker, the use of public monies to advance Chattanooga's reputation as a place where "healthy, intelligent people want to live," rather than a city marked by "crime, decay, and blight" seemed intuitive: the cost of using public investment to catalyze private development, particularly when the funds weren't coming out of the city's general coffers, would be greatly outweighed by its benefits, especially once private-driven revitalization took hold. "It is not acceptable for (residents) to have to live in neighborhoods where they are burdened by the fear of crime, decay, and blight that result from the irresponsible acts of those who live outside their neighborhood."[6]

Between May and December 2002, Mayor Corker engaged almost singlehandedly in a fundraising campaign that secured another $51 million in private support toward the implementation of the *21st Century Waterfront Plan*'s vision. The projects included in the $120 million budget were allocated accordingly: the redevelopment of Ross's Landing ($25.9 million), the steps connecting the Hunter Museum to Market Street ($6.35 million), $5.5 million for land acquisition, $30 million for the aquarium expansion, $19.5 for the Hunter Museum expansion, $3 million for the Creative Discovery Museum expansion, $15 million for parking, $13.5 million for Roper Park, and $1.1 million for miscellaneous expenses. Also during this time, the Southside Redevelopment Corporation was renamed the Chattanooga Downtown Redevelopment Corporation and charged with overseeing the implementation of the 21st Century Waterfront Plan, while the Community Foundation was assigned to serve as the fiscal agent.[7]

In October 2002, the City of Chattanooga announced the sale of $55 million in public bonds to front the public segment of the funding, vowing to use the revenues gained through the local hotel-motel tax to repay the bond. Local decision makers agreed that Phase 1 of implementation should include $46 million to improve Ross's Landing, create a connection between the Hunter Museum and Market Street, and construct a new public park on the North Shore.

Correspondingly, several major downtown tourist attractions announced their plans to use private capital to expand their facilities alongside the city-backed public space improvements: the Tennessee Aquarium announced a $30 million expansion, the Hunter Museum pledged to give itself a $19.5 million "facelift," and the Creative Discovery Museum set aside $3 million for renovations.[8]

Interpreting Ross's Landing

As mentioned in the previous chapter, the original site of Ross's Landing was added to the National Register of Historic Places in 1972—though little happened with it in the ensuing decades. With the announcement of the *21st Century Waterfront Plan* three decades later, local planners and placemakers returned their attention to the historically significant site.

Knowing that any redevelopment of the landing would be subject to regulations stated in Section 106 of the National Historic Preservation Act, the 21st Century Waterfront Plan's design team established a formal participation process for determining the future use of Ross's Landing as well as the appropriate historical interpretation of the space. Because the *21st Century Waterfront Plan* drew connections between Ross's Landing and long-standing efforts to have the archaeological sites at Moccasin Bend designated as a National Historic Park, River City Company initially reached out to the National Park Service (NPS), who offered the services of an in-house consultant to help interpret the site. A *Times Free Press* story published several weeks later stated that the consultant had presented "several ideas on how to interpret the Trail of Tears in the riverfront plans. These range from having two-dimensional cutouts of a Cherokee detachment walking down Market Street to a maritime exhibit at Ross's Landing depicting the flatboats some of the Cherokees were forced into as they were sent west on the river."[9]

When asked to comment on the NPS proposals, members of a small, but organized local Native American community agreed that city plans to honor the area's Trail of Tears history were "long overdue," but contended that efforts "need to involve Native American artists and architects in the plans."[10] Section 106 of the National Historic Preservation Act sets special provisions regarding engaging Native American governmental organizations, so River City Company staff, who felt uncomfortable with the encounter exhibits proposed by the NPS and wanted further guidance, organized a series of meetings between leaders of the Cherokee Nation (Tahlequah, Oklahoma), the Eastern Band of Cherokee (Cherokee, North Carolina), and the National Park Service.

During these conversations it became clear that the Park Service's proposals for the space were inadequate to deal with the traumatic events that had occurred at the site 160 years prior. At the heart of Native consultants' critiques of the proposals were concerns about Cherokee self-determination and cultural awareness—specifically, how the symbols and time frame chosen by NPS consultants emphasized narratives of extermination and defeat rather than Native survival and resilience. In an interview with the *Chattanooga Times Free Press*, Dr. Richard Allen, a policy analyst with the Cherokee Nation in Tahlequah, Oklahoma, who had participated in the initial planning meetings, recalled a turning-point conversation between the different stakeholder groups: "We politely thanked the park service but rejected their idea. [Ross's Landing] wasn't theirs to interpret. . . . In order for

Chattanooga to understand its history, it would have to go back into the pre-contact era and bring it forward. It's not a reversal of the Trail of Tears, but it does acknowledge that we were there. I think people will know the things sacred to us. The mountains, the river, the landscape. All of that belonged to us. It's a sacred place."[11]

For Allen and other Native advocates, the construction of the stockades and barges would infuse the downtown landscape with a neo-colonial narrative of dislocation and displacement. The reconstruction of these structures of trauma implied the impossibility for a return, either symbolically or materially, of a people to their historic homeland.

In contrast, Native participants articulated a positive, living, contemporary vision for the revitalization of Ross's Landing—one that would infuse the riverfront with a richer historical and cultural meaning. Participants wanted the space to remind visitors that, although the Trail of Tears changed the courses of history for both the Cherokee Nation and the United States forever, the event did not weaken the Cherokee's culture or define them as a people. On the contrary, Native people have persevered and thrived despite the injustices wreaked against them, adapting their communities in order to survive, and even thrive, as a dynamic and diverse set of people.

The Passage at Ross's Landing

The idea for The Passage at Ross's Landing had several origins. The plan recommended substantial pedestrian access, public space, and public art improvements along the riverfront, especially in the areas between the aquarium and the river which were physically disconnected by Riverside Drive. To help realize the recommendations, Mayor Corker funded $1.2 million for acquisitions and appointed a thirteen-member committee to manage the city's public arts agenda. In November 2002, the city, working with Allied Arts of Greater Chattanooga, organized a series of community input sessions which attracted more than five hundred participants. Several months later, the Allied Arts of Greater Chattanooga released a Public Art Plan intended to establish a policy framework for making use of the substantial public arts allocation.[12]

Additionally, Governor Don Sundquist announced a $2.55 million federal transportation grant to the City of Chattanooga to support pedestrian connections on the waterfront. The *21st Century Waterfront Plan* called for an underground passage connecting the public space and aquarium to the river and planners agreed: "The area [would] also serve as the trail head for the Trail of Tears and feature some interpretive elements and fountains."[13] Corker boasted that Chattanooga's riverfront would add to the city's cultured, cosmopolitan feel during the press conference where he announced the public arts allocation: "I am confident that the pier and the passage will become very visible landmarks, and when completed will cause our community to be distinguished around the nation for our commitment to public art."[14]

The sentiments expressed by Native consultants advising the redevelopment of Ross's Landing were considered by the Public Art Committee, and ultimately formed the basis for the Request for Qualifications (RFQ) related to the passageway site. Arts educator, and former executive director of Public Arts Chattanooga, Peggy Townsend recalled the RFQ development process, which ultimately garnered twelve submissions. "They wanted something that was more celebratory that nodded to the past but also celebrated a very alive and thriving culture and a place of joy but not so somber.... *That prompted us to really write that kind of language in the* RFQ *and also require that team members that were selected be Native American....* I think we ended up having about five or six teams that were shortlisted.... They were all really different and really wonderful.... The winning team was Gadugi. They're all from Locust Grove, Oklahoma."[15]

Each of the shortlisted artists was awarded a $2,500 stipend, plus travel expenses, to develop a proposal for the passageway site. Ultimately, the committee chose a collective of Cherokee craftsmen and artists who called themselves *Gadugi* (ᏍᏯᏯ)—a traditional Cherokee term meaning "to come [or work] together."[16] Gadugi's incorporation of circles and pre-Cherokee, Mississippian, and Muskogee references compelled local organizers, who wanted the site to tell a much longer story than the events leading up to and surrounding the Trail of Tears. Gadugi wanted the space to suggest the potential for both symbolic and physical return. In Cherokee culture, the circle signifies reconciliation and return. Gadugi team members argued the Passage would "[complete] a circle of return that began with the removal of their culture from this area over one hundred and fifty years ago."[17]

The number seven is sacred within Cherokee culture, representing the seven original clans of the Cherokee people, and it became a central theme in Gadugi's design proposal.

Townsend recalled how, out of all of the proposals, Gadugi's vision for the passageway best encompassed the narratives of cultural survival and resilience that the earlier Native American participants had called for. "*Kudos to the committee for really thinking that through. It was the right thing to do.* Just little, wonderful kinds of poetic things happened throughout that project. The Gadugi talked a lot about the prophecy of coming home. . . . They use the circle a lot in the imagery there. When they were selected and we got to know them a little bit, they told us that this was a prophetic project because they are coming back to Chattanooga to work on this thing in this place, which is pretty huge. None of them were professional public artists. One of them is a school teacher. One of them is a potter. One of them is a metal worker. They're all incredible artists but they had never worked in a large public art setting."[18]

In an interview for the *Times Free Press*, Gadugi member Knokovtee Scott emphasized that Chattanooga had been a cultural epicenter long before the arrival of colonial settlers, and the Passage would take this longer view of local history: "visitors will find out that Chattanooga has an amazing past. One thousand years before Chattanooga existed, it was an epicenter for the Southeast of a culture that was flowering."[19]

But, while the celebrations of Cherokee and pre-Cherokee culture were to be the presiding narratives at The Passage at Ross's Landing, the Gadugi team did want to acknowledge and memorialize the space as a central deportation center during the forced removal of the southeastern tribes. An editorial published in the *Chattanooga Times Free Press* supporting the project described Gadugi's inspiration for the design of the public space: "entering the Passage from Market Street, people will approach seven doorways. From the lintel of each, water will trickle down like tears, for the tears along this cruel trail began as the Cherokee were taken from their doorways of their homes. The trickle will fall into a stream of water dropping toward the river in a growing cascade that recalls the chaos of the brutal roundup and stockading which preceded the removal. The water will come to rest in a reflection pool beneath the parkway."[20]

The final design for the Passage contained four areas, each with a distinct water feature. By late 2003, construction on the site was underway, with the Gadugi team serving as creative consultants during the building phase. The first section is adjacent to the Tennessee Aquarium, and contains seven doors. Water drips from each of these doorframes, signifying that the Trail of Tears began at the front doors of the homes of the Cherokee people.

The second section is comprised of seven descending landings connected by stairs. As the walkway descends below Riverside Drive, the Passage widens and a cascade of water rushes down the right wall toward the Tennessee River. Seven, six-foot-tall clay discs are mounted on the left wall along the descent; each contains a cultural symbol based on artifacts discovered in the ruins of three local Mississippian era settlements. the Hixson, Dallas, and Citico sites. At the bottom terrace of the space, a large steel disc with a carving of the Water Spider—an ancient symbol of prophecy, who is said to have foretold the forced removal of Native communities from the southeast—rises from a large pool of water opening up to the river and Ross's Landing. The fourth section of the site is comprised of a twenty-foot-tall wall containing seven mounted steel figures of Cherokee stickball players.[21]

The theme of reconciliation is apparent both in the design of the site and the artists' statement, which is inscribed on a plaque at the entrance to the passageway under Riverside Drive: "It is our team's honor and privilege to complete the circle begun by our ancestors so many years ago by bringing back to this area the vitality and visual strengths of our Cherokee forefathers' artwork. Through this art installation, we feel as though we are symbolically returning to our ancestral homeland."[22]

These symbolic and discursive efforts at reconciliation were further supported during a private ceremonial blessing of the site, and a day-long public festival, which highlighted Cherokee history and culture through music, dance, sports, and storytelling. During the ceremonial blessing, which was held at dawn in January 2005, and attended by individuals closely involved with the project, a sacred fire was lit from seven special types of wood brought to Chattanooga from Oklahoma. The smoke was used to cleanse the site and put the ancestral spirits who had long remained "unsettled" in the space "at peace."[23] In a way, this blessing signaled an emotional reconciliation with the trauma and upheaval that had occurred at the site, and across the city, nearly two centuries prior.

On May 13, 2005, the city organized a series of events related to the grand opening of The Passage at Ross's Landing. The dedication of the Passage was significant because it marked one of the few post-removal occasions where the chiefs of all three Cherokee nations (the Cherokee Nation, Eastern Band of Cherokee, and United Keetowah Band of Cherokee) were present together. One Cherokee participant who traveled to Chattanooga to attend the opening ceremony observed, "Watching the little Cherokee children play in the water was like looking into the future, which is the direction we need to go for the Cherokee people."[24]

In his opening remarks to festival-goers, Eastern Band Chief Michell Hicks described the power of The Passage at Ross's Landing to reinscribe Chattanooga's downtown with narratives of Cherokee rootedness and return: "many years ago this passage divided us, broke our nation apart. . . . This place remembers before we were divided, when we were one great nation, the Cherokee Nation. The water holds our tears of joy and sorrow. The rocks hold the sounds of our great Cherokee language. This soil has absorbed our blood and continues to clutch at our footsteps. How great for a passage that once tore us apart to finally bring us together. No amount of removal or federal policy can strip this land of the memories it embraces. We have traveled today from all different directions but we can know Chattanooga today as our home."[25]

Chief Hicks's discussion rooted Cherokee cultural memory and meaning firmly in place, arguing that the connection between her people and the land on which present-day Chattanooga was settled preceded and persisted despite the colonial encounters and experience of dispossession. Discussing the economic history of Ross's Landing, Hicks described the settlement as a place where Cherokee "entrepreneurs" transformed a small trading post into the "economic force of the frontier," only to be forced to give up "that which they had been told they were too savage to be a part of." Hicks commended the city for its ability to accomplish such a level of "inclusive" revitalization without "the displacement of the heart and soul of this community, its people and its history." "It is our team's honor and privilege to bring back to this area the artistic vitality and visual strengths of our forefathers' symbolic designs and return the native to its ancestral home."[26]

Ann Coulter, an urban designer and planner who prepared the documentation of public art at the Passage, described the significance of the site in a report submitted to the Allied Arts of Greater Chattanooga. In it, she linked the revitalization of Cherokee culture directly to the economic transformation of the new tourism-driven downtown: "the art installation in The Passage is presently the only large public installation of contemporary Southeastern Native American art in the United States, possibly in the world. The motifs and themes represented in the art are not well known outside of small circles of artists and craftspeople, archaeologists or historians. The art in The Passage, due to its location in a heavily traveled tourist venue, has the opportunity to help whole generations of visitors learn about and appreciate the rich artistic heritage of Southeastern Native American tribes."[27]

Place-markers and signs located across the downtown area are printed in both English and the Cherokee language, and at Ross's Landing are inscribed with quotes from Cherokee and U.S. leaders during the eighteenth and nineteenth centuries, showing the evolution of discourses of sovereignty, property rights, and legal entitlement which ultimately culminated

in the passage of the Indian Removal Act and the Trail of Tears. This site
for public education, art, and civic interaction has become a form of socio-
spatial cultural recognition and repentance. The Passage advances a political reconciliation narrative, whereby the city acknowledges its hand in
dispossession and displacement and uses the mechanisms of urban reinvestment and cultural revitalization to produce a site honoring the Cherokee
as a resilient, thriving, contemporary people.

Additional Features of the
21st Century Waterfront Plan

Several landscapes along the north bank of the riverfront also acknowledge the historical injustices that have occurred in the city. Directly across
the river from The Passage at Ross's Landing sits Renaissance Park, another
large public space to grow out of the 21st Century Waterfront Plan. Renaissance Park is built atop the original site of "Camp Contraband," Chattanooga's Civil War-era free black settlement.

By the time the construction of the Passage had begun, public attention
turned to a 23.5-acre industrial site on the north bank of the Tennessee
River that had been identified in the *21st Century Waterfront Plan* for a second public space adjacent to Coolidge Park. In early April 2004, the City of
Chattanooga announced their plan to develop a $13 million park on the site.
The 23.5-acre site was purchased from GE-Roper Corporation, a stove and
stovepipe manufacturing company which had been operating on the site
since the 1920s. The project's $15 million price tag included $450,000 for
purchase, approximately $2 million for land remediation, and about $10 million to design and build the park. Although planners focused primarily on
the site as a wetlands restoration and ecological park, urban designers also
emphasized the historical significance of the space, which was an original
section of Camp Contraband: "On this park site, former slaves who joined
the Union army and later settled on the north shore were bivouacked. There
is evidence of Native Americans there before written history, and the site
was crossed by some of the Cherokee forced from their homes on the Trail
of Tears. Chattanooga will symbolically commemorate that sad history in
the design of the Passage under Riverfront Parkway."[28]

Today, historic place-making signage and a riverfront picnic area marks
the location of Camp Contraband's quarters. Several winding footpaths that
wander through the space are designed to symbolize the passage of the Cherokee through the space during the departing steps of the Trail of Tears.

Finally, in the shadow of the John Ross Bridge and Lookout Mountain stands a sculpture called *Ascending Path*, which depicts several individuals traversing an elevated structure. Louisiana-based sculptor Aaron Hussey described his intent with the project accordingly: "Weary travelers move across the land upon man-made structures that rise above our reach but in our view. Many people have traversed this site going west; some by choice, some by force, and others in fear. This crossing holds the spirit of silent travelers."[29]

Declaring Repentance

On October 16, 2006, Chattanooga city officials took their efforts further when Chattanooga mayor Ron Littlefield and Chadwick Smith, principal chief of the Cherokee Nation, signed a Memorandum of Understanding (MOU) which recognized that the "City of Chattanooga is located within the boundary of the Cherokee Nation before the forced removal in 1839," and that both parties had an interest in the "preservation and interpretation of Cherokee Historic Sites in and around Chattanooga." "In the spirit of repentance," this contract intended to bind the parties "together in a relationship expressed in the Cherokee language as *Du-na-li-i-yv* and described in the English language as 'a friendship between groups.'"[30]

Mayor Littlefield recalled the trip to Tahlequah, Oklahoma, to present the document: "That was a very emotional trip. The proclamation of repentance there that was very carefully written and very . . . I recall I said out there that no one has ever said we're sorry and that's what we did. That proclamation is signed by myself and Leamon Pierce, who was the chairman of the council at the time. The point was, first of all we acknowledge all these things that shouldn't have happened, happened. Wasn't on our watch, we didn't do it, but it's a stain on the land, it was a commitment that was not . . . it was a promise that was not kept because they weren't supposed to be uprooted and taken out."[31]

When asked to reflect on the significance of community history to his place-making work, Lyndhurst Foundation vice president Bruz Clark discussed a need to collectively reckon with the complexities of local social life, of the city's dark episodes and legacies of injustice as well as its innovations and successes. Clark sees his role at the Lyndhurst Foundation, which is and has been one of the premier institutions supporting local arts and cultural development for half a century, as providing the financial and technical resources to local and regional actors who are willing to take these complexities on in creative and innovative ways.

I think it means a lot. Again, so much of our investment has been on identifying, remembering, celebrating our past, and I don't just mean our Anglo-Saxon past. It has been the past. As a great example, our Native American past and present as well.

History is an interesting thing. I think there is a fine line between being nostalgic and recognizing history as the foundation for what happens next. Honoring that, if it is to be honored, or maybe regretting it if it was not such a great chapter in our history . . . the Trail of Tears, for instance, but recognizing that as important and figuring out what to do with it is more—the History Center, from what I understand to be their storylines, I think, they are really going to do a great job at lifting out some of that history, community history, and having that tell us how that has influenced our behavior and decisions, feelings for each other, and that sort of thing. It is very complex.[32]

Without a doubt, Chattanooga's thirty-year homecoming to the Tennessee Riverfront is full of powerful examples of what can be achieved when public, private, and nonprofit sectors team up with empowered citizens to collaboratively envision and plan for their community's future. But, what comments such as Clark's statement above do not clarify are the racialized politics undergirding notions of citizen- and stakeholdership in a city with a three-hundred-year-long history of racism and uneven geographic development. In Chattanooga, where the success of planning is measured by the large numbers of people who show up and participate, local boosters do not push to ask themselves who shows up and participates in these early discussions, and who does not; what stakes these participants have—or do not have—in the redevelopment game, or whether their visions and priorities have historically been promised, supported, or implemented.

Citizen participation in the Moccasin Bend Task Force, Vision 2000, and the 21st Century Waterfront planning efforts have been internationally lauded, and the priorities, goals, and recommendations in each have been palatable to many middle-class, white, "back to the city" urban cosmopolitanism enthusiasts. Certainly, the Passage and other public gestures of reconciliation and repentance offer compelling models for planners and place makers to consider as part of a local social agenda.

But unignorably, the visions enacted through policy and planning over the past three decades have not been representative of the historic downtown population, which, at the time that revitalization efforts kicked off in the early 1980s, was predominantly working class and majority black. Vannice Hughley, a lifelong resident of Chattanooga and president of the Lincoln Park Neighborhood Association, argued that the priorities established during these early riverfront and downtown revitalization efforts were hardly the priorities and values held by most working-class African American communities in Chattanooga at that time.

Referring to the Tennessee Aquarium, which is hailed by many contemporary boosters as the cornerstone of the downtown millennial renaissance, Ms. Hughley stated plainly that, for many of the working-class African American residents who cannot afford the facility's expensive admission fee, the aquarium has long been referred to sardonically as the "catfish pond." Challenging the mainstream narrative of progressive downtown revival, Hughley emphasized the ethical and political limits of a public sector that invests hundreds of millions of dollars in tourism-related development projects when local residents, and working-class African American residents in particular, cannot access quality education systems or creative, fulfilling economic opportunities that are spurred by new investments. "How are you going to let the schools fall apart," she exclaimed, "but yet you're going to put all that money down in the catfish pond?"[33] Similarly, a local resident who was interviewed by the *Times Free Press* during a visit to the Passage argued that Chattanooga's reinvestment is highly uneven. "This Passage area, the tribute to the Trail of Tears, is a great thing they've done," Henry Slayton told the *Times Free Press*, "but the rest of the city is dealing with potholes and bad sidewalks. This stuff is good, but it should happen in other neighborhoods [as well]."[34]

Conclusion: Flipping the Script on Cultural Organizing

Presently, there are several popular organizations counteracting mainstream revitalization discourse in Chattanooga. These largely volunteer-based movements illuminate the highly uneven terrain of urban reinvestment and call for a more equitably developed city. Volunteer-based groups such as Concerned Citizens for Justice (CCJ), Mercy Junction, Chattanooga Organized for Action (COA), the Westside Community Association, Idle No More Chattanooga, and the Grove Street Settlement House have problematized Chattanooga's storybook tale of urban progress through a range of creative, place-based public activities and initiatives, including marches, history tours, protests, street theater, justice schools, skill sharing, storytelling, spoken word, free stores, discussions with community elders, and solidarity fundraisers.[35]

Importantly, these groups integrate the typically cultural and symbolic work of placemaking with an economic justice-based vision for community planning and development, demonstrating the inextricability of these two elements to a transformative urban social justice movement in a diverse city comprised of several overlapping diasporic communities. In their understanding of cultural development, art is not a set of relics; it is the active production of communities of security and belonging.

In October 2011, local antiracism activists Concerned Citizens for Justice organized two marches against police brutality along Chattanooga's riverfront. Organizers planned for the march to coincide with one of the city's major outdoor sports festivals called "River Rocks," which is held at Ross's Landing and attracts thousands of tourists to the city. As part of the demonstration, participants marched to key sites of local Cherokee and African American exploitation and resistance, including the former city jail, the Passage, and the Walnut Street Bridge.

Organizers drew attention to the historical significance of the sites and connected these legacies to ongoing struggles for social justice across downtown Chattanooga. During the march, organizers reclaimed and recast sites of exploitation into sites of empowerment by highlighting the long histories of local social and racial justice organizing in downtown Chattanooga. One of CCJ's central messages, "poverty is violence," disrupted the myth that urban reinvestment had been shared by everyone in the city and that racial reconciliation had been achieved.

The CCJ marches against racism and police brutality did more than publicly call out social inequalities: they also helped to forge spaces where diasporic citizens could come together to creatively imagine and create alternative worlds based on mutuality, trust, and respect. For example, CCJ organizers used The Chattanooga Body Count Quilt as their banner during the march. The Chattanooga Body Count Quilt was begun by CCJ founding member Maxine Cousins as a way to process, heal, and memorialize the men and women whose lives had been lost while in police custody in Chattanooga since the mid-1970s. Each quilt square contains the name and face of one person. Cousins described her motivation behind starting the quilt several years ago: "You know, I really think you have to build relationships. I think you have to feel—from me to you—*that you have my best interest at heart and that I have your best interest at heart.* And that— you have to build that. That's why I started the Body Count Quilt. I think that if you have a *space where people can come to talk about their problems* and do a quilt or whatever—for whatever reason, you build relationships. *You begin to care about each other.* And then you start doing other things. . . . If you've got those gardens on the Westside, teach people how to grow food and can! But do it at a big assembly—not individually. That will teach people to care about each other. That's what needs to happen."[36]

Cousin's Body Count Quilt illuminates some of the conditions that are prerequisites for moving beyond symbolic to substantive reconciliation in twenty-first-century urban planning and community development. It is not simply about bringing people together in a space and letting them hash out differences. More fundamentally, we planners and urban practitioners should support and enable spaces and processes that allow participants to creatively process and potentially heal from trauma, collaboratively design community-based solutions, and practice the arts of interpersonal empathy and self-care.

Idle No More!

The Chattanooga riverfront and The Passage at Ross's Landing have also recently become a central gathering space for Native activists involved in the southeastern Idle No More! movement. Idle No More! is a growing global Native/First Nations movement that began in late 2012, after Attawapiskat First Nation chief Theresa Spence began a six-week hunger strike to protest the Canadian government's treatment of First Nation citizens. Spence's protest quickly gained the attention of Native American activists and their allies across the western hemisphere, who responded by launching marches, walks, prayer vigils, and flash mob "round dances" in public spaces across the United States and Canada. The purpose of these actions have been to call attention to the apartheid-like conditions affecting Native communities living on federal tribal lands and demand renewed commitments to legal and cultural tribal sovereignty.

On January 20, 2013, nearly one hundred primarily Native residents from across the Chattanooga region gathered at Ross's Landing for a prayer vigil to honor Chief Spence. During this event, organizers made speeches, issued prayers, sang and played music, danced, and celebrated the Native American heritage of Chattanooga and southern Appalachia. Their collective message to one another, and to onlookers, was clear: United States-Native relations have come a long way since the days of forced removal, but the legacies of racialized violence and dispossession endure. Public spaces such as the Passage tell important stories about resilience and symbolic home-coming, but they are only the beginning of conversations about how place-making and community development can best support and enable a more equitable and racially just world.

The Tennessee Riverfront and areas immediately surrounding Ross's Landing are historic sites of multiracial diasporic placemaking—spaces where overlapping cultural groups have worked with and against one another to carve out communities of material security and cultural belonging for more than four centuries. While mainstream planning efforts have produced new collaborations and deeper affinities, they have also produced greater contestation over physical space and cultural place in the city. By exploring the 21st Century Waterfront Plan, this chapter demonstrated how public and civic leaders in Chattanooga have used planning and placemaking to acknowledge and attempt to reconcile local historical violence and trauma through diverse place-making and policy initiatives. Yet, the contestability of Chattanooga's mainstream interracial tolerance and reconciliation narratives are evident in two grassroots movements' creative, direct action claims to the riverfront and the surrounding historic core.

CHAPTER EIGHT

From Rabble-Rousing to SPARCing Community Transformation

The Evolution of Chattanooga Organized for Action

Chattanooga Organized for Action (COA) began with a simple yet elusive mission. According to former executive director Perrin Lance, "We decided that we wanted to bring protest culture back into the City of Chattanooga."[1] Over the next several months, the group staged demonstrations against the BP oil spill, bank bailouts, and political corruption, occasionally capturing press coverage, but for the most part flying under the radar of the general public and local elected officials. At the same time that COA organizers were using public assembly, street theater, and creative protest to call out local problems, members of the group were looking for longer-term, community-based projects to advance social justice in the city.

The scope and scale of COA's resident organizing efforts took new form during the fall of 2011, when Roxann Larson, president of the Dogwood Apartments Residents Council, notified Lance about a letter she had received earlier that week from the Chattanooga Housing Authority. The letter invited Larson to an early morning meeting to hear from Mayor Littlefield and the Housing Authority about an exciting new planning opportunity for the Westside neighborhood. Lance immediately sought out the other tenants' council leaders from across the Westside and discovered that Leroy and Gloria Griffith, who ran the Westside Community Association next to College Hill Courts, had not been invited to the meeting.

Lance, Larsen, and Joe Clark (president of Boynton Terrace Senior Apartments) decided to attend the meeting and see what the city and its housing authority had in store for the neighborhood. Lance described the eeriness of walking into a room full of powerful local development players and being completely ignored: "So, we roll up and . . . there's forty to fifty white dudes and some women. And everyone is there, like everyone in town is there, except guess who? People from the Westside . . . who found out about it at the last minute. And I will never forget this. . . . We just sit down at this table and get our coffee. No one is coming to us or talking to us, that's expected, all right. Then a white guy in a suit gets up, opens the whole affair and says something to the extent of, "I know we're all really excited about what we're going to do here for our community." And thunderous applause ... [*The Westside*] *ain't seen any of these people there ... ever.*"[2]

As the event began, Lance and his colleagues learned that Mayor Littlefield wanted to bring Atlanta-based nonprofit Purpose Built Communities into Chattanooga to redevelop College Hill Courts into a mixed-income, new urbanist community. The presenters argued that tearing down College Hill Courts and replacing it with mixed-income housing would improve the overall quality of the neighborhood. They cited statistics about improved educational attainment and income levels.

Considering that the Westside is primarily seniors and families living on fixed, very low incomes, it was obvious to Lance and Westside leaders present that the planners pitching the initiative were not talking about improving the qualities of life among the residents who already lived there. Lance continued: "Purpose Built Communities gets up and they go over their plan and they're pitching it to everybody here. Littlefield said that he invited these people from Atlanta a couple of years ago to give this presentation. And they are talking about wanting to tear down the Westside as it is and make it into a mixed-income development. They're saying—they are coming out with all these statistics saying—after mixed-income developments, the education levels of the children rise. [But what they don't say is that they rise because] they're counting different children!"[3]

After the meeting, the COA members convened a meeting with Westside leaders to share the information they learned and begin to plan their campaign to save College Hill Courts.

Neighborhood leaders took the information and began to research policy and planning tools and benchmarks for preserving affordable housing, including historic preservation designation and inclusionary housing ordinances.

Westside Community Association president Leroy Griffith compiled his research into an inclusionary housing ordinance for the City of Chattanooga. The ordinance outlined several measures to mandate affordable housing development and preservation in the city's urban core, including a one-to-one replacement of all public and subsidized units sold or demolished by the Chattanooga Housing Authority, and a 10 percent affordability inclusion requirement for all new construction and multiunit rehabilitation in downtown Chattanooga. "[The Westside leaders] made their own independent decision [to fight back]," Lance continued. "Then Leroy and Gloria and Roxanne and Joe and all them, well, they came to us and said, 'Okay, what can we do together? What can you all help us with to fight this?' So we worked with them to develop a strategic campaign. The campaign was called the 'Not for Sale Campaign,' and it basically stated, not only, no to this destruction of College Hills on the West Side, [it also] said no to Purpose Built anywhere in the city. It [also] laid out a vision crafted by the people of the Westside."[4]

Equipped with knowledge about inclusionary housing, and an ordinance crafted by and for the low-income people of Chattanooga, COA organizers worked with the Westside Community Association to develop a citizens' petition based on the housing legislation. Over the next three months, the coalition gathered more than twelve hundred signatures on "The Petition to Save Our Homes."

Although they were promised opportunities to address the City Council several times during this period, their efforts to play by the rules were always obstructed. Lance recalled what led the group to finally take matters into their own hands:

> So, everything kind of got going very quickly. The Westside had several discussions, several meetings. They knew that Purpose Built was going to give a presentation to the City Council. The Westside had to get on the agenda. Sally Robinson, the chair of the Housing Committee, said, "Sure." We had it in an email. This is their community, right? [The resident leaders] wanted to have a say. And we roll up and, again, everybody is there in their suits and . . . Sally Robinson says, "No you all can't stay, you all can't stay." She didn't give a reason as to why the decision changed. She said it is a public information hearing. . . . So there's a certain point where you have to make a decision to shut things down.
>
> So, after Purpose Built gave their wonderful presentation meeting . . . Leroy stood up in full minister's regalia and cried out, "When will we be heard? When will the Westside be heard?" And then everybody chimed in exactly, "When are we going to be heard?" The Westside shut it down and immediately walked out, and held a press conference right there. We shut everything down. Sometimes you have to make those decisions.[5]

In the weeks that followed, Mayor Littlefield and the Chattanooga Housing Authority made no efforts to budge in their support for Purpose Built Communities and the destruction of College Hill Courts. In response, COA and the Westside Community Association continued to collect signatures on their petition for affordable housing.

On April 12, 2012, the "Not for Sale" campaign's efforts culminated in a march from College Hill Courts to the City Council's chambers to present the petition and demand an end to Purpose Built's plan for the redevelopment of College Hill Courts. Organizers began with a press conference that was televised by three local television stations. Then, more than one hundred people participated in the march to the Council's chambers. When the protestors arrived at City Hall, they packed the chamber so that it was standing room only. During the public comment period, four seasoned Westside activists spoke out against Purpose Built Communities and in favor of the inclusionary ordinance developed by their neighbors.

Within two weeks of the march, the Housing Authority issued a statement to say it no longer supported Purpose Built Communities' proposal for College Hill Courts. The mayor persisted but ultimately lost after Purpose Built Communities pulled out. Although the Westside Community Association has not been successful in having the Chattanooga City Council adopt their inclusionary housing ordinance, they promote inclusionary practices via the People's Coalition for Affordable Housing. The "Not for Sale" Campaign had an indisputable effect on the politics of affordable housing in downtown Chattanooga that continues to play out today.[6]

Out of Crisis, Opportunity

For two years, COA's members organized defensively, using direct action techniques to voice dissent against unjust local plans and policies, bringing awareness to the issues and occasionally obstructing their passage. Their ability to draw working-class people together presented a very real form of political power, but in terms of their ability to transform urban policy and development outcomes, direct actions had only gotten them so far. To be sure, gathering twelve hundred signatures, warding off Purpose Built Communities, and saving College Hill Courts from mixed-income redevelopment were remarkable wins, especially considering how rapidly public housing was being lost across the urban core.

But, while green community organizers pointed to this victory as a turning point, residents of the Westside knew their security was tenuous and relative at best. The case of Purpose Built had not been unique, but rather was the continuation of a legacy of racist and paternalistic planning in Chattanooga, where low-income communities and communities of color were "planned for" rather than "planned with." Longtime Westside leaders knew that, because they were constantly defending their community from outsiders' visions and improvement plans, there had not been an opportunity for the neighborhood to plan proactively.

Chattanooga Organized for Action Reimagined

By early January 2013, COA had canvassed and begun conversations about resident councils in two publicly subsidized housing developments: College Hill Courts on the Westside and Cromwell Apartments in East Brainerd, over Missionary Ridge. Additionally, COA staff began to discuss forming a City Wide Tenants Council with several community leaders residing in public and project-based Section 8 housing. Based on community meetings and conversations that door-to-door canvassers had with tenants at several of the Housing Authority-managed properties, it was obvious to COA that subsidized housing tenants needed political space and structure to voice their issues and collaboratively discover solutions to the common problems they faced as low-income residents living in a rapidly gentrifying city.

The Support function of COA was organized to help neighborhood-based associations build personal and group capacity vis-à-vis Organizational Growth Plans. The Support team "develops and implements both individual and organizational support services and serves to connect the needs of the grassroots organizations with the resources of social service providers and COA volunteers."[7] Since its early days, COA had had a relationship with faculty in UTC's Department of Social Work. By late 2012, COA was working closely with social workers at UTC and Southern Adventist University to develop a new framework for supporting neighborhood-based movements. Dr. Valerie Radu, an assistant professor of social work at UTC and the founder of the Grove Street Settlement House, advised that COA engage in human needs assessments with its partner communities in order to maximize its ability to provide meaningful support. This assessment would measure the strengths, abilities, and needs of the different grassroots communities through an "asset-based community development" approach.[8]

Launched in January 2013, the Support arm of COA began two data collection initiatives: one focused on gathering personal needs information from individual community leaders ("Individual Assessments"), and a second focused on group or "Organizational Assessments." These assessments would provide capacity information about the human and social infrastructure in neighborhoods and particular housing developments—information that could serve as baselines for place-based strategies to increase leadership development and organizational strength across Chattanooga's urban core.

Individual Assessments were conducted by Catharine Whiting, a UTC Social Work graduate student; they involved a series of interviews about the participant's immediate, intermediate, and long-term personal needs, his or her use of social and public services, life goals and interests, and potential contributions to the COA Volunteer Corps team. Organizational assessments involved meetings with association leaders to discuss opportunities and barriers experienced while doing grassroots organizing in predominantly low-income, politically marginalized communities.[9]

At the same time that the COA Works Support team was collecting information about its partner communities, another tool was developed to measure the "strengths and abilities" of COA's significant volunteer reserve. Having nearly three thousand members subscribing to COA's online newsletter and blog updates, COA issued a call for its subscribers to join the Volunteer Corps. Literature was developed explaining the need for volunteers, a tool was created for assessing individual skills and potential contributions, and planning began for a Volunteer training workshop where volunteers' "assets, talents, and personalities [would be] uncovered and catalogued."[10]

Additionally, the COA Support team decided to strengthen and expand the Westside Free Store—a free exchange market grounded in "radical hospitality" and launched by the Grove Street Settlement House in partnership with COA and the Renaissance Presbyterian Church. Finally, the Support team recommitted themselves to their original community partners: the Westside Community Association.[11] During the later winter/early spring, the Westside Community Association had been enduring capacity challenges, as some members had dropped out, others had less time to be involved, and the few remaining felt increasingly disempowered. An important component of COA's Support agenda involved the establishment of neighborhood Free Stores. These biweekly swap meets are supported by volunteer labor and donated goods, but their value to residents should not be underestimated. In addition to giving low-income community members a place to find gently used clothing, housewares, and children's goods at no cost, Free Stores employ volunteers who help administer resident surveys, recruit participants to a women's support group, and provide social service referrals. Instead of defaulting to public bureaucracies and private charities to address basic social needs, COA's asset-based community development framework begins with an assessment of how residents living in low-income communities across the urban core are *already* meeting certain needs indigenously.

These internal support networks, which include transportation, health care, food sharing, child care, and more, form the bedrock of COA's Support framework. In emphasizing the existing relationships, outside volunteer and institutional service provisions assume secondary and tertiary roles. This is not to say that the public and nonprofit sectors don't play critical roles supporting low-income communities through a variety of social programs. Rather, COA's process suggests that institutional and outside, charity-based solutions need not be the de facto approaches to social service provision in the twenty-first century. With strong foundations in resident cooperation and mutual aid, the COA Support framework allowed volunteers to assume deeper, more focused roles, whereby public and private institutions potentially became enablers of social welfare and resident empowerment rather than (real and/or perceived) obstructionists.

The portion of COA's new mission most directly related to urban planning, and that I personally made contributions to, was their "Connect" agenda, which charged itself with: "[Working] with membership to develop and implement the SPARC Initiative, a tool by which base membership organizations will arrive at a common vision, goals, and a shared strategy for real material change in their communities."[12] The Sustaining People and Reclaiming Communities (SPARC) Initiative was a grassroots, capacity-building and community planning process grounded in popular education, traditional community organizing, urban planning, and social work practice.

During its pilot phase, SPARC involved a series of monthly trainings and information gathering sessions, wherein a cohort of neighborhood leaders (typically members of registered neighborhood associations) worked with COA staff and volunteers to learn the skills necessary to develop a block leader network, collect residents' stories and concerns for the community, articulate a neighborhood vision, and implement strategy to achieve the visions and goals described.

Importantly, the SPARC Initiative took the time upfront to support the human infrastructure necessary for launching a bottom-up, resident-driven process. As block leaders were identified and trained to become community liaisons between their neighbors and neighborhood associations, they were also invited to enroll in neighborhood assessment workshops to produce data to undergird the SPARC planning process, and ultimately the action plans. As the process progressed, the monthly trainings also provided a space to collaboratively analyze community data which had been collected in order to explore how the different neighborhoods might work together to achieve common visions and goals for equitable community development vis-à-vis a People's Coalition Vision and Action plan for Chattanooga's urban core.

The SPARC Initiative differed from traditional neighborhood planning initiatives because it approached comprehensive planning and community development through a resident-driven process. Rather than impose expert-driven comprehensive plans for a set of diverse urban neighborhoods, the SPARC Initiative sought to train and work with grassroots community leaders to facilitate neighborhood planning processes with their neighbors. Though the initiative began on the neighborhood scale, it connected neighborhood plans together via the People's Coalition and planning process, and therefore offered a potential model for expanding practices of community self-determination and negotiating neighborhoods' interdependence across the city of Chattanooga.

Moreover, the SPARC Initiative took a holistic and bottom-up view of community development, accounting for and cultivating not only the typical physical, social, and economic development infrastructures in place, but also the human infrastructure (i.e., civic participation, the strength of interpersonal relationships, ability and willingness to offer mutual aid and neighborhood support) that sustains them.

An advertisement developed to attract neighborhood participants into the program described the intent of the SPARC Initiative accordingly: "The purpose of the SPARC Initiative is to partner with grassroots community organizations so that they can become powerful, sustainable, and capable of enacting their own visions for their communities. To accomplish this, COA will work with community leaders to produce Community Stories, Visions, and Plans that articulate the wishes of a community and turn them into tangible and measurable goals. These goals are then tracked to timelines, prioritized, and translated into accessible Community Organization Plans."[13]

Over the course of several months, three neighborhoods in East Chattanooga committed to developing community plans vis-à-vis the SPARC Initiative and People's Coalition: Lincoln Park, Avondale, and Churchville. Each of these neighborhoods joined the initiative with a preexisting organizational capacity and need for a community plan: Glenwood, for example, was a highly empowered neighborhood, with nearly forty active block leaders and a recently updated neighborhood plan. Lincoln Park, in contrast, had a neighborhood association but no active block leaders, had not had a neighborhood plan update in decades, and chose to team up with COA because it was facing an existential threat to its historical and cultural assets. Avondale and Churchville, also both historically African American neighborhoods, joined because they experienced the less immediate threat of gentrification creeping across the urban core and into East Chattanooga.

The varying capacities of COA's partner organizations created both complications and opportunities with respect to launching the SPARC Initiative in East Chattanooga. One opportunity took the form of working with the Glenwood Neighborhood Association to develop the block leader training module, and integrating that capacity-building session into overall SPARC Initiative structure. During the spring and summer of 2013, COA organizers worked with leaders from the remaining three neighborhoods to identify and train block leaders, and in the cases of Lincoln Park and Glenwood, to administer their Comprehensive Neighborhood Assessments.

During this period, however, it became apparent that, in Avondale and Churchville, more basic community-building activities and infrastructure would be needed before developing a block leader cohort. This led to the neighborhood associations' decisions to launch Free Stores. Although organizing the Free Stores has set both neighborhoods back in their overall community planning timeline, both remain committed to working with the People's Coalition to create neighborhood and community-wide visions and plans once a strong human infrastructure in the neighborhood is in place.

The Planning Free School of Chattanooga

In developing the Sustaining People and Reclaiming Communities (SPARC) Initiative discussed above, we quickly realized that it would not suffice to merely invite grassroots communities into a citizen-driven process without also working with residents to develop the planning research and public engagement skills necessary to pull off such an initiative. To this end, I collaborated with COA and staff from the Chattanooga Public Library to launch the Planning Free School of Chattanooga: an experimental planning engagement and capacity-building initiative dedicated to "coordinating action toward a just and sustainable city."[14]

Free schools emerged in the 1960s and 1970s as parent- and community-based responses to highly unequal K-12 public education systems in U.S. cities. While the planning free school was influenced by the traditional K-12 free school model, it much more closely resembled the anarchistic free school (or "free skool") model of popular education that is prevalent in cities across the United States, Canada, and parts of Europe today. These schools are typically volunteer-based-and-driven workshops organized around topics determined to be significant by local residents. The pedagogical philosophy behind this movement is driven by the belief that every person, regardless of their educational background or attainment, has something to teach and to learn from their neighbors and fellow local citizens. Anarchistic free schools are marked by their decentralized, asset-based approaches to programming, and by the responsibilities that they place on both educators and learners to self-organize.[15]

The school was structured with two desired outcomes in mind, to enable historically underrepresented residents to: (1) develop technical capacity to participate in informal, institution-backed planning and development conversations and initiatives; and (2) use this new capacity to launch independent, community-based visioning and planning processes. Through their combined participation in the Planning Free School and SPARC Initiative, we hoped to support and enable new forms of neighborhood autonomy, self-determination, mutual aid, and community interdependence through the creation of neighborhood- and coalition-wide community stories, visions, and action plans.

These guiding principles grew out of a recognition that, for many local residents, knowing how to navigate local bureaucracies did not guarantee personal or community gains from development investments and outcomes over the long term. For this reason, although the free school was promoted as an opportunity open to all residents, organizers made it clear that the purpose of the school would be to center the voices from the community who had historically been marginalized or excluded.

Related to the Planning Free School's motto was its mission statement. Broadly speaking, we sought to bring residents and activists together to discuss critical issues affecting Chattanooga and to create opportunities for sharing skills and stories in the pursuit of a more just and sustainable city. Specifically, we did this by building a planning education and engagement curriculum with the following four objectives:

1. Engage organizations and individuals in critical discussions about Chattanooga and its most pressing socioeconomic issues;
2. Democratize technical planning and community development knowledge through participant-driven skill-sharing workshops;
3. Collect and produce publicly available, community-level data supporting social justice organizing across the city; and
4. Catalyze a "people's" planning process within and between neighborhoods that had been historically left out of citizen planning and development initiatives and reinvestment initiatives.

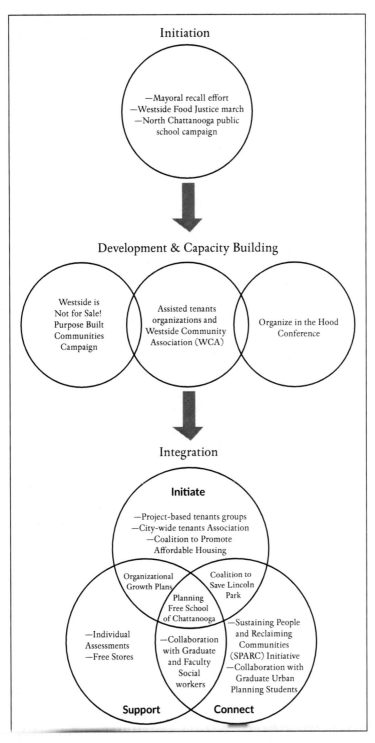

The evolution of Chattanooga Organized for Action.

We adopted a free school model because its horizontal, participant-driven format signaled a clear departure from the mainstream, institutionally backed initiatives that had historically been implemented in the city. Organizers further distinguished the program by being forthright about the initiative's commitments to community self-determination and equitable development across downtown Chattanooga. By framing the Planning Free School as a social justice initiative, potential participants came to see the school as an alternative space where the hopes and concerns of historically marginalized and underrepresented residents would be centered, and where they might come to expand their technical skills and social networks to help them realize their visions for their neighborhoods and the broader community.

The Planning Free School was offered at no cost, with flexible meeting space, marketing assistance, and collaborative research instruction from library staff. All workshops were advertised as open to the public, and organizers recruited participants through several channels: the Chattanooga Bicentennial Public Library's online Public Events calendar, a website and Facebook page, printed posters, and multiple email invitations distributed across Chattanooga Organized for Action's 2,500-plus-member online list serve.

Though we knew that the specific content of the free school curriculum would be decided by participants who attended the workshops, they devised a curriculum structure organized into four broad categories: skill-shares, critical conversations, issue-based discussion groups, and transformative place-making workshops. Skill-Shares were technical trainings designed to build planning capacity among Chattanooga residents. Critical Conversations were discussions meant to help local activists grapple with privilege and politics in Chattanooga. Issue-Based Discussion Groups were workshops organized around four planning topics: housing, employment and workforce development, the arts and cultural development, and transportation and mobility. Transformative Place-Making Workshops were activities designed to introduce participants to a range of nontraditional planning techniques that integrated music, visual art, model building, and play.

Organized in tandem with the Planning Free School of Chattanooga, the SPARC Initiative helped to catalyze a transformative, citizen-led planning movement within the city's underrepresented and marginalized neighborhoods. Through coordinated collaboration with urban planners, educators, librarians, community organizers, and social workers, neighborhood associations and other grassroots community groups explored and exercised self-determination and interdependence through the development of neighborhood and coalition-based community visions and action plans.

Residents and community activists who participated in the Free School were invited to join the SPARC Initiative, while existing SPARC participants attended Free School workshops to join discussion groups and get trained in information gathering and analysis. Chattanooga Organized for Action director Perrin Lance described how his participation in the Free School helped him to rethink COA's role as a local nonprofit dedicated to amplifying the voices of the city's marginalized and oppressed through a combination of grassroots organizing, social work and empowerment, and urban planning:

> I've developed and designed, in collaboration with you and some other folks, the SPARC initiative ... by participating in the Planning Free School ... that helped us to see that you can look at what you're doing in communities in terms of, "Well, I do environmental justice work"; OK, that's great. "I do income inequality work," or "I do antiracism work." But *no, it's all the same damn thing. The problem is that people don't own their own communities.* . . . But here is where people get a little lost, and where you've got to be really politically and philosophically careful. . . . You *arrive at a place of autonomy and self-determination through a process of mutual aid and mutual cooperation.* You arrive at this place by understanding how your needs are bound up with "the other."
>
> In the Free School, we created this assessment tool, and we were out the other day with it going through Glenwood, where we talked to a block leader, who is a component of the human infrastructure of that particular community. . . . We talked to this woman, and she knew all of her neighbors; but when we asked her to describe the relationships between the neighbors themselves, she said that they don't do too much visiting; they don't really talk to each other; people just sort of go to their homes, and so forth and so on.
>
> Well—if our goal is to go beyond, to break free and liberate ourselves and each other from these oppressions, we're not going to do it individually, because our oppressions intersect. We need to do this ... through a strategy of collaboration. You're not going to be able to do that unless you understand how your needs are bound up with one another's; that your needs can be met by the community.[10]

By moving from the personal to the neighborhood-wide to the inter-neighborhood scales, resident-driven community planning and development processes such as the SPARC Initiative have the potential to help community organizers counter mainstream comprehensive urban planning processes by working with directly impacted residents to develop capacity and "scale out" the geographic and technical scopes of their analyses. The result, in theory, is a form of bottom-up, comprehensive planning, where seemingly disconnected communities move through these processes together, enacting social interdependence and looking toward their neighbors to help devise neighborhood-based solutions to citywide problems.

The purpose of Free School workshops was to do more than share experiences or air grievances. Organizers also wanted to work with participants to collect and analyze existing community reports and demographic data so that they could substantiate their claims with concrete evidence. For example, a registered landscape architect employed with the City of Chattanooga attended the four-part geographic information software (GIS) course in order to gain basic mapping skills so that she could make a case to her department to have GIS installed on her work computer. Another participant enrolled in the course to learn GIS in anticipation of applying to graduate programs in urban planning. During a Transportation and Mobility session, participants were shown a map of the existing bus routes and asked to compare service quality and accessibility along the different routes.

One person whose physical disabilities prevented her from having a driver's license stood up, approached the map, and began describing inconsistencies in service. As an individual who relied exclusively on the bus and walking to get around the city, she had firsthand experience riding almost every one of the local bus routes. Pointing to a portion of the St. Elmo neighborhood in South Chattanooga, she emphasized the social immobility and isolation of a low-income, primarily senior population living outside of the bus service area.

> They're trapped. You've got about three miles in St. Elmo where a lot of elderly people live, and they will have to walk all the way up here to the edge to catch the bus; this is where the incline is located. They have service to the incline and that's it. The St. Elmo bus doesn't run often, and if you go out to St. Elmo you've got to walk up and over to here, to where the Alton Park bus picks up, because that picks up more often. And as it gets later in the day, the more chance there is that the Alton Park bus won't come at all. The later in the night-

time—if the bus breaks down or it's having problems—they won't send a new bus out. They'll just haul the bus back to the depot. You're standing there waiting for the last bus and the bus never shows up. You pretty much have to make other arrangements to get home.[17]

Following this open discussion, the facilitator of the meeting showed participants how to use an online census mapping program to collect the demographic information for the St. Elmo neighborhood in question. The group also discussed tools for evaluating discrepancies in public transit service access and quality.

The most fruitful Skill Share workshop, both in terms of its appeal to a broad, diverse group of participants, and its ability to produce tangible and intangible community-based outcomes, was the two-part "Developing a Neighborhood Assessment Tool" session. On the afternoon of Saturday, March 30, 2012, fifteen participants gathered for an extended session focused on exploring the uses and benefits of neighborhood assessments. Participants included neighborhood association leaders, professionally trained planners, retirees, community activists, artists, workforce development specialists, and a formerly incarcerated individual looking for ways to plug back into his community.

A draft tool had been constructed prior to the meeting based on assessment categories and measurements outlined in a standard community development textbook. To begin, participants systematically reviewed the indicators and were encouraged to discuss, refine, add to, or replace existing categories. The resulting conversation, which lasted more than three hours—more than twice as long as it had been scheduled for—succeeded in fine-tuning these measurements—and much more: fostering new personal and professional relationships between neighborhood activists, developing an easily administered template for assessing community infrastructure, reframing the metrics of community infrastructure through a diasporic perspective, and setting the ground for an additional action research partnership between Chattanooga Organized for Action, the Glenwood Neighborhood Association, and Southern Adventist University's graduate program in Social Work.

The assessment was organized into four broad infrastructure categories: physical, social, economic development, and human. Participants quickly pointed out relevant measures that were missing from the list. During a review of the housing indicators, one participant suggested that "tent cities," or homeless camps, be added to the housing stock assessment checklist, arguing that hidden, informal means of shelter are as important to account for as the ones in plain sight: "Speaking about housing stuff, maybe there should be some kind of taking account of homelessness in the communities, specifically tent cities, campsites. Not that I would encourage anybody to disturb anybody who's there, leave them alone, but if you know something, if you see something, that should be taken into account too. Often times they're very, very well hidden, but in plain sight."[18]

In other words, while housing assessments typically focus on measures that can be easily quantified, a more socially responsible assessment must also account for the intangible, extra- market factors contributing to housing (in)security in the city, including homelessness, the prevalence of informal housing settlements ("tent cities"), and illegal squatting. This participant went on to acknowledge the complexity of assessing social life in marginalized spaces, stating that part of their invisibility is intentional because it offers a degree of protection from revanchist urban policy makers. He stressed the importance of treating vulnerable populations with humanity and respect, and taking their lead with respect to whether and how their communities are accounted for.

Debating and Discussing High Stakes Issues in a Low Stakes Setting

The initial assessment tool workshop also provided space for participants to discuss and debate contentious social issues like squatting. Early in the workshop, one participant, the president of a neighborhood association in a predominantly middle-class neighborhood in East Chattanooga, suggested that "vandalism" be added to the housing stock assessment checklist. Her point was that community assessors should account for vacant homes that have been broken into and/or damaged by illegal tenants because these properties have a negative impact on the surrounding environment.

At the time of her suggestion, the point had not seemed debatable. However, several minutes later, when the issue of squatting arose in the context of Chattanooga's large homeless population, the following conversation took place:

cb: When Hamilton County released the list of houses that they were putting on the sale block, [my partner] and I went around and looked at a lot of them and almost 100 percent of the ones we looked at had squatters in them that you totally would have no idea about [if you didn't visit the property].

EH: That's the vandalism I was talking about.

CB: I don't think that's vandalism. I think that's people appropriately using housing that is just left. When people just abandon these properties and they live out of state and people are using them in their community, because we have a lot of folks who don't have access to any sort of emergency shelters or any sort of temporary housing. I don't have any moral problem with it. I'm just saying, you know, but that's a big thing that I didn't realize was there until I went to the actual houses and looked inside of them because you wouldn't have any idea.

EH: We had one on Derby Street. We called it vandalism, went to environmental court and as a result that property was sold and . . . now . . . they have people living there.[19]

What is notable about this conversation is not just that the two participants had different opinions about the moral acceptability of illegal squatting—though the workshop did provide an important space to allow ethical disagreements to be collaboratively explored without pressure to reach consensus. More importantly, the conversation illustrates an attempt (by CB) to go deeper—to understand the issue of illegal squatting in relation to the local housing affordability crisis, absentee landlordism, and class politics.

Their discussion led to the refinement of the assessment tool, but it also illuminated how illegal squatting, which many people consider outright vandalism, is a symptom of the grossly inadequate stock of emergency, temporary, and very-low-income housing. Finally, this conversation is significant because it illustrates how peer-to-peer education can aid grassroots communities in diagnosing and solving their own problems. Rather than wait and see if further damage occurred, EH, the leader of a highly active and empowered neighborhood association, chose to take action on the "vandalized" house on Derby Street and work with the City of Chattanooga to get the property sold to an individual who could rehabilitate the structure and lease it out to new tenants.

Connecting the Personal and the Political

The conversations that produced the neighborhood assessment tool allowed participants to explore complex dimensions of urban social life in highly personal and affective ways. During a review of public health infrastructure, for example, one participant proclaimed that mental health was a crucial indicator of urban health and sustainability, particularly in communities where people have endured generations of racist and sexist exclusion, violence, and trauma:

> I was at a community get-together Thursday and there was a young woman who was part of a violent crime. She was shot twice in the stomach, her sister was shot in the wrist. It was a violent crime. She's a mother of seven. She has four biological children, she has temporary custody of two relatives' children that's in her family and legally adopted child that's in her family. She's a mother of seven, single parent and she has been denied disability twice.
>
> Also, I talked to her about her kids because her kids had witnessed the shooting. They were at home, but neither one of those individuals has received counseling. I think that's a very important aspect of it because you've got to be able [to cope] mentally—maybe make it available as support counseling. At least in the urban areas where we shelf counseling and put it on the churches, but I think professional counseling should play a part.[20]

This participant had built his career around helping formerly incarcerated individuals reintegrate into society. In his view, it is impossible to devise sustainable solutions to deep-seated social and cultural urban problems until people of all backgrounds are willing to deeply reckon with the realities experienced by society's most economically and socially vulnerable community members. Participants seemed to agree that this reckoning must involve acknowledging that centuries of racist violence and exclusion have produced deep inequality as well as personal wounds in dire need of attention, care, and healing.

Relatedly, employment data analysis and discussions about first-source hiring and community benefits agreements has helped local community organizers launch several labor and housing-related campaigns around the city. For example, the People's Coalition for Affordable Housing endorsed a community benefits agreement (CBA) for any redevelopment of the former Harriet Tubman public housing site. Although no formal CBA has been negotiated, this pressure did compel the City of Chattanooga to announce a first-source hiring program, which will ensure that East Chattanooga residents receive a percentage of all temporary and permanent jobs connected with any redevelopment of the site. Equipped with analysis skills and the ability to discuss a range of progressive urban policy tools, social justice advocates today are better equipped to participate in and critique local planning and development initiatives.

Participants also increased their capacity to launch their own visioning and action planning processes. For example, the Planning Free School, in collaboration with COA, helped resident leaders from the Coalition to Save Lincoln Park develop a strategy to halt the allocation of state and federal transportation funds for the Central Avenue extension. Discussed at length in the final chapter, the Planning Free School dedicated several workshops exclusively to planning and development issues in Lincoln Park, including discussions about participation laws, neighborhood assessments, land trusts, historic preservation, tourism, and community economic development. Out of these conversations, neighborhood leaders decided to adopt the "No to Central Avenue/Yes to Lincoln Park" campaign. The Coalition's central demand has been to have the remaining historic park land put into public trust and used as the basis for African American tourism and economic development, and they used some of the tools and processes that they developed through SPARC and Planning Free School workshops to articulate and visualize this vision.

The Politics of Black Self-Determination and Neighborhood Preservation in Lincoln Park

If the historical development of Lincoln Park during the first half of the twentieth century illustrated the public sector's power to provide high-quality services and facilities for Chattanooga's black community, the postwar decades showed its power to just as quickly redirect and withdraw that support. Several chapters of this book have discussed the complex relationship that some black Chattanoogans have to the effects of legal desegregation in the city. While newfound freedoms in housing and education presented opportunities to escape the inner city, on the one hand, the result of African American outmigration included the breakdown of what had been historical, centralized, tight-knit communities.

An unintended outcome of legal desegregation was systematic disinvestment in black-only public facilities and spaces across the South. On September 24, 1963, newly elected mayor Ralph H. Kelley (1963–69) declared that all public buildings, parks, playgrounds, swimming pools, golf courses, and community centers were "open to all." This announcement, made nearly a decade after the *Brown v. Board of Education* Supreme Court ruling, marked the beginning of formal desegregation in Chattanooga.[1]

Over the next decade, the City redirected funds from Lincoln Park into nearby Warner Park. The concession stand was the first facility to close, followed by the pool in 1966. During segregation, Warner Park had been the white counterpart to Lincoln Park, containing a swimming pool, playground, and extensive sports facilities. Local planners and policy makers justified their decision by arguing that it did not make sense to invest in two major city parks when African Americans could now use Warner Park instead.

Institutional Encroachment and Land Swapping

In late 1974, Hensley-Schmidt Inc., an engineering consulting firm working for the State of Tennessee, requested that the City of Chattanooga declare Lincoln Park as "surplus" land in order to facilitate the approval and construction of a Central Avenue freeway. Historically, East End (now Central) Avenue had marked the eastern border of the city, and its northern terminus is located just past East Third Street, at the entrance to Lincoln Park and its adjacent neighborhood. After Interstate I-24 was constructed through the Southside of downtown Chattanooga in the late 1960s, Central Avenue transformed into a thoroughfare to connect cars exiting the freeway with the central city and eastern neighborhoods. The Central Avenue freeway proposal recommended that the avenue be further extended to connect with North Chattanooga by way of a new bridge over the Tennessee River. In response to their request to declare Lincoln Park surplus property, County Commissioner Conrad issued the following statement: "After studying all aspects I feel compelled to reject the destruction of Lincoln Park and the devastation of the Fairhills-Riverview section of North Chattanooga. I am flatly opposed to this route for several reasons. First, people are my top priority. Secondly, there are other, better alternatives. Third, we must preserve and improve existing park space in our city. Most people want progress. So do I. But at what price? I am not willing, in the guise of progress, to desecrate our environment."[2] Conrad's emphasis on Lincoln Park as a people-oriented, community space was perhaps the last time a member of the white political establishment publicly defended the park as a public end in itself. Ultimately, the proposal for the extension and bridge was abandoned and alternative routes were adopted for bridges to connect the northern and southern shores of the city.

But, just because state transportation planners had shifted their focus away from Lincoln Park for the time being, this did not mean that it was safe from institutional encroachment. On November 3, 1979, the City announced its plan to engage in a public land swap with neighboring Erlanger Hospital. The hospital was planning to expand its campus and needed a place to store construction equipment during the construction phase. In exchange for the ten-acre Lincoln Park property, the hospital planned to give the Department of Parks and Recreation an eight-acre site in Glenwood, a middle-class neighborhood located in East Chattanooga.

The City announced that they would build a park where the old children's hospital had once stood. The *Chattanooga Times* reported: "The City Commissioner said the use of Lincoln Park has been gradually phased out, except for two ball fields there, with the recreational needs of the community being served at the nearby Carver Center and Warner Park. The Lincoln Park swimming pool has been long closed. The tennis courts have not been repaired because new and better ones are available at Carver Center and

Warner Park. And the little-used recreation center at Lincoln Park has finally been closed."[3]

In making the case for the land swap, city officials argued that the park and its facilities had been declining for years. Only a fraction of its original amenities remained, they argued, and most of them had deteriorated substantially after years of prioritizing the Carver Center and Warner Park for resources. Though the Commissioner argued that the African American community's recreational needs were being met by Warner Park and the Carver Recreation Center, he did not acknowledge that many black Chattanoogans felt uncomfortable or unsafe using the facilities at Warner Park, where they had been legally excluded for decades. Nor did he discuss the historical and cultural value of the park to the black community. Finally, while the newly constructed Carver Recreation Center did not have the same history of exclusion, its facilities were not equipped to serve the nearly ten thousand children and youth living on the eastside of town. Instead, the Commissioner offered an economic rationale for systematic neglect and disinvestment of one of the region's most historically significant black cultural destinations.

With the land negotiated, the City first allowed Erlanger to store their equipment on a portion of the site. But in 1979, the City transferred ownership over one portion of the park to the Hamilton County Hospital Authority, and the remainder of it was deeded to them in 1981. By 1985, Erlanger Medical Center's campus had expanded by 500,000 square feet. The additional square footage included a 1,200-car parking garage, two multipurpose buildings, five additional floors above the Children's Hospital, a combination energy plant and laundry facility, and six additional floors to the west wing of the medical center.[4]

Lincoln Park Neighborhood Improvement League

During the same time period, Erlanger Hospital purchased nearly a dozen additional residential and commercial properties in the adjacent Lincoln Park neighborhood and along East Third Street. Realizing the extent of the hospital's encroachment and fearing for their own homes, several neighborhood residents sprang into action. In 1982, they organized the Lincoln Park Neighborhood Improvement League and immediately began negotiating with Erlanger Hospital on an institutional expansion moratorium.

The Improvement League was successful in reaching an agreement—but its efforts continued beyond the initial negotiation. The League's president,

Bessie "Mother" Smith, convinced her co-organizers to apply for Community Development Block Grant funds from the U.S. Department of Housing and Urban Development to begin neighborhood stabilization efforts throughout the Lincoln Park neighborhood. The League was awarded their first grant one year later (1983–84). By 1985, the group had received half a million dollars in CDBG funds, which they prioritized for street, sidewalk, curb, and gutter improvements. Based on their success, the neighborhood was also selected to participate in a "comprehensive housing rehabilitation program" sponsored by the City and funded through the CDBG program.[5]

The Lincoln Park Improvement League also launched important cooperative and mutual aid initiatives that did not rely on public funds. In 1986, the League organized a citywide fundraiser to help Alberta Sorrell, a seventy-one-year-old widow who had lived in a rented house in the neighborhood for seventeen years, to purchase the rental home she was in risk of being evicted from by an absentee landlord who wanted to sell the property. In response, the Improvement League organized teas and bake sales and solicited donations from local churches. Through these activities, they raised the $4,000 asking price and were able to offer Sorrell an interest-free, affordable loan so that she could purchase her home from her landlord. Additionally, the League negotiated with local housing nonprofit developers Chattanooga Neighborhood Enterprise to offer Sorrell a no-interest home improvement loan so that she could make necessary upgrades to the house. The group planned to use the monies repaid by Sorrell to start a revolving loan fund so that they could offer similar services to other low-income households in the neighborhood.[6]

Piloting the Community Impact Initiative in Lincoln Park

The Lincoln Park Neighborhood Improvement League's model for cooperative, resident-driven community development caught the attention of both local and national community development practitioners. Chattanooga Neighborhood Enterprise had formed after the famous urban designer and real estate developer James Rouse visited Chattanooga and challenged city leaders to combat the widespread housing deterioration plaguing the historic core (see chapter 6).

Some CNE staff approached Lincoln Park's leaders to be a pilot neighborhood for their Community Impact Initiative—a program that evolved from the Venture 2000 Initiative and was intended to eliminate all substandard housing citywide within a decade. The organization commended the League for their collaborative, cooperative approach, calling it a model for sustainable neighborhood development: "That's the key to the Enterprise program: neighborhoods working together to meet the housing needs of their residents, and receiving support from the foundation and other interested agencies and individuals to structure rehabilitation programs and financing packages that get the job done while keeping the price of housing within the means of the poor."[7]

Same, Same—No Change

While on paper and in the press the Lincoln Park Neighborhood Improvement League's partnership with CNE was touted as a model for successful neighborhood revitalization, descriptions of the collaboration from neighborhood leaders who participated in the initiative paint a less optimistic scene. Lincoln Park homeowner and Neighborhood Association president Vannice Hughley first got involved with neighborhood organizing and community development during CNE's pilot program. She offered the following extended description of her role in an initiative, which she believed ultimately caused more damage to neighborhood trust and civic morale than good:

> The community has been 'empowered' by a number of organizations.
> The more things change, the more they remain same. Same, same—no
> change. Lincoln Park was a pilot area for Chattanooga Neighborhood
> Enterprise. . . . Mother [Bessie Smith] was in charge. CNE got down
> in here and was walking and talking from house to house. There was
> a lot of resistance, especially from the older people. A lot of "I'm not
> dealing with this!" And me really believing what I was being told,
> that this was the way it had always been. If you say it, we believe it
> until proven different. I was under the impression that this was going
> to happen! This was going to happen. People could sign up, and
> they'd sign up, enthused, after we talked to them. Me, especially—I
> sold the thing to them. Me, walking with Mayor Bob Corker and
> Mother, on the street, talking to people.
>
> Now, after it was all over, there were people who—well, who were
> homeowners, and who made too much money. But you don't remem-
> ber when they said, "Low to moderate income"? Well, by what
> scales? Anyway, no money came. My husband and I didn't qualify.
> They had you thinking that there were home improvement loans.

People said, "Oh, I want that." But to no avail . . . I would say the renters, they probably got over good. Because a lot of their properties were repaired. Other than that, I didn't see anything happening. Every time a person would try to ask for a loan or qualify for a loan, there was nothing happening. There was a man . . . [Matt Piles] I was just giving him a fit. He stopped taking my calls. Because he would talk the talk, but wouldn't walk the walk. So finally I said, "I don't want to deal with this anymore. I don't want to deal with it because it's not what it was supposed to be." . . . I was just over it. I said, "This is not fair." I told him, "You've got some nerve coming down here and getting people emotionally invested, when you knew you weren't going to do anything about it." I was so mad at him. . . . So that's what was happening then. Nothing happened. Same, same—no change.[8]

Hughley believes that she and other neighborhood leaders were used by CNE staff and city officials to build community buy-in for an incentive program that was never meant to directly benefit the longtime working-class homeowners living in Lincoln Park. Absentee landlords who owned rental properties in the neighborhood often qualified for rental rehabilitation loans based on the incomes of their tenants, but the owner-occupied households that needed improvement capital most of all rarely qualified for assistance. In consequence, many longtime residents had their hopes built up only to be let down. This exacerbated residents' distrust of city government, as well as their trust of leaders in the Lincoln Park Neighborhood Improvement League, whose members did most of the grassroots organizing for CNE. Further, Hughley's story underscores the relativity and fuzziness of the terms *low* and *moderate income*, and illustrates how planners often use the language of community empowerment to catalyze economic gentrification.

Besides the issue of non-qualifying residents, Hughley criticized CNE's work in Lincoln Park on the basis that they never completed many of the streetscape improvements that they started. By the late 1980s, CNE's money for work in Lincoln Park had dried up. Today, two decades after the CNE pilot program was launched, many sidewalks remain half-completed, and are inaccessible to people with limited physical mobility. Several streets are without nighttime lighting, there are no public trash or recycling cans, and storm water management issues continue to affect residents whenever it rains.[9]

Erlanger in the Age of Community Partnerships

By the late 1980s, Erlanger Hospital had purchased most of the available land along the UTC-Erlanger East Third Street corridor and several properties in the Lincoln Park neighborhood. In the past, the relationship between the hospital and the Improvement League had been contentious. In an effort to rebuild some of the trust that had been lost during the previous decade, Erlanger began conversations with CNE about "adopting" the neighborhood in order to market it as a desirable place for doctors and hospital employees to purchase homes. "What we're doing," one spokesman from CNE told *Chattanooga Times*, "is turning an adversarial relationship into a kind of cooperative one."[10]

Likewise, representatives from Erlanger signaled a turning point in hospital-neighborhood relations. Carolyn Gilliam, a spokeswoman for Erlanger, characterized their efforts as an olive branch: "It's a different picture today. We want our neighbors to be as beautiful as we're trying to be. Mrs. Smith has been battling for a long time. She may have some scars from those battles."[11]

In the early 1990s, the hospital launched the Erlanger Community Partnership, an initiative focused on restoring a portion of the historic park into a usable "public" space. Over the next twenty-four months, Mayor Gene Roberts, the City's Department of Economic and Community Development, and CNE got involved. The group secured $30,000 in CDBG funds and used the money to make several improvements to the park. First, they commissioned a replica of Lincoln Park's original stone archway and had it installed on a parcel of land that Erlanger deeded back to the city. Additionally, they installed tennis courts, a basketball court, picnic tables, and grills. In exchange for these improvements, the Lincoln Park Neighborhood Improvement League assumed responsibility for maintaining some of the landscaping on the grounds.

Over the next fifteen years, little public attention was focused on Lincoln Park or its surrounding neighborhood. The Improvement League renamed itself the Lincoln Park Neighborhood Association and continued to uphold its end of the Erlanger Partnership by maintaining the landscaping where the archway had been constructed. The hospital maintained its end of the bargain by not encroaching further into the neighborhood, while CNE and the city turned their attention away from Lincoln Park and toward other neighborhoods in the urban core as they began to focus more on market rate housing development.

The Shifting Scope of Riverside Revitalization

Although city and institutional planners never achieved the sort of New Urbanist, mixed-income economic revitalization they had envisioned in the 1980s, the Lincoln Park neighborhood remained relatively unchanged through the first decade of the twenty-first century. Over the past twenty years, the historically black neighborhood remained small but stable, with 270 residents, 91.5 percent of whom were African American, and with 47 black households (42.3 percent) owning their own homes. The most dramatic demographic shift has been the aging of its population: between 2000 and 2010, the population over the age of sixty-five more than doubled, and the population over eighty nearly tripled. Whereas in 2000, senior citizens comprised 20.1 percent of the total population, in 2010, 43.7 percent of residents were over the age of sixty-five. Residents over the age of eighty alone comprised nearly 30 percent (28.7 percent) of the total population in Lincoln Park. Correspondingly, there has been a significant decrease in the number of working-age adults living in the neighborhood: between 2000 and 2010, the number of eighteen- to sixty-four-year-olds dropped by 39 percent.[12]

As the neighborhood's population has aged in place, the focus of the Lincoln Park Neighborhood Association has shifted. The vast majority of the Neighborhood Association's members today are senior citizens concerned about noise, public safety, and youth violence. The park had historically been a space for intergenerational community building, but today is perceived as unsafe by many senior residents. Despite their concerns about safety, there is widespread agreement that the park is a valuable historical community asset that ought to be preserved and enhanced, specifically by and for Chattanooga's African American community. These commitments have ramped up significantly in the past several years, as it has slowly come to light that the City has its own vision for the historic park and its namesake neighborhood.

Although the politically contentious Central Avenue freeway project proposed in the early 1970s was ultimately abandoned, recent history revealed that plans for a Central Avenue extension were only shelved. In late 2011, the City announced their plan to use federal funds to construct an extension of Central Avenue north to Amnicola Highway. The proposal was championed by the Regional Planning Agency and UTC Chancellor Richard Brown as a project consistent with the university's long-term Master Plan to provide student housing and other university amenities in and along the Third Street corridor.[13]

Tiffany Rankins, vice president of the Neighborhood Association, described how she and Hughley first learned that the City was revisiting their plans for a roadway to bisect their neighborhood. Although Hughley had been the president of the Neighborhood Association for several years, she and Rankins learned about the extension the same way that everyone else in the city did: by reading about it in the *Times Free Press*.

Furious that neighborhood residents had been left out of the conversations leading up to the decision to reintroduce the Central Avenue extension project, Hughley and Rankins reached out to the public officials mentioned in Smith's newspaper article to get a better sense of the scope and scale of the extension project. But, instead of having a frank conversation about how the road would impact the park space and adjacent neighborhood, they were shown architectural drawings and assured that they were only "conceptual" plans for the extension. In Rankins's recollection, the politics were palpable:

> There was an article in the paper in 2011, with an image of a map, and it mentioned the extension. So basically, Mom started calling the mayor's office, and I got on the phone and asked someone to explain the maps. The city engineer agreed to host a meeting downtown to provide details about the plan. He [the city engineer] didn't show, but some other people showed: the architect showed, and Ellis Smith, the reporter. So we were sort of twiddling our thumbs, going back and forth. What was kind of weird was Ellis Smith got up and asked the architect whether he had said anything that made them mad. I thought, why would he say that?
>
> So then we called the mayor's office and told them that nobody had showed up to the meeting. So they said they'd come down [to Lincoln Park]. But we had no idea [of] the kind of entourage they'd bring in. So basically each individual was getting up and saying a little of this, a little of that. They were showing concepts at the time, which ended up being the actual design, but they kept calling it a "concept." Every time [Mayor] Littlefield spoke, he would turn to his colleagues rather than to us. They didn't tell us about the NEPA application or any of those things. We were basically . . . we didn't know what to ask. . . . So then they left, and the next thing we heard was when Councilor McGary called one morning to say that they would be voting on the project that evening. We got up [to the Council meeting] and said, "What can

we do about this?" And [Chattanooga City Councilor] Pam Ladd said, "Basically, nothing."[14]

Though the Central Avenue extension was slated to use state and federal transportation dollars and was therefore subject to the National Environmental Protection Act (NEPA) and Title VI antidiscrimination stipulations, city officials and their consultants had not made neighborhood residents explicitly aware of the public comment period leading up to the approval of public funds. When leaders of the Neighborhood Association subsequently expressed their surprise and disapproval of the proposed route through their historic park, they were told that the project had been in the works for forty years and was unstoppable. Even though the funds had not yet been approved at the time of the 2013 City Council meeting described by Rankins, Chief Engineer Bill Payne was quoted in the *Times Free Press* as saying, "The goal isn't for residents to say if they want the Central Avenue extension but to help the city determine the community impact it will have. It's not necessarily a question of 'do you want this or not.'"[15]

For Rankins and Hughley, the meeting with Mayor Littlefield and his entourage was further evidence that professional planners in Chattanooga had no real commitment to the needs and desires of the local African American community—especially when they concerned low-income and socially vulnerable residents, as was the case in Lincoln Park, where the majority are renters, and most are elderly and living on fixed incomes. Rankins described the distrust that was cemented because of these encounters: "Mom says it all the time: when someone is getting shot, murdered, or when the houses are burning, it's 'your community,' but when I want to take something in there and build it up, it's 'our community.' [Mayor] Littlefield came up in here and said this has been going on for forty years! What has? What's been going on? And it's not just him. When it was going through the City Council there were councilors up there telling us, 'There's nothing you can do about it.' I was sitting there like, 'Wow. *This is how they talk to us.*' You know your voice doesn't mean a thing. They say, 'We'll come and get your input.' But what for? You're not going to do anything with it or about it."[16]

The double standard in outreach and engagement described by Rankins underscores the racialized politics of stakeholdership in a city that has long tried to cover up its more sinister practices with liberal multicultural discourse and cosmetic place-making improvements. Her statement also underscores the paternalism that many city officials display toward low-income residents of color and their neighborhoods. In Chattanooga, where black poverty is pathologized, and residents are told they must "take their own neighborhoods back" from criminals and other "undesirables," statements such as those made during the early Central Avenue meetings connote a failure on the City's part to acknowledge historical legacies of racism and exclusion against black Chattanoogans. As gentrification expands beyond the central business district and real estate pressures create new frontiers of capital accumulation in historically neglected parts of the city, public discourse shifts. Suddenly, impoverished inner-city neighborhoods are treated not as local residents' responsibilities, but as underutilized urban assets, ripe for the taking. The onus is no longer on existing residents to take their communities back, but on city officials and private developers to save these neighborhoods from themselves.

A Neighborhood Fights Back, Again

The outcomes of these double standards are evident in policy and planning documents used by planners and urban technicians to rationalize their expansions into new gentrification frontiers. In her statements above, Rankins mentioned that city officials did not explain the NEPA process or the criteria that they used to assess the environmental and social impacts of the Central Avenue extension. Had they done so, neighborhood leaders maintain, residents would have submitted comments describing how the further destruction of the park would significantly and negatively impact the historic and cultural integrity of their community.

But the process was not transparent to neighborhood leaders, who immediately began to explore options for stopping it and/or changing its route after learning about the extension plan. At the same time that city-hired consultants URS Corporation were completing an "Assessment of Historical/Architectural Resources" as part of the required NEPA documentation, Rankins discovered that the designation of the park as an historic site might exclude the use of public monies for the project. Unaware that the City had already been in conversation with the state historic preservation office, Rankins compiled and submitted an application to the State to have the park designated as a historic place. Her argument focused on the Olympic-sized swimming pool, built with WPA funds, and the baseball fields where the Negro Leagues had practiced and played: "[Lincoln Park] is a historical place, and basically I wanted to just try to put a hold, as far as getting the federal money, any way I could. . . . If they're asking for federal money, then my tax money . . . goes to supporting that hospital. It's not private. So I should have some sort of say-so. It's the same thing with the land swap. It went on, and it was all undercover. Who knew? Who knew? I'm not trying to get all upset about it, but let's preserve what's left as an African American park. Because there's still a lot that can be done with it."[17]

After submitting their application, Rankins received a letter from the state preservation office thanking her for her claim but rejecting it. Their rejection was based on two points: state officers determined that the site had been irreparably altered, and that the property owners (Erlanger Hospital) were not in support of such a designation, and the State had no power to impose the historic designation on an unwilling property owner.[18]

On receiving the rejection letter from the State, Rankins and Hughley approached Erlanger Hospital, who owns the property. They emphasized the historic and cultural significance of the park to the African American community, and inquired whether the hospital might be willing to get on board with a plan to save what was left of the park and build a community economic development agenda around the preservation of one of the few remaining African American historical assets in the city. Unwilling to budge, the hospital initially recalled the same talking points as the City and State. When Rankins and Hughley realized they would be unsuccessful at inspiring a change of heart, they asked the hospital permission to host a Lincoln Park Reunion so that the local African American community could come together to celebrate their memories of the historic public space.

Initially, their suggestion was rejected because of the liability it posed to the hospital. But, as Lincoln Park organizers persisted, another rationale emerged. Rankins and Hughley recalled how they were told during a meeting with hospital administrators, most of whom were white, that Erlanger was uncomfortable with having one of their properties associated with the United Negro League of professional baseball because of the word "Negro." Rather than place the term in its historical context and celebrate the site as a critical space of African American placemaking during the Jim Crow period, administrators and board members preferred to disassociate themselves with the realities of historic race relations in the city. The denial of this place-based history stands in stark contrast to the work that has been done to acknowledge, repent, and reconcile with the public sector's role in the forced removal of the Cherokee vis-à-vis the Trail of Tears.[19]

Lincoln Park and the Planning
Free School of Chattanooga

When the *Times Free Press* reported on the five-lane Central Avenue extension in early March 2013, one frequent Planning Free School participant brought the article to a Transportation and Mobility discussion group meeting and suggested that Chattanooga Organized for Action and the Planning Free School engage Lincoln Park leaders to see if they might be able to assist them in their efforts to halt the road extension through the park space. Then COA organizers sprang into action; they quickly engaged neighborhood association leaders from all neighborhoods potentially affected by the Central Avenue extension, and invited them to a meeting to discuss the current transportation proposal. After hearing from members of the Lincoln Park neighborhood, neighboring community leaders agreed that the plan was myopic: an extension through Lincoln Park would destroy one of the few remaining African American historical assets in Chattanooga.

These neighborhood associations, which included the more affluent areas of Fort Wood and Highland Park, banded together to form the Coalition to Save Lincoln Park. The Coalition began to meet with representatives from Erlanger, the City of Chattanooga, and the Hamilton County Regional Planning Agency. They insisted that the extension proposal and public monies had been approved without having engaged any directly impacted residents, which is a direct violation of federal Title VI antidiscrimination legislation.

Simultaneously, COA organizers encouraged neighborhood leaders from Lincoln Park to attend Planning Free School workshops (discussed in the previous chapter) to gain further research and technical planning skills to aid in their negotiation efforts. Several members of the neighborhood, including Rankins and Hughley, began to attend Arts and Cultural Development and Housing discussion group meetings.[20] To accommodate their real-time planning needs, the Planning Free School adapted its curriculum to make Lincoln Park a case study for ongoing collaborative analysis. The City had recently posted a memo with the preliminary Assessment of Historical/Architectural Resources document completed by their consultants. It concluded that:

> The preliminary assessment is that Lincoln Park does not meet
> National Register of Historic Places (NRHP) eligibility because it
> does not retain its historic size and features. The park has been

reduced in size by over half. Additionally, the only historic features that remain on the subject piece of land are: (1) the old gate post, which stands at the southern edge of the park along Cleveland Street; (2) and the concession stand, which has been altered. Extant features in the park date to the 1980s and 1990s. While the tennis courts may be at or near their historic location, the current ballfield is not.

Lincoln Park Neighborhood—The preliminary assessment is that the Lincoln Park neighborhood does not meet NRHP eligibility because development has eroded the neighborhood edges to the west and south, numerous homes have been demolished leaving vacant lots throughout the neighborhood, a number of new houses have been built and many older homes have been altered by substantial renovations and additions. Additionally, the small neighborhood lacks a cohesive feel architecturally as it was built out in different eras and there are many vacant lots and two relatively large paved parking lots adjacent to the neighborhood churches.[21]

Though cloaked in politically neutral, seemingly objective language, consultants essentially argued that decades of institutional neglect and municipal disinvestment in the park justified the determination that the park lacked historical and architectural integrity, and was therefore ineligible for designation and the protections that accompanied it. Nowhere in their assessment had the authors contextualized the physical deterioration occurring in the neighborhood, nor did they acknowledge the neighborhood's advocacy for the preservation of the park. The judgment illustrates the authors' lack of intimate or first-hand knowledge of the historic park space. Had residents who knew and remembered the park been part of NEPA evaluation, they would have quickly pointed out that the "old gate post" was a reproduction constructed in the 1990s during the era of Erlanger's community partnership, and that the original WPA-era pool and bathhouse, though significantly altered, were still intact on the site.

During one of the Arts and Cultural Development Planning Free School workshops, Lincoln Park leaders were given the floor to make their case for historic preservation and discuss how the restoration of the park might catalyze future economic revitalization for Chattanooga's black community. The themes of this conversation were unmistakable: the park had been a critical site of diasporic placemaking for African Americans across the Southeast, and its historical significance had implications for social justice and equitable development in Chattanooga in the future. Furthermore, the park and its namesake residential community were inseparable: what impacted one impacted the other; the destruction of one implies the destruction of the other; survival and cultural preservation of both are inextricable.

During another Transformative Placemaking workshop focused on linking cultural development to community economic justice agendas, Hughley described her motivation for opposing the Central Avenue extension: "I think, I really do . . . we have something to be very, very . . . I don't use the word 'proud'—but we have something to be thankful for and grateful for. Because we are connected to a historical area; the Lincoln Park and the Lincoln Park Community join together. This park was famous and had notoriety, and we ought to be the same way. It used to be better. This community used to be a better community. It was all about . . . see people . . . took care of their . . . we had rentals where everybody took care of the house and took care of the children. You knew you were in Lincoln Park and it was about something."[22]

For Hughley, her family, and many of her neighbors, stopping the extension was about much more than preserving the physical integrity of the historic park space, or preventing upticks in noise or traffic. The park has deep symbolic meaning for many longtime residents, not to mention Chattanooga's black community at large, many of whom remember the once vibrant and tight-knit neighborhood, of which the park was the social and economic centerpiece. For them, stopping the Central Avenue extension is even more fundamentally about preserving the cultural integrity of Lincoln Park as this sort of place, as a neighborhood "about something."

Out of this series of Planning Free School workshops, the Coalition to Save Lincoln Park developed the motto of its campaign: "No to Central Avenue—Yes to Lincoln Park!" At its core, the message was not merely a rejection of the road extension. More fundamentally, it was an affirmation of the people who knew and loved the neighborhood and called it their home. Besides using the Planning Free School as an organizing space, Lincoln Park leaders participated in Skill Shares and Issue-Based Discussion Groups in order to increase their technical planning vocabulary and capacity. They did this in part to participate more aptly in discussions with the mayor's office and staff from the Regional Planning Agency.

More importantly, though, Lincoln Park leaders attended Skill Shares to develop expertise to launch a neighborhood planning initiative independent from these institutional actors, using the Sustaining People and Reclaiming Communities (SPARC) model of planning described in the previous chapter. Several residents and their allies attended the Planning Free School's Comprehensive Neighborhood Assessment training, which they then used to collect parcel-level land use and quality of life data, and, ultimately, diagnose their neighborhood's planning strengths and opportunities.

Having the ability to collect, analyze, and represent their own neighborhood-level data gave resident leaders power over Lincoln Park's narrative of place and vision for its urban change, which had up until then been dominated by university and local transportation planners who stressed greater connectivity, road network efficiency, and institutional expansion. During one Housing discussion focused on exploring cooperative land models, for example, participants explored community land trusts (CLTs) as a tool for removing property from the speculative market, and promoting place-based community development.

To contextualize the potential of CLTs, participants assessed parcel maps and neighborhood housing data and explored whether and how a CLT might help Lincoln Park practice self-determination in the context of short- and long-term gentrification planning across Chattanooga's historic core. Neighborhood leaders debated strategies to promote CLT conversion of neighborhood housing, which included acquiring vacancies and working with elderly homeowners to potentially put their properties into community trust. They ultimately chose to pursue the land trust model for the historic park space, which they thought could help preserve the park as public space, in perpetuity, while also introducing residents to the land trust model and making them comfortable with the nontraditional ownership structure.[23]

Tentative Wins

Shortly thereafter, the Coalition to Save Lincoln Park began carrying their message "No to Central Avenue/Yes to Lincoln Park!" into hospital, city, and regional planning agency board rooms. At the same time, resident leaders from the Lincoln Park neighborhood continued to develop engagement skills, and collect and analyze community-level data to substantiate the claims they were making vis-à-vis the Planning Free School. They used these skills to apply pressure to local leaders, forcing them to clarify their intentions and be transparent about how authorization and spending decisions were made.

During one Chattanooga-Hamilton County/North Georgia Transportation Planning Organization (TPO) Board meeting, for example, a group of activists led by Lincoln Park leaders arrived with signs and demanded deeper accountability from local decision makers. During this meeting, COA organizers mentioned the possibility of a Title VI antidiscrimination complaint; then deputy chief of staff Jeff Cannon ultimately conceded that the City had been given more than fifteen different options for the Central Avenue extension by consultants, several of which did not bisect the historic park space, and promised to share them with concerned residents.[24]

Within days, the mayor's office organized a press conference to release a public resolution, declaring that no money would be drawn for the Central Avenue extension project until an authentic public engagement process was implemented for directly impacted communities. In his resolution, Mayor Berke made the following promise: "I want to say loud and clear to the residents of Lincoln Park and surrounding neighborhoods: we will make you part of any process that affects your neighborhood. We want and need your input."[25]

Lincoln Park leaders also began to gain some traction with Erlanger Hospital, who owned the property. By early summer 2013, Erlanger Hospital had agreed to sponsor the "first annual" Lincoln Park reunion later that summer and cover the cost of liability insurance for the event. In late June, the Neighborhood Association hosted a Reunion Planning meeting with neighborhood residents at the Gethsemane Missionary Baptist Church. The goal of the meeting was to engage neighborhood residents in a discussion about how to best structure the reunion event. Facilitators adapted a "City as Play" workshop inspired by planner James Rojas's "Place It!" participation model, which they had completed during the Planning Free School; they used this activity to prompt residents to create models of their "ideal reunion" for Lincoln Park.[26] They then used those stories of place to create a list of participants' desires for the reunion event.

At this meeting, residents invited administrators from Erlanger Hospital to hear directly from Lincoln Park residents, as well as other residents from across the city, about the historical and cultural significance of the park. In addition to the "ideal reunion" exercise, neighborhood leaders led hospital officials on a transect walk of Erlanger's property to point out existing historic infrastructure, including the bathhouse constructed as part of the WPA program. The walk had been inspired by a Planning Free School Skill Share workshop that several Coalition members attended on transect walks earlier that spring. The interactive, highly participatory exercise helped residents clarify inaccuracies stated in the draft Assessment of Historical/Architectural Resources, and allowed hospital administrators to understand more deeply the significance of the park and neighborhood to the local and regional African American population.

SPARCing a New Era of Community Self-Determination in Lincoln Park?

As Lincoln Park leaders worked closely with Chattanooga Organized for Action on the Coalition to Save Lincoln Park, a trust in COA's intentions and organizing tactics began to form. Unlike the mid-1980s so-called partnerships with Chattanooga Neighborhood Enterprise, Erlanger Hospital, and the East Chattanooga Improvement League's Weed and Seed program, leaders came to believe that COA has no motive other than to help their neighborhood exercise community self-determination in the face of institutional encroachment and mounting gentrification pressure. When asked how their collaboration with COA was different from previous partnerships, Rankins and Hughley replied that:

HUGHLEY: For one thing, it's more involved.

RANKINS: [And] there is more action . . .

HUGHLEY: And that's something that we never had before. [To have] somebody who is on your side; who is for your cause. That's something we've never had before. And so that's why I'm just amazed by [Perrin Lance, executive director of COA] being up there, jumping on them people. Oh man.

RANKINS: It's good to have someone who's not afraid of their job. You know what I mean? That's the only thing.

HUGHLEY: That's the whole thing.[27]

COA organizers demonstrated their willingness to take political risks and speak truth to power; in effect, neighborhood leaders in historically marginalized communities like Lincoln Park began to see collaboration with the group as something distinctive from previous community planning initiatives. But the proof of this difference lies not only in its process; it also lies in COA's ability to help local communities leverage tangible benefits and outcomes. Rankins summarized the importance of showing commitment through outcomes, linking it to building trust: "You've got to make sure each step is a winning step, and for it to be shown as a winning step. You have to keep [directly impacted residents] involved in the process; you can't, basically, do things without keeping them involved. Because now you're basically at a point where, for so many years, people have seen that nothing has been done. They really believe that 'these white folks do what they want to do.' That's their phrase. So I am telling them, 'No, you have a voice in all of this—you just need to speak it well.' They have to listen."[28]

The COA goal to help enable community self-determination and inter-dependence inspired leaders in Lincoln Park to commit to participating in the Sustaining People and Reclaiming Communities planning initiative. On June 23, 2013, Yolanda Putnam of the *Times Free Press* published an article announcing Lincoln Park's plan to develop a neighborhood vision and action plan vis-à-vis the SPARC initiative.[29] This announcement was critical for two reasons. First, it placed pressure on the Berke administration, which had previously promised meaningful community input but had not issued any details about what that process would actually look like. Second, it flipped the direction of traditional engagement and community planning processes in the city: instead of having a City or regional planning agency-controlled process where residents were invited into the process, residents announced that they would be organizing and managing their own community engagement process, and the City and hospital would be the stakeholders invited to the neighborhood's decision-making table.

Two months later, the Coalition to Save Lincoln Park gained what appeared to be a monumental win. Mayor Andy Berke organized a press conference in the neighborhood, during which time he announced that the City would no longer pursue its original road extension through the park. Additionally, Berke promised to work with Erlanger Hospital and the Trust for Public Land to return the property to public use and ensure that the site was preserved as a site of black history and placemaking in perpetuity.[30] Two months later, the City announced that it had reached a land swap deal with Erlanger Hospital. In exchange for 5.3 acres of the Lincoln Park property, Erlanger would receive a parcel in Alton Park for the construction of a new community health center.[31]

Over the next year, the Lincoln Park neighborhood participated in an abridged version of the SPARC Initiative described in the previous chapter. As part of this process, they collected and analyzed baseline neighborhood data and worked with local architecture nonprofit The Glass House Collective to develop housing, economic development, cultural development and tourism, and transportation solutions for the neighborhood. Features of their proposal and site plan for the park space include the conversion of the historic bathhouse structure into an African American Heritage Museum, planting community gardens and hosting a farmer's market, a "Wall of Fame" tribute to the United Negro League baseball players who played at the park, restored baseball and basketball facilities, a community pavilion, and a number of additional streetscape and public urban amenity improvements.[32]

Despite these gains, more recent announcements from the City have left residents skeptical about the true intentions of the Berke administration. In March 2014, the City released new drawings of the Central Avenue extension. Although the route changed slightly from previous drawings, it still appeared that the extension bisected and encroached on a small section of the park.[33] Resident leaders protested, eventually threatening the City with a Title VI complaint, and representatives from the mayor's office threatened to pull the plug on the land swap and park restoration.

Resident leaders had hoped that, by developing their own neighborhood vision and plan, they would preempt the entrance of regional planning staff, who stated that they would begin a comprehensive planning process in the neighborhood beginning in 2017. In reality, the regional planning agency began this process much sooner, when they launched the Third to Riverside Neighborhood Planning process after winning an EPA Brownfield Area Wide Planning Grant in late 2013. This initiative has a broader geographic scope than the historic Lincoln Park neighborhood, but the primary residential district is the historic neighborhood.

Notably, in addition to the park and neighborhood, the NEPA Assessment of Historical/Architectural Resources had included a third site of potential impact: the Cumberland Corporation site (constructed in 1941/1947), which is located directly to the north of the park and adjacent to the Lincoln Park neighborhood. The NEPA evaluators concluded that, unlike Lincoln Park, the Cumberland Corporation site is eligible for historic preservation status because it has retained its architectural integrity—a designation that would enable developers to access a range of historic tax credits and related financial incentives.[34]

The Cumberland Corporation facility has been eyed by local planners as a potential adaptive reuse site for several years. The hospital and university in particular had identified the property for potential redevelopment into high-end housing and commercial space because of its interesting industrial architecture and proximity to their facilities. To these ends, the Environmental Protection Agency (US EPA) selected Enterprise Center, Inc. as one of its FY 2013 "Area Wide Planning Grant" recipients. The $200,000 award was to develop a planning assessment of the Third Street corridor, including the Cannon/Cumberland Corporation and Lincoln Park neighborhoods. Concurrently, the *Times Free Press* reported that a private developer was very interested in redeveloping the factory into a multifamily condo and apartment project.[35]

Over the next two years, staff of the Chattanooga-Hamilton County Regional Planning Agency (RPA) developed a research and engagement strategy to complete the Brownfield area planning study. Though traditional in their participation strategy (staff organized a charrette as well as a series of exercises, including transect walks and a visual preference survey), these planners encouraged Lincoln Park leaders to participate in the activities, and gave them time during one public meeting to present the vision for the park and neighborhood that they had developed, in part, through their participation with the SPARC Initiative and Planning Free School.

Considering the redevelopment potential of the Cumberland Corporation site, which the EPA-funded study ultimately concluded was a key "catalyst site" for the continued revitalization of the Tennessee Riverfront and Third Street corridor, the motivations driving the Central Avenue extension are clearly about more than connecting two thoroughfares and offering better ambulance access to the hospital. The proposed extension, as well as Lincoln Park residents' opposition to the development, ought to be understood in the context of short-, middle-, and long-range gentrification planning in the city. The Cumberland Corporation site, perceived as an attractive adaptive reuse project, is considered eligible for historic designation and revitalization, despite the presumption of high levels of site contamination. Yet, the historic assets associated with a working-class black neighborhood and Chattanooga's African American community at large have been deemed ineligible because decades of neglect on the part of the hospital authority have deteriorated the historic facilities.

The threat of displacement that some residents feel was further cemented in 2014, after the River City Company expanded its redevelopment priority area to include the Third Street corridor and the Lincoln Park neighborhood. Though the Third Street Neighborhood Plan calls for greater urban equity through the preservation and construction of new affordable housing, these goals were not operationalized, and little else in the document suggests that local institutional actors are invested in seeing the Lincoln Park neighborhood preserved as a working- class community.

The Neighborhood Association's vision was included as an appendix in their draft plan, and several of the report's key recommendations responded directly to the concerns that the Coalition to Save Lincoln Park had regularly raised, including the preservation of the park, cultural programming and tourism, senior housing and affordability, placemaking, and economic development:

> The plan recommends retaining and enhancing the existing Lincoln Park area that is bordered by Cleveland Avenue to the south and Central Avenue to the west. The conceptual design indicated on the plan map illustrates how the current area could be designed to accommodate a small ball field, tennis courts, basketball courts, playground, a pedestrian path, and a community pavilion space. These proposed elements were derived from the features noted in the schematic park design submitted by the residents at one of the public workshops. Residents have also expressed an interest in repurposing the original Lincoln Park bathhouse into an African American Heritage Museum and Community Center which is located across Central Avenue to the west. The bathhouse is currently owned, managed, and used by Erlanger Hospital as a grounds maintenance building. It is strongly recommended that future designs prominently celebrate the history of Lincoln Park as a regional African American recreational center. When a park program plan is developed for Lincoln Park these elements, including restoration of the original bathhouse, should be explored.[36]

However, the document also firmly advocates for the Central Avenue extension project, which the RPA sees as essential to unlocking the economic and housing potential of the Cumberland site. The neighborhood rejects this stance, and again, cooperation has dissolved and negotiations are at an impasse. The Coalition to Save Lincoln Park has used this time lag to establish relationships with local Native American activists, who also challenge the road extension on the basis that it would further desecrate Citico Mound, a Mississippian-era burial complex that was razed in the early twentieth century to construct Riverfront Parkway. In September 2017, the Keeper of the Park Service determined that the eastern portion of the historic park space is indeed eligible for historical designation—a decision that has boosted the organizing efforts of the Coalition and forced the city to revisit their original environmental impact reports.

Tellingly, the mayor's office linked the land deal to the approval of the Central Avenue extension, which, because of the community's ongoing protest, still has not been completed, more than three years after Mayor Berke made the announcement. In October 2017, the city announced $2 million in funding to "revitalize" the historic park space but provided no indication that funds would also be applied to the preservation of housing affordability within the adjacent residential neighborhood. These political decisions have the potential to exacerbate uneven geographic development in Chattanooga even further by using placemaking to create a façade of tolerance and equality while simultaneously co-opting African American historical and cultural infrastructure for the sake of social and economic "progress" that almost exclusively benefits middle- to upper-class white, "back to the city" enthusiasts.

In short, the City of Chattanooga's land swap with Erlanger Hospital has yet to demonstrate whether Lincoln Park neighborhood's demands for the space will be realized. As time goes on, Coalition members are losing what little semblance of trust they felt toward the mayor's office and RPA planners. What has unequivocally changed, though, is the direction in which this engagement was instigated. The Coalition's campaign combined collaborative research, creative placemaking, and direct organizing to make the case for the inseparability of the park and neighborhood. Rather than wait for the City to outline an engagement plan and invite residents to their decision-making table, Lincoln Park residents proactively developed a vision, collected and analyzed data to substantiate their claims for change, and attended institutional meetings, prepared to discuss their desires for the future. Public sector planners, in turn, had no choice but to acknowledge the Coalition's competent work, and incorporate elements of their vision into the official plan for the neighborhood.

Ultimately, Lincoln Park is an illustrative case for thinking through the politics of diasporic placemaking for three important reasons. It is one of the oldest and most historically significant black neighborhoods in Chattanooga—the product of more than a century of cooperative placemaking and community building. Though significantly altered by years of city and county neglect, key elements of the historic civic infrastructure remain, and the park clearly retains its historic and cultural significance to the local black community. Nevertheless, the neighborhood is changing, as institutional pressures carry over into housing markets and planned improvements for the neighborhood result in a more diverse and "desirable" place to live. The neighborhood and its namesake park cannot go back in time, they can only move forward. Residents see the potential for the park to catalyze African American tourism and economic development in the future, and time will tell to what extent these visions are realized.

Second, although most of these place-making efforts have happened outside of formal, institution-backed initiatives, several have occurred inside or because of them. For this reason, Lincoln Park provides a case for better understanding how spatial collaborations, contestations, and negotiations take place in communities comprised of multiple, overlapping diasporic populations.

Finally, members of the Lincoln Park Neighborhood Association are working with Chattanooga Organized for Action and the Coalition to Save Lincoln Park to preserve what remains of their historic public space. They continue to face political and administrative hurdles in making their case for the historical integrity of a long neglected site that is partially designated for hospital facility expansion. Their struggle reveals the complicated politics of local historical preservation in communities impacted by racism, institutional encroachment, disinvestment, and long-term public sector neglect.

Conclusion

To return to the opening pages of this book, the five-hundred-year-long history of urban development and change in Chattanooga, Tennessee, has been complex, heterogeneous, and uneven. At its core, the city's evolution has been propelled by different uprooted and migratory populations carving out communities of material security and cultural belonging from their shared and often contested spatial environments. From Dragging Canoe and the Chickamauga Confederacy's struggle to preserve Cherokee landholdings against encroaching white settlers prior to and during the American Revolutionary War, to Camp Contraband and the Big Nine, multiracial solidarity during the civil rights and black power movements, and contemporary struggles over the right to the city—in all of these stories, urban growth and change have been propelled by spatial collaborations and contestations between different people who, at their core, wanted the same things: places of security and belonging to call "home."

People, regardless of who they are or where they hail from, want to feel safe and secure; they desire to see their personal and shared values represented in their local socio-spatial landscapes. What unites disparate worldviews and encounters are the shared experiences of uprootedness and outsider-ness, as well as the human desires to forge places of belonging regardless of how hostile the environment is. *Diasporic placemaking*— conceived as the vast set of creative, everyday place-making practices through which [historically] uprooted people plant cultural and material roots, offers a practical framework to help us better understand how Chattanooga and cities like it have evolved, and will continue to evolve in the future.

The history of development and change in Chattanooga also shows us how differentiated urban space has been, and continues to be, racialized and socially stratified. In Chattanooga, the contestations and collaborations between different diasporic populations have been shaped by a deeply racialized paternalism, which is enacted largely through place-based public policies and urban development. Institutional political and economic power in Chattanooga is distributed along a spectrum of privilege and opportunity stacked largely in favor of middle-class and property-owning whites, and residents of color living downtown, and in working-class African

American neighborhoods in particular, have endured more than three centuries of expert-driven, so-called rational policy making and planning *to* and *for*, as opposed to *with*, their communities. Wealthy and middle-class white residents, in contrast, have been at the helm of political and development decision making, and over the past forty years the city has become known as a national leader in the realm of participatory planning.

Although we should acknowledge exceptions to this trend, counterexamples are not proof that Chattanooga—or many cities in colonial settler societies—is equitable, fair, or post-racist. To the contrary, this book joins a growing body of historically grounded literature which demonstrates how liberal multicultural politics and place-making efforts typically do little to change unequal, racist social structures. Instead, they inadvertently reinforce concentrations of spatial power and privilege into the hands of middle- and upper-class whites while creating a public image and narrative about racial equality and reconciliation. Though Chattanooga's mainstream place narrative recognizes the contributions of people of color to Chattanooga's city-building efforts, and speak to some efforts, such as the Cherokee and African American placemaking that occurred through the 21st Century Waterfront Plan, these efforts obfuscate persistent racialized inequality in the city by presenting a public façade of celebration, tolerance, and racial reconciliation while failing to substantively enact changes to preserve cultural assets and redistribute material power and resources into working-class black neighborhoods. In short, these place-making efforts interpret but ultimately do not substantively counteract or dismantle legacies of racism and inequality that plague the city.

As described in detail in Appendix 1, "Theorizing Diasporic Placemaking," reconsidering urban development and change through a multidiasporic placemaking frame can help to illuminate patterns of development and stories of place that have been racialized and otherwise differentiated and ordered across a vast network of political and economic opportunity structures. Such a reconsideration demands that our analyses go deeper than the cosmetic, surface levels of urban multiculturalism and place-identity work and focus instead on the everyday collaborations and conflicts that drive the city's ever-evolving networks of place-based, racialized inclusion and exclusion. To say that cities evolve through diasporic placemaking is to demand that we take seriously the "-making" in "placemaking": that we value actions at least as much as we do the words and cultural artifacts produced through them. I have emphasized diasporic "place" and "making" in the context of urban development and change to underscore how unique local and regional environments evolve through complex social interactions, even as they are certainly not limited to transformative multiracial alliances.

Using this frame does more than historically contextualize present-day patterns of social inequality and uneven geographic development. It also helps one uncover and understand place-based legacies of resistance and alternative world-building which may inspire hope and provide wayfaring, if not blueprints, to guide radical community planning in the twenty-first century. From Jewish communists organizing alongside African American laborers in the 1930s, to Chattanooga Organized for Action's alliance with the Westside Community Association and Lincoln Park Neighborhood Association today, this book has presented cases of placemaking, planning, and urban development in Chattanooga over more than several centuries to reveal complex histories of multiracial solidarity that both confirm and defy stereotypes about race, place, and multiethnic social togetherness in the city and across the American South.

Reconstructing stories and structures of place involves the ongoing and sustainable cultivation of community power. In very tangible ways, collective urban storytelling—both its discursive and material forms—is political praxis. In Chattanooga, excavating and reconstructing spaces of multiracial solidarity and togetherness can help community-based organizers wrestle local legacies of antiracist practice away from city boosters who, whether intentionally or not, use idealistic narratives of political liberalism and racial tolerance to conceal ongoing racialized exclusion and growing local social inequality.

Diasporic placemaking extends mainstream definitions of placemaking by demanding that cultural processes of storytelling be treated as inseparable from material processes of structural transformation. In the context of twenty-first-century urban revitalization, this book demonstrates how creativity and cultural development undergird both local social justice practice and sustained inequality. It teaches us that placemaking has the potential to radically transform communities in directions both closer to and further away from racial justice and social equity, and that doing so involves much more than inscribing space with a particular story: it is, quite literally, social in/justice in action.

Lessons for Urban Practitioners

To dig beneath the cosmetic level of place-making practice, then, this book suggests that one must ask oneself who owns and controls local urban storytelling practices, and who benefits from or is burdened by that telling. Often times, the answers to these questions are extremely complex. They are most certainly connected to truths about local political, cultural, and economic infrastructures. Understanding the politics of diasporic placemaking on a deeper level therefore requires us to learn about histories of community agency-making, self-determination, cooperation and interdependence, paternalism, co-optation, and commodification, which are often subtle, multifaceted, and hidden from plain view.

First and foremost, planners and urban practitioners must renew their commitments to engaging historically marginalized and other directly impacted residents in all stages of neighborhood visioning, planning, and development. The outcomes of these processes may point to expanded tourism and cultural development, or they may emphasize other community development goals and strategies that are not aligned with the local planning and development machine. What matters most is that poor and working-class communities of color must *have a direct and ongoing say in matters, and benefit directly from* improved urban opportunity structures in the city in ways that they have personally articulated as being beneficial. This is particularly true in the case of cultural tourism, for, as Clyde Woods warned, "In the absence of a tourism agenda that has emerged from community-based decision making, a community's heritage can be turned against it and used to reproduce and expand the existing structures of exploitation."[1]

Fortunately, such a transformative shift does not require starting from scratch. On the contrary, one only has to look back at the history of community building in the Southside or Hill City over the past one hundred and fifty years to discover a treasure trove of examples of creative, cooperative community building that both defied and subverted de facto and de jure racism and segregation in the pursuit of a more equitable society.

Urban planning is one of the few spatial professions with a code of ethics that explicitly links our work to the advancement of socially just and socioeconomically equitable places. Despite this ethical mandate, many professional planners are left scratching their heads or pointing to cosmetic (as opposed to substantive) urban improvements when asked how the field might play a more proactive role in advancing racially diverse and socially equitable communities. Despite the myriad experiences of and attitudes toward Chattanooga's present-day urban renaissance, local planning and development arenas continue to operate according to narrow definitions of gentrification and placemaking. When asked to reflect on the unevenness of the city's revitalization, those leaders often plead ignorance about how to actively mitigate displacement and dislocation—or they argue that the ends of gentrification outweigh its means. As a result of these narrow understandings, urban inequality in Chattanooga and cities like it continues to grow, reinforcing highly uneven investment patterns and opportunities structures vis-à-vis housing, education and workforce training, economic development, and arts and cultural planning priorities. When seemingly disconnected disparities are explicitly linked together, troubling patterns of environmental, economic, and cultural inequality emerge.

Unsurprisingly, working-class communities of color have borne disproportionate burdens from shortsighted and narrow-minded planning and development decision making since the city's earliest days. To be sure, professional planners are culpable in the making of uneven access and development. We are responsible insofar as we develop and facilitate the participation processes meant to generate public interest, foster capacity building, and ensure buy-in. We analyze community data and write up ethically loaded reports meant to serve and justify community development interventions in the cities and regions where we are employed.

In Chattanooga, local planners and elected officials also operate according to narrow and historically racialized definitions of public participation and stakeholdership. These views severely limit the potential for citizen-based community development movements to transform the city into a more just and sustainable place for all its residents. For historically marginalized and excluded Chattanoogans, time has demonstrated repeatedly that just because a person figures out how to navigate public and/or institutional bureaucracies does not mean she or he will get a fair share in the benefits of planning and development decisions.

This book has argued that so little has changed in Chattanooga, in part, because existing participation methods have not transformed engagement, analysis, and political decision-making processes. While participation methods like town hall meetings and charrettes usually afford some degree of citizen input, they do little to ensure fair and widespread civic representation. With some important exceptions, most of which involve some degree of participatory action research, public participation schemes rarely put the powers of data collection, summary, and analysis into the hands of directly impacted and historically marginalized residents themselves. In many cities, including Chattanooga, new participation technologies and techniques actually inadvertently exacerbate social inequality by further empowering the already-engaged, obscuring inequities with respect to access, capacity, and political power, and creating the illusion of more widespread democratic decision making.

However, this project has also revealed the power of people to create alternatives. As participants in the Planning Free School and SPARC Initiative seized their new urban analysis capacities, mainstream planners and policy makers felt pressure to respond in ways that they had not before. Fortunately for local social justice advocates, Chattanooga Neighborhood Enterprise (CNE), the leading nonprofit housing developers in the city, hired a new executive director in late 2013 who has previously worked for a community land trust and has extensive knowledge about and connections to the community benefits agreement movement. Although it is still too early to evaluate the effects of this hire, the new director's seat at the helm of CNE may have a transformative effect on local planners' and policy makers' attitudes toward supporting deep and widespread affordability within the local housing stock, and equitable community development practices in the city more generally.

In an effort to rise to Woods and McKittrick's challenge to reimagine placemaking as "spatial liberation," this book proposes that we ask ourselves how we might come to better support and enable diasporic placemaking. Urban historiography can help us identify the processes and conditions through which multidiasporic placemaking occurs. Through this work, we can come to reckon deeply with how local legacies of labor, economic development, housing, and urban expansion have produced landscapes of urban and regional (in)opportunity, and where we might most effectively intervene to change these persistent patterns of socio-spatial inequality.

In the first chapters of this book, I explored the construction of Chattanooga's public urban cosmopolitanism narrative, paying special attention to how local histories of Native American and African American placemaking were differently incorporated into—or against—mainstream discourses about cultural diversity and interracial harmony. In doing so, I illuminated how the history of urban development and change in downtown Chattanooga was propelled by processes of collaborative and contested community building that set the foundation for urban planning and creative/cultural development-based revitalization initiatives today.

In the middle chapters, I explored contemporary case studies of diasporic placemaking in downtown Chattanooga, including the ongoing revitalization of the East Ninth Street/East MLK Boulevard corridor and the city's return to the Tennessee Riverfront. These chapters explored ideas of racial reconciliation and justice vis-à-vis placemaking and urban development to further illuminate how historic patterns of racialized paternalism both persist, and are challenged by, culture-based revitalization projects across the city. By exploring creative placemaking and cultural development programs in these neighborhoods, I hope the case studies will contribute to a growing subfield of planning scholarship which explores how creative and cultural development can have restorative and reparative, as well as damaging, powers in historically marginalized communities.

The most important lesson from the final two chapters of the book is that, in order for creative and cultural development to have transformative effects on socio-spatial development, directly impacted and historically excluded citizens should have as close to complete control over the planning and creative processes as possible. This imperative should hold whether the project involves public art, cultural events, or historic preservation. Asserting the imperative of community self-determination is not akin to saying that so long as a struggle is place- and consensus-based, anything goes. Communities are not homogenous; nor are they static. Chattanooga's own history has shown how suburban priorities and struggles over space and place, for example, often differ from inner-city ones, and that the Westside is not the Southside is not North or East Chattanooga.

But it is here that the impulse of diasporic placemaking becomes crucial to remember. At our cores, we share similar desires to create home spaces of cultural belonging and material security. And, as much as we sometimes like to think that we operate independently and away from those who are different than us, we are fundamentally psychically and socio-spatially interdependent beings. Our communities evolve according to how we negotiate (i.e., avoid, deny, embrace) our interdependencies with one another across social and spatial differences.

An important consideration to these effects is geographic scale. While most of the cases explored in this book focused on micro- or neighborhood-level politics in Chattanooga's urban core, other examples, including the recently formed citywide Coalition for Affordable Housing, the Sustaining People and Reclaiming Communities (SPARC) Initiative, and the growing Free Store movement, demonstrate that it is possible to connect seemingly isolated struggles across space. The SPARC Initiative's community-planning efforts, in particular, tried to understand and leverage the scaling up and out of community self-determination qua interdependence. By starting with personal stories, visions, and plans, and using facilitated dialogue and creative expression to help individuals connect their stories to others in the room, we initiated a process that honored the personal while also honoring the social or collective. We then used this interpersonal recognition to cultivate solidarity and political power so that neighborhoods could develop and implement both community- and coalition-based visions and action plans.

The SPARC Initiative and Planning Free School began in Chattanooga, but they need not be limited to it. One can imagine how it would be possible to create visions and action plans that encompass ever-increasing scales of community, from neighbors to neighborhoods, urban cores to cities, and ultimately regions that transcend superficially imposed political boundaries such as county and state lines. In this sense, the community engagement and spatial professions have much to learn about how better to support and enable diasporic placemaking, which is a trans-local and even transnational phenomenon.

A separate note for individuals and institutions who want to better support and enable multiracial diasporic placemaking: the goal of cultural recognition projects like the Passage and the revitalization of Lincoln Park are not about the feelings of reconciliation that they might produce in mainstream (i.e., white, property-owning) society. The goal of supporting and enabling diasporic placemaking is not to make white residents and urban professionals feel more comfortable or at ease with local histories of racism and uneven geographic development. To the contrary, in many cases, the end result of public art and cultural development initiatives may be precisely to produce an opposite effect.

Most fundamentally, the value in these projects lies in the sense of belonging and potential for justice that gets cultivated by and for the directly impacted population whose story is being told. In the case of The Passage at Ross's Landing, the Cherokee artists who designed the space focused on their people as strong and resilient despite enduring the Trail of Tears. In Lincoln Park, resident activists emphasized the significance of the park to the United Negro baseball league as a Jim Crow-era cultural institution despite protests from hospital administrators who did not want to be associated with the racially charged language of the Jim Crow period. These stories suggest to those who are committed to expanding multiethnic placemaking in complex urban environments that we ought to strive to help realize projects that produce dissonance and even discomfort among locals and visitors instead of anesthetized narratives of racial harmony and urban progress.

The diasporic place-making approach warrants inter- and transdisciplinary scholarship as well as a commitment to collaborative, popular education. When together we reconstruct stories of urban diasporic place-making, long and instructive histories of antiracist and anticolonial practice emerge. Locating moments of self-determination qua interdependence within historical legacies of place-based resistance and alternative world-building allows contemporary struggles for social justice and equitable community development to be understood not as aberrations, but as links in a chain of multiracial solidarity work which can, in the case of Chattanooga, be traced back more than three centuries.

Considering these long histories, the challenge for social justice-minded activists and spatial professionals shifts from imagining entirely new modes of urban spatial consciousness to locating, excavating, cultivating, and enabling the critical spatial awareness which has been present and active in historically uprooted communities since the dawn of modern colonialism and the so-called discovery of the New World. When we fail to place current struggles over space and place in their local historical contexts, we risk missing profound opportunities to enable and support culturally-based citizen-driven equitable community development.

Theorizing Diasporic Placemaking

This theoretical appendix draws from literature across several disciplines to clarify what I mean by *diasporic placemaking* as discursive, analytical, and political frames. By connecting theories of socio-spatial production with diasporic identity formation, placemaking, and participatory planning, I lay the conceptual ground for this book and subsequent studies that seek to know how multidiasporic negotiations produce complex urban environments in communities across the world.

Activating Space

Placing diasporic placemaking in the context of critical social theory's "spatial turn" adds theoretical depth. For four decades, critical social theory has been revolutionized by the recognition that space and spatial production are central to theories of social change and development progress. Arguments that space "matters"—not only in a normative, ideological sense, but in an everyday *lived, material* sense of the word—have resounded from across the academic disciplines, transforming not only the historically spatial fields of geography, city planning, and architecture, but also unusual suspects within the humanities, including history, literary theory, anthropology, and semiotics.

Lefebvre famously asserted that social practice is comprised of three distinct, interrelated, trajectories of production: spatial production, representations of space, and representational spaces. At the cornerstone of his unified theory of social production, Lefebvre maintained that the "perceived-conceived-lived triad"[1] must grasp this multidimensional spatiality of social life.

Lefebvre's unified triad of spatial production rested on the idea that modern socio-spatial practice is dominated by *monocentric strategies* that flatten, homogenize, compartmentalize, and, ultimately, annihilate place from space. The destructive social consequences of annihilation-through-abstraction throughout the course of modern history are manifold. Dispossession, exile, slavery, and war are all symptoms of the annihilation-through-abstraction logic of spatial production. To combat these nihilistic impulses, Lefebvre's "science of space" depended on "the bringing-together of disassociated aspects, the unification of disparate tendencies and factors. . . . It sets itself up in clear opposition to . . . homogenizing efforts. . . . It implies the mobilization of differences in a single movement . . . differences of regime, country, location, ethnic group, natural resources, and so on."[2] The connection between knowledge and power suggested by the concept of spatial hegemony promises both oppressive and emancipatory potential for spatial practice, depending on whether knowledge production is exercised as *savior* or *connaissance*. Lefebvre wrote: "The connection between knowledge (*savior*) and power is thus made manifest, although this in no way interdicts a critical and subversive form of knowledge (*connaissance*); on the contrary, it points up the antagonism between a knowledge which serves power and a form of knowing which refuses to acknowledge power."[3]

He later defined the former (*savior*) as abstract conceptualization—theory that is understood as preceding and guiding social practice—and the latter (*connaissance*) as "knowing" through practice and everyday lived experience. "Like all social practice," Lefebvre reminded us, "spatial practice is lived directly before it is conceptualized; but the speculative primacy of the conceived over the lived causes practice to disappear along with life."[4]

The Politics of Place

Massey characterized space as an ever-unfolding "simultaneity—of-stories-so-far,"[5] and established three axioms upon which her theory of heterogeneous socio-spatial production and possibility resided. First, space is the product of interrelations which constitute and are constituted by interactions; it is fundamentally about the relationships and power dynamics between different beings and objects rather than the beings or objects themselves. Second, space is characterized by "coexisting heterogeneity" and "contemporaneous plurality."[6] Third, space is in a process of ever-becoming, and for this reason it is inherently a-teleological, having neither destiny nor end. For Massey, the second and third propositions were of particular interest, for they suggested a range of political and cultural opportunities for linking social change to spatial production through everyday creative/imaginative and political acts.

For Massey, the openness of space suggests possibility, "loose ends and missing links," rather than containers for "always-already constituted identities."[7] This potentiality and openness inspired an optimism that saved her theory of post-modern space from the nihilistic tendencies that many post-modern political and social philosophers adopted when faced with the immense challenge of articulating a unified theory about a fragmented world. Later in her text, Massey defined this optimism as an "open attitude of being; for the (potential) *outwardlookingness* of practiced subjectivity."[8] The motivation for imagining time (history) and space (geography) as open and always changing is simple: "only if we conceive of the future as open can we seriously accept or engage in any genuine notion of politics. Only if the future is open is there any ground for a politics which can make a difference."[9] Now characterized as an active process of always-becoming, space escapes objectification: no longer understood as a "thing" or even a series of "things," space is reconceived as an "event."

Soja developed a theory of socio-spatial dialecticism that asserted the "mutual constitutive-ness" of social and spatial life, declaring "spatiality situates social life in an active arena where purposeful human agency jostles problematically with tendential social determinations to shape everyday activity, particularize social change, and etch into place the course of time and the making of history."[10] Space both produces and is produced by social life; social life produces and is produced through space. This "mutual *constitutive-ness*" of social and spatial practice forms the common bedrock of the "spatial turn" in critical social theory, grounding and connecting an otherwise disparate set of intellectual and political projects together through their common emphasis on the social production of space vis-à-vis everyday, lived experience.

Soja later termed this awareness a "new spatial consciousness"[11]—an awareness rooted in an understanding that, if space is socially constructed, it can be deconstructed and reconstructed according to multiple socio-spatial logics—including equitable and emancipatory ones. He declared that "we make our geographies, for good or bad, just or unjust, in much the same way it can be said that we make our histories, under conditions not of our own choosing but in real-world contexts already shaped by socio-spatial processes in the past and the enveloping historically and socially constituted geographies of the present."[12] Insofar as space is an actively unfolding, dynamic, heterogeneous process of social becoming, there exists the potential for making and remaking our communities in more just and sustainable ways.

In her 1985 essay "New Directions in Space," Massey mapped the historical roots of the spatial turn in critical social theory, locating the origin of this shift in the cultural, ideological, and geopolitical transformations of the 1960s. Prior to this decade, professional and academic geography focused on regions, and specifically their differences—in other words, on the "uniqueness" of places. For Massey, the "place-based unit was overthrown" during the positivist "White Heat" revolution of the 1960s—a movement which had emerged during an epoch of unprecedented wealth accumulation and technological innovation, and was driven by the belief in "saving the world through the application of neutral science and technology."[13]

However, the global political and economic restructuring that drove American deindustrialization during the 1970s and 1980s underscored the fact that space itself was a sociopolitical construct. This recognition led to the "radical critique" of the 1970s, an intellectual and practical movement tasked with "unraveling the underlying causes of a variety of outcomes in the world" by examining everyday socio-spatial practices with the goal of discovering patterns across time and space. For Massey, the "the unique is back on the agenda ... and much of this particularity is spatially constructed ... [for this reason] it is vital that we accept and continue to insist upon the importance of space and spatial variations in concrete analysis."[14]

Theorizing Diaspora

Literature produced from within and across the global diasporas have long demanded historically grounded, critically nuanced assessments of the racialization of space and place.[15] The term *diaspora* itself is an expansive concept, applying to diverse people in a variety of unique geographic, political, sociocultural, and historical contexts. Entomologically, the term is derived from the Greek word *diasperien: dia-* "across," and *-sperien* "to sow or scatter seeds." Braziel and Mannur argued the term has historically had a negative connotation, signifying the forced dislocation and displacement of subjects from their homelands due to religious exile, slavery, and war.[16] In its most literal sense, however, diaspora has a more benign meaning, signifying movement, dispersion, and migration.

McKittrick and Woods challenged their readers to assume a new take on an old question—"how are black bodies implicated in the production of urban space?"—arguing that, rather than take an essentialist view, scholars ought to conceptualize race space to production in terms of the personal and community power that communities of color regularly exercise despite enduring centuries of structural and spatial exclusion and violence.[17] McKittrick and Woods rejected claims that black diasporic experiences are limited to dislocation, catastrophe, migration, and abandonment, but acknowledged that these forces must be considered when we think about the how "the lives of subaltern subjects are shaped by, and are shaping, the imaginative, three-dimensional, social, and political contours of human geographies."[18] To this end, they challenged their readers to turn inward and ask themselves, "how [our own] geographic desires might be bound up in conquest?"—prompting their readers to reimagine placemaking as "spatial liberation and other emancipatory strategies [that] can perhaps move us away from territoriality, the normative practice of staking a claim to space."[19]

Articulating Diasporic Belonging and Citizenship

Questions about territoriality and claim-staking are critical because of the enduring legacies of settler colonialism, extermination, dispossession, slavery, and exile. Forced and induced migration dominated the movement of people around the world between the late fifteenth and mid-nineteenth centuries, and therefore must be central to any conceptualization of *diaspora* as a tool for historical and social analysis. Inikori examined the economic dynamics of the African slave trades across the Atlantic Ocean, Sahara Desert, Red Sea, and Indian Ocean during the first four hundred years of modern Western expansion and development. He assessed the extent to which slave labor and the slave trade "accelerated or retarded" political-economic shifts from "primarily agrarian/agricultural to primarily industrial" modes of spatial production, both in terms of European and New World accumulation and the extractive pressures on labor and natural resources within continental Africa during this four-hundred-year time period.[20]

Inikori estimated the percentage of economic development transactions that depended on or were in some way supported by slave labor/trade during this time, demonstrating how the transatlantic slave economy produced a sophisticated division of and demand for labor specialization, including trade and finance, transportation, manufacturing, mining, export staple agriculture in plantations, commercial agriculture in medium freehold farms, and the sale of labor. These divisions were ordered regionally, producing varied political and economic landscapes that reflected the specialized economic infrastructures taking root across the New World.

The middle Atlantic and Northeast regions of the United States developed their economies around commercial foodstuffs for export to plantations in the West Indies, finance and credit, import/export trades, shipbuilding, lumber production, fishing, and industrial manufacturing. The southern United States, in contrast, with its agrarian and plantation-based economies, dominated global tobacco and cotton production. Through this structural transformation, indigenous economic structures and practices in the West Indies were replaced with export-oriented, cash crop plantations, primarily sugar, coffee, cotton, and indigo. Continental Africa, in contrast, received virtually no share of the global industrial investment during this time. Its function in the global economy was limited almost exclusively to the extraction of enslaved people. Industries associated with the slave trade included shipbuilding; guns, ammunition, and the manufacturing of special metal goods; sugar; and most significantly, the cotton textile industry. Taken together, these economic innovations and specializations produced "favorable demand conditions" for rapid urbanization across the United States. In other words, African slavery formed the cornerstone of European and North World global economic expansion and development for the first four hundred years of modern history.[21]

Though reckoning with historical trauma is necessary, scholars who theorize diaspora in more positive and generative terms warn against default victimhood narratives, which may foreclose possibilities for reimagining the regional and global movement of people and ideas between places as the basis for socio-spatial justice and liberation. Hamilton, for example, warned that the "scope, analysis, and interpretation of the diaspora must exceed the narrow view of slavery and its aftermath."[22] Similarly, Boyce Davies and M'Bow challenged their readers to consider how voluntary migration and movement has influenced the evolution of transnational diasporic communities and identities before, during, and after the transatlantic slave trade. Together, these three forms of migration have resulted in the "relocation and redefinition of diasporic peoples in a range of international locations." They wrote that "the African diaspora—the dispersion of African peoples all over the world—is in effect an *already existing* globalization of African peoples. Created through centuries of migration, it *preceded*, at the level of demographics, the economic and communications structures now defined as globalization."[23]

For Boyce Davies and M'Bow, the multiple modes and products of human migration form the bedrock of a theory and potential "geopolitical reality" of diasporic belonging and citizenship for the twenty-first century. The history of treating Africans as "deportable subjects," they argued, has produced a sense of "statelessness" among the people of the global African diaspora. But as members of a self-identified group who seek political and economic legitimacy in a geopolitical arena that demands the terms of nationhood, some terms of diasporic "sovereignty" must be articulated. To this end, Boyce Davies and M'Bow propose a theory of diasporic national belonging that radically departs from Western traditions of citizenship by using voices from across the African diaspora to frame the terms of self, community, spatial practice, and progress. In their views, the politicization of African diaspora citizenship would put into practice a central intent of pan-Africanist thinkers: to create an international network of ideas and practices that can then be positioned as a usable political body for the benefit of common yet distinct, and geographically dispersed, communities.

Self-Determination and Interdependence

For many individuals writing from a position of diasporic "statelessness," spatial control and land reform are at the heart of any truly transformative equitable development process. Fanon described this spatial imperative accordingly: "for a colonized people the most essential value, because the most concrete, is first and foremost the land: the land which will bring them bread and, above all, dignity."[24] Similarly, Woods argued that land reform is "the only solution to the question of guaranteeing subsistence, formalizing the group economy, and gaining political, cultural, and personal dignity and freedom."[25]

In addition to a spatial imperative, diasporic placemaking involves personal and interpersonal articulations of community belonging. Hamilton argued that "the ongoing struggle of black people for human dignity and liberation is a creative process. It embodies contradictory crosscurrents and conflicts such as the dialectical relationship between creativity and action, travail and reaction."[26] She pointed to the "shared historical experiences" of dislocation and marginalization, as well as the shared experiences of resilience and resistance, as constitutive elements uniting otherwise vastly diverse people and communities together as members of the global black diaspora.

Patterson and Kelley argued that *diaspora* is a shared process and condition experienced by diverse colonized people living across the world, brought on by experiences with imperial expansion and modern empire building, and also arguably solidarity, adaptation, and transformation. Many who theorize about diasporas place great emphasis on *articulation* as the creative process through which diasporic identities and cultures are manifested. The processes and conditions of diaspora are ultimately generative and creative in nature; they are actions and declarations of survival and resilience. To this point, Patterson and Kelley highlighted the dialectical nature of diasporic being and becoming, arguing that, for as much as the diasporic experience is one of uprooting and oppression, it is more importantly characterized by kinship and community building. This dual understanding of diaspora allows for imagining diasporic sites where connected histories and "overlapping migrations" produce places rooted in transformative intercultural exchange and political- economic solidarity.[27]

Tiya Miles traced the migration of one Cherokee-African American family from northern Georgia (less than twenty miles from present-day Chattanooga) during the period between Cherokee national formation and their forced removal to Oklahoma. The Shoe Boots family saga sheds light on the long, deep entwinement of Native American and African American socio-spatial histories—both in the Southeast and later west of the Mississippi River. Recent moves to create cultural and political discourses around Native American-African American ontological "indivisibility," for instance, are two examples of reimagining new ontologies of cultural belonging and togetherness in the context of multiple and overlapping diasporas. Narratives of creolization and multiracial solidarity can be traced back to all regionalized spaces of colonial encounters; it is only recently that critical scholarship has turned to the deeply intertwined cultural, political, and socio-spatial histories of indigenous and African American people living in the United States and its antecedent territories. These narratives complement a more substantial canon of black-indigenous cultural history in Latin America and the Caribbean, and represent a growing interdisciplinary field focused on cultural rootedness and relational belonging in sites of multiple and overlapping diasporas.[28]

Stuart Hall described the unique processes of diasporic identity formation as "a matter of 'becoming' as well as 'being' . . . belonging to the future as much as to the past . . . undergoing constant transformation . . . subject to the continuous play of culture, history, and power."[29] Citing Hall's earlier ideas about diasporic migration and cultural belonging, Patterson and Kelley argued that, insofar as there is no inherent "belongingness" for diasporic citizens, relationships must be deliberately articulated. This idea—that belonging is not always already bound to a particular place or community, and that it is up to directly impacted people to articulate their own terms of attachment and togetherness—has great emancipatory potential for local antiracism and anticolonial struggles. Recent moves to create a cultural and political discourse around Native American-African American "indivisibility" is one example of reimagining cultural belonging, kinship, and togetherness in the context of multidiasporic placemaking.[30]

In this book, I suggested that *diasporic placemaking* can provide an analytical frame to enrich mainstream diversity planning and equitable community development discussions. The history of multiethnic placemaking in Chattanooga provides insight into how collaborations and contestations can generate urban social and spatial orders. By exploring stories of urban diasporic placemaking, we find long and instructive histories of antiracist and anticolonial practice. Reframing local development in these terms may help planners and other urban and spatial actors understand how to integrate antiracism agendas into urban planning and redevelopment in different and potentially transformative ways.

In defense of these abolitionist place-making practices, McKittrick and Woods wrote:

The act of making corners, neighborhoods, communities, cities, rural lands, rivers, and mountains sacred is central to their defense and the defense of the communities that love and cherish them. . . . The people of urban and rural communities that are undergoing gentrification, the prisoners, refugees, and orphans, and all displaced persons from Africa to Africville have different desires for home. They want to build new homes in places that have barred their entry. They also want to explore and reimagine the politics of place. The realization of these desires can transform the world when these visions are based in traditions that see place as the location of co-operation, stewardship, and social justice rather than just sites to be dominated, enclosed, commodified, exploited, and segregated. Black geographies will play a central role in the reconstruction of the global community.[31]

In this sense, the challenge for social justice-minded spatial practitioners shifts from imagining entirely new modes of urban spatial consciousness, and toward locating, excavating, and enabling the critical spatial awarenesses that have been present and active in uprooted and migratory communities for centuries.

Place and Placemaking

Increasingly, planners, architects, and urban designers have subscribed to place-based approaches to urban and regional (re)development, emphasizing their professions' need to tap into and plan in accordance with the unique identities of neighborhoods, cities, and regions. Questions about how to "make" places, whether through preservation, new development, or renewal, have been explored for the past half century. One of the earliest and most well-known works is Jacobs's *The Life and Death of Great American Cities*. Her focus on the qualitative, phenomenological aspects of urban life, including the street and sidewalk, social encounter and interaction, design vernaculars, adaptation, and improvisation formed the bedrock for her outspoken support for the preservation of pedestrian-scaled cities during the era of large-scale federal Urban Renewal.[32]

Lynch also discussed the importance of communities having a strong sense of place in the opening pages of his urban design classic *The Image of the City*. In it, he argued that a sense of place is achieved through a combination of organic and planned spatial interventions. Without going so far as to name *placemaking* as a professional practice, Lynch recognized the unique responsibilities of an emerging field dedicated to shaping ever-evolving cities for diverse "sensuous enjoyment": "Not only is the city an object which is perceived (and perhaps enjoyed) by millions of people in widely diverse class and character, but it is the product of many builders who are constantly modifying the structure for reasons of their own. While it may be stable in general outlines for some time, it is ever-changing in detail. Only partial control can be exercised over its growth and form. There is no final result, only a continuous succession of phases. No wonder, then, that the art of shaping cities for sensuous enjoyment is an art quite separate from architecture or music or literature. It may learn a great deal from these other arts, but it cannot imitate them."[33]

While Lynch realized that successful cities were as much the result of nonphysical interactions as they were the physical design of nodes, edges, pathways, landmarks, and districts, his focus on visual *legibility* inspired subsequent generations of designers and placemakers to fixate on physical design as the means through which dynamic social life is achieved. Whyte's popular ethnographic account of small urban public spaces in Manhattan reinforced the idea that a key set of physical interventions (lighting, seating, water features, access to natural elements, food, and landmark "triangulation") had the potential to activate the social life of underutilized spaces.[34] More recently, conversations have focused on the role of public art[35] and historical preservation[36] in local place-making efforts, arguing that placemaking is key to unlocking a community's economic potential in the postindustrial, creative economic era.

Though the planned design and physical characteristics of spaces matter, placemaking in its most fundamental practice is not developed exclusively through professional training or expertise in the arts or urban design. As Lynch pointed out, it can only be partially controlled through institutional land use planning and development decision. Schneekloth and Shibley defined *placemaking* as the universal human impulse to forge community, and "transform the places in which we find ourselves into places in which we live. . . . It is fundamental human activity that is sometimes almost invisible and sometimes dramatic . . . it can be done with the support of others or can be an act of defiance in the face of power. . . . The making of places—our homes, our neighborhoods, our places of work and play—not only changes and maintains the physical world of living; it also is a way we can make our communities and connect with other people."[37]

The notion that placemaking is a universal human practice begs questions about the appropriate role of trained professionals in relation to the local community that they are working in. Ben-Joseph argued that placemaking is increasingly regulated through zoning, design reviews, and general standardization, yet Crawford suggested that placemaking standardization stands in contrast to the "everyday urbanism" that ordinary people enact through their interactions with one another and their environments.[38] To respond to this tension, Schneekloth and Shibley proposed "enabling placemaking," which focuses on people in places, relationship building, and collaborative processes characterized by openness and mutual learning.[39]

But how is enabling placemaking achieved? Martin studied how place relates to collective action framing, arguing that "organizations discursively relate the conditions of the place . . . to their different agendas for collective action. In doing so, they construct the local scale of the neighborhood and its organizations as the appropriate sphere for political activism, consolidating the 'neighborhood' as a salient political place."[40]

Despite such advances in theory and more radical practice, mainstream placemaking practice continues to be preoccupied with standardization, which appeals to experts' technical sensibilities but does not necessarily reflect the needs or desires of non-experts who will be directly impacted by changes to the space. Beauregard argued that, although places are imbued with multiple narratives, they are typically dominated by the techno-professional vision for what is considered to work.[41]

In his call for a return to "phenomenological placemaking," Arefi wrote that placemaking evolved out of experience of spaces, but increasingly has been defined according to urban design standards and criteria: "The question [then] is who is more qualified: the experts whose training and expertise allows them to regulate placemaking, or the lay people whose lived experiences and not their formal training authorizes them to place or engage in placemaking?"[42] The ironic result is that, in the pursuit of a stronger place-based identity, communities surrender to conforming standards, and further homogenization ensues. Moreover, fundamental issues related to civic participation, representation, and democratic decision making remain largely unresolved.

Diasporic Space

If the term *diaspora* signifies physical migration as well as a set of conditions and processes, articulations, and radical democratic possibilities, what then are diasporic spaces? In short, they are spaces of action and complexity, of hybridity and contradiction. Diasporic spaces are sites of expropriation, displacement, containment, and deportation: the master's house, the missionary schoolhouse, the stockade pen, prison, and public workhouse. In another sense, they are abstracted and commodified space; places emptied of community landscapes—the "abstract, cadastral grid"—reconfigured into property available for the taking. Diasporic space is, using the words of Nicholas Blomley, "settled" or colonized space, for it was through land enclosure and urban economic development that people of color across the New World have been uprooted, relocated, and forced underground to seek refuge from the social relations that were designed to exploit their land and labor.[43]

McKittrick and Woods alluded to a subterranean space: the half-hidden "tension between the mapped and the unknown,"[44] Ang-I ygate described diasporic spaces as "(un)locations—spaces where experiences of diaspora reside that are invisible, largely unacknowledged, and therefore under-theorized."[45] In the context of property, diasporic spaces are spaces of tenuousness—a constant reminder of the potential for the "profound loss of land and livelihood."[46] Oftentimes these are the spaces that have been neglected or abandoned by the structural forces of capitalism: the lowlands in a global landscape characterized by racialized, uneven geographic development.

However, diasporic spaces are also radically decolonized places, characterized by vitality, resilience, and creative improvisation. Woods and Scott described these spaces of cultural production as sites of subaltern epistemologies and locally situated knowledge; spaces charged with vigilant attention to memory, and hope for a radically different future.[47] Diasporic spaces are spaces of real and potential overlapping cultural togetherness: places with the potential to subvert and bypass, if not counteract, the isolation of living in an exploitative economic system. McKittrick and Woods referred to these critical sites of diasporic cultural belonging and material security as "ethical spaces of geographic reform."[48]

Diasporic Placemaking

How do diasporic spaces, having the potential for both liberation and subjugation, become diasporic *places*, in the sense of being actively transformed into sites of anti-racist, decolonized material security and cultural belonging? McKittrick and Woods defined *place* as "the location of cooperation, stewardship, and social justice"[49]—in short, the antithesis to abstracted, colonized space. Similarly, Thu Su'o'ng Thi Nguyên characterized "diasporic placemaking" in three ways: as the production of hybridical spaces, as the shedding of light on (un)locations, and as active resistance to flows of global capital. Nguyên argued that peripheral spaces provided critical opportunities for Vietnamese residents living in Austin, Texas, to access services and promote cultural belonging, and it is within these diasporic places that counter-hegemonic discourses and practices were cultivated, and where home and community spaces for these otherwise socially isolated immigrant residents were forged.[50]

Blomley's theory of urban decolonization helps to clarify the theoretical aim of this book. Rejecting the myths of Manifest Destiny and Terra Nullius ("no-man's-land"), he argued that these two spatial representations have dominated settlers' geopolitical imaginations since the nineteenth century, and serve as political and ethical rationales for ongoing indigenous dispossession and displacement in the twenty-first century. Blomley conceived landscapes as spaces composed not only of "bricks and mortar, but also discursive representations."[51] Insofar as landscapes are sociocultural as well as physical places, they're in a persistent state of *contestory becoming*.[52] Contestory becoming, like the previously discussed relationship between place and belonging, opens up a range of political, cultural, and material possibilities for people engaged in on-the-ground struggles over space and place.

Furthermore, Blomley drew a clear distinction between dispossession and displacement. He characterized the former as the physical removal of people from land or space that they claim as their home, and the latter as the sociocultural processes through which a person or community's presence, history, and ties to the land are written out of official narratives of place. He described this cultural process accordingly: "The creation of the city requires active placemaking that relies upon certain forgettings of the past, as well as some creative reconstructions. This is a positive and a negative project of effacement and of production. Urban displacement . . . seems to entail two related maneuvers. First, native people must be conceptually removed from urban space. . . . Second, displacement requires the concomitant emplacement of a settler society: This place is to be made into a white place through physical settlement and occupation."[53]

What is most important about the distinction between dispossession and displacement is that, while dispossession can be complete in the sense that a person or group can be physically removed and excluded from a particular space, displacement, as an erasure of cultural ties and relations, can never be a complete or wholly exclusionary process. For this reason, the notion of disruption or, to borrow Sandercock's term, *insurgent* placemaking, suggests possibilities for reclaiming and decolonizing community spaces through political organizing, occupation, and direct action.[54]

Lightweis-Goff argued that insofar as placemaking and development are key culprits in forgetting, they are also crucial to remembering. "You cannot wash away a bloodstain. Attempts to scrub the stain repeat its dimensions in a frenzy of repetition that changes the surface and texture that surround it."[55] She posited a form of placemaking that wrestles the power of landscape repetition away from actors and institutions who want people to forget the sinister chapters in our nation's history, and places it into the hands of those who are desperate to confront and process the connections between place, violence, and belonging in deeper ways: "At the sites of lynchings, the space—rather than the spectacle—should be the emphasis, because the critique of publicness and consensus disrupts the tourist's relationship to the ground on which he is standing, or the resident's relationship to the community in which he is embedded. . . . The repetition of the landscape . . . can be interrupted with matter out of place that resists seamless replication: the plaque we never notice until the day we notice nothing else."[56]

In response to anesthetized versions of placemaking, a growing number of critics argue for subaltern and insurgent forms of spatial practice—forms that acknowledge the intersectionality and hybridity of diasporic identity, the contingency of history, the contradictions of territory, and the exceptions to "American Exceptionalism." Sandercock summarized the importance of—and challenges associated with—adopting an embodied, critically nuanced, and politically transformative approach to placemaking, writing: "We need theories of space and of place, theories of the state and of the role of planning within the state apparatus; theories of power and knowledge; theories of gender and race inequalities; theories of bodies as social constructions; and so on. The list can never be complete, or completed, for two reasons. First, because each new generation rewrites history according to its own interests and issues. . . . Second, because the boundaries we draw around the object of planning history are determined in the first place by how we define planning. That is, and always will be, a political and strategic decision."[57]

Reframing planning and community development as processes of multidiasporic placemaking extends place-making literature by explicitly linking the cultural identity work of socio-spatial storytelling to human movement and migration and a local economic justice agenda. To this end, this project explored the long history of diasporic placemaking in downtown Chattanooga in order to better understand how planning and place-making practitioners might come to support and enable processes that create everyday places of material and cultural belonging, while also acknowledging and transforming historically unequal structures embedded in urban space.

APPENDIX 2

Methodology

This book contributes to conversations about how to better plan for and develop more just and sustainable multicultural places by exploring three centuries of multiethnic placemaking in the southeastern U.S. city of Chattanooga, Tennessee. To do so, I employed a multi-method, transdisciplinary research design. I do so in the spirit of Leonie Sandercock's call to move beyond "mainstream planning history" and explore the "transformative possibilities" found in "insurgent planning histories," assembling stories that "puncture" and "demythologize" the "heroic image of planning history" by centering the voices of women, people of color, and members of the gay and lesbian communities.[1] Sandercock reminded her readers that "professions, like nations, keep their shape by moulding their members'/citizens' understanding of the past, causing them to forget those events which do not accord with a righteous image, while keeping alive those memories that do.... The boundaries of planning history are not a given. These boundaries shift in relation to the definition of planning (as both ideas and practices) and in relation to the historian's purpose.... In emphasizing planning as a regulatory or disciplinary practice, we may miss its transformative possibilities, which in turn may be connected to histories of resistance to specific planning practices and regulatory regimes."[2]

To this end, I paid special attention to the interplays between official, city- and institution-backed planning initiatives and those organized by ordinary citizens, including artists, activists, neighborhood leaders, students, educators, and others. In this sense, this book contributes to a growing collection of insurgent planning historiographies by reconstructing a diverse and complex history of local community building in Chattanooga that falls outside of and against what is considered mainstream planning history and practice.

This research combined traditional ethnographic techniques with a participatory action research design. I chose this unconventional approach because I had hoped to develop a project that would both deconstruct and disrupt mainstream representations of urban development and change in the city. In the introduction to their influential text *Black Geographies and the Politics of Place*, McKittrick and Woods argued that an emancipatory approach to racialized spatial production requires interdisciplinary tools and perspectives. "To critically view and imagine black geographies as interdisciplinary sites," they wrote, "from the diaspora and prisons to grassroots activists and housing patterns—brings into focus networks and relations of power, resistance, histories, and the everyday, rather than locations that are simply subjugated, perpetually ghettoized, or ungeographic."[3]

Choosing an action-oriented, narrative-based approach made sense given the theoretical and practical goals of the project. Jerome Bruner described narrative inquiry as a search for meaning that can't be captured by traditional quantitative or even standard qualitative methods. Narrative inquiry focuses on rich, detailed storytelling. Bruner argued that, methodologically, narrative inquiry is concerned with the construction of dual landscapes: landscapes of action and landscapes of consciousness.[4] Insofar as this research sought to produce relevant, action-oriented accounts of how diasporic placemaking has, continues to, and might come to unfold across downtown Chattanooga, a storied approach to data collection and analysis was a natural choice of methods.

Archival Analysis

A major goal of this project was to understand how actors not trained in professional urban planning or design engaged in creative placemaking. To this end, the most chapters of this book wove together news reports, historical maps, planning documents, and other official representations of development and urban change with unofficial and nontechnical representations of life in Chattanooga, including footage of and artifacts from direct actions and community events, photography and film, poetry, and musical traditions such as the blues. While the majority of archival work related to this project was conducted personally, more participatory modes of archival co-inquiry and analysis were employed during the action research phase of the project.[5]

Semi-structured, Narrative-Based Interviews with Local Placemakers

Narrative inquiry has the power to bring contested hi/stories to light, provide entry points for making sense of complicated, contradictory stories about self and community, and serve as a basis for personal empowerment.[6] Chase argued that part of narrative inquiry's power lay in its ability to capture subjects as they attempt to make sense of themselves through the lens of personal experience. The subject recounts her own story, by and for herself and in her own terms—in this sense narrative inquiry involves "constructing and communicating meaning."[7] Storytelling involves subjectification—agency-making—even when the story being uttered recalls experiences of exclusion or trauma. Forester pointed out that storytelling can transform both the speaker and the listener, noting the potential powers of utterance and discourse when he contended that "what's said is often more important for what it *does* as a practical performance (making a promise or offering reassurance, for example) than for whatever it *labels*, describes, or names."[8]

I designed the placemaker interviews as modified "in-depth, phenomenologically-based" interviews. The goal of the phenomenological approach was to invoke detailed stories in three areas: personal experience and life history, experience and process (stories of practice), and critical reflection.[9] In total, forty-seven (N=47) local placemakers living and/or working in downtown Chattanooga were interviewed for this project. A *placemaker* was defined broadly as a person whose professional or personal work involved actively inscribing the local urban environment with some sort of story or identity. Participants included planners, architects, artists, activists, neighborhood leaders, nonprofit executives, foundation officers, and elected officials.

The standard placemaker interview guide was developed and organized into three content areas: (1) personal background and experiences; (2) process-oriented questions/stories of practice; and (3) critical reflection. Within the first category, participants were asked to reflect on four topics: their personal background and connection to Chattanooga, the factors leading to and motivating their place-making work, their perceptions of urban change in the city, and the historical events and moments that they believe have most significantly shaped the identity of the city.

Within stories of practice, participants were asked to paint pictures of their work by commenting on the following content areas: (1) their role in local place-making and community development initiatives; (2) their experiences with stakeholder engagement and reaching "unusual suspects"; (3) their experiences with local partnerships and coalition building; (4) their techniques for negotiating local politics; (5) the social message of their work and any visioning processes that helped form that narrative; and lastly, (6) any lessons learned from past professional mistakes.

In the final section of the interview, participants were asked to reflect on the meaning of four topics: (1) the existing and potential roles of art and cultural development for advancing urban transformation; (2) the significance of community history to their specific place-making practices; (3) any barriers and challenges that inhibit their work; and finally, (4) what sort of "place" Chattanooga is. These interviews were transcribed and thematically coded using Atlas TI software. Passages from some of these interviews are included in several chapters of this book.

Participant Observation

Due to the people and place-oriented nature of this research, it was important to engage directly with the neighborhoods and sites studied. Over the course of twelve months (July 2012 to July 2013) that I lived full time in Chattanooga, I regularly visited and participated in public and community events on the Tennessee Riverfront, several neighborhoods in East Chattanooga (especially Glenwood and Lincoln Park), East Martin Luther King Boulevard (formerly East Ninth Street), and the Central Business District. I regularly attended city council and planning-related meetings. I paid special attention to how people used the spaces and how they interacted with others using them for similar or different purposes. I also participated in regular meetings with the Westside Community Association, Occupy Chattanooga, Chattanooga Organized for Action, Concerned Citizens for Justice, and the Coalition to Save Lincoln Park.

From Diagnosis to Action Planning:
Two Experimental Planning Interventions

Action research-oriented, community-based planning is one tried (and occasionally proven) method for tackling neighborhood issues while also working to improve residents' sense of self-worth and democratic agency.[10] Instead of deferring to the technical expertise of professionals who may be unconcerned with the particular needs, hopes, and concerns of a neighborhood (especially if it lacks a large property tax base), participatory planning focuses on building capacity among residents themselves to negotiate the terms of planning in their neighborhoods. Several scholars have pointed to the potential for increased social capital across social difference as an important benefit of resident-driven planning.[11] By bringing many voices around the table and using the spaces created to discuss, deliberate, make decisions, and above all, develop mutual expertise, the potential of citizen planning transforms into the promise of just and equitable community movement. Ken Reardon described this transformation as "actually transferring skills and power through the process of doing the neighborhood plan."[12]

Processes that engage historically excluded citizens in sustained, meaningful planning deliberations have myriad potential benefits. Discussing the transformative potential of participation in public deliberations, Forester wrote: "Much more is at stake in dialogic and argumentative processes than claims about what is or is not true.... At stake too are issues of political membership and identity, memory and hope, confidence and competence, appreciation and respect, acknowledgment and the ability to act together. The transformations at stake are those not only of knowledge or of class structure, but of people more or less able to act practically together to better their lives, people we might call citizens."[13]

As an urban researcher and activist with professional experience working as a public space, economic development, and affordable housing planner, I felt upon arriving in Chattanooga in July 2012 that I could not in good conscience limit the research project to the promises and limits of existing diasporic placemaking across downtown Chattanooga. In the spirit of the participatory action research tradition, this research project intervened and expanded current conversations underway in downtown Chattanooga about race, place, culture, history, and equitable development by launching two experimental grassroots capacity-building and community planning initiatives: the Sustaining People and Reclaiming Communities (SPARC) Initiative, and the Planning Free School of Chattanooga (PFSC).

Both experiments were designed as alternatives to mainstream planning practice underway across the city. As described elsewhere in this book, the participatory action research component of this project evolved out of a partnership between myself, a doctoral candidate in the Department of City and Regional Planning at Cornell University, members of Chattanooga Organized for Action (COA), a community-based nonprofit working to "initiate, support, and connect" place-based social justice movements in Chattanooga, and staff from the main branch of the Chattanooga Public Library.

My relationship with COA organizers began to gel after an initial site visit to downtown Chattanooga in July 2011. During this trip, I made appointments with and introduced myself to as many local community development and place-making actors as I could arrange during the week-long trip. One of these conversations included a spirited discussion with COA co-founder Perrin Lance, who described for me his organization's early trials and tribulations to organize around and illuminate the daily experiences of the "other Chattanooga"—which is to say, those historically uprooted and oppressed residents whom the current urban renaissance had exploited and/or left behind.

It became obvious to both Lance and myself that our meeting had been serendipitous, and that an action research partnership might provide mutual benefit and gain. Lance and his co-organizers considered working with me to be an opportunity to have someone with credentials, training, and experience working as an urban planner lend their eyes and ears to the local social justice struggle in downtown Chattanooga. I saw collaboration with COA as potentially connecting me to an existing network of social justice-oriented placemakers organizing across the city.

The purpose of the action research component of this book was twofold. First, we sought to recruit and train citizen planners from historically uprooted and marginalized communities by inviting them to attend free workshops vis-à-vis the Planning Free School of Chattanooga.[14] Second, we engaged residents and local stakeholders in alternative community visioning and strategic planning processes with the goal of producing culturally relevant, equitable community development plans for participating neighborhoods.

The Planning Free School ran between January and May 2013, while the SPARC Initiative ran through the middle of 2014. We designed both interventions with two broad, overarching goals in mind: (1) to increase resident leaders' capacity to participate in formal, citywide design, planning, and development conversations; and (2) to support and enable low- and moderate-income residents to exercise new forms of place-based autonomy, self-determination, mutual aid, and interdependence through neighborhood- and a "People's Coalition"-based visioning and action planning.

The action research initiative utilized an asset-based community development model combining urban planning, popular education, traditional community organizing, and social work to produce bottom-up comprehensive community plans. Although this initiative focused on neighborhoods located within the urban core, we recognized that diasporic placemaking occurs across a range of local and trans-local/regional geographic scales. This multimodal, multi-scalar understanding of community planning suggests the importance of devising creative solutions to place-based problems, including multidisciplinary collaboration and regional coalition building.[15]

Through their participation in this engaged research initiative, Chattanooga Organized for Action has ramped up their efforts even further by working with historically marginalized neighborhoods to develop neighborhood and coalition-based community plans. These initiatives are grounded in the premise that cultural and creative expressions are central to the projects of equitable development and community self-determination in socially complex, culturally diverse cities like Chattanooga. The stories of diasporic placemaking in Chattanooga explored in this book suggest that racial reconciliation and reparation work in the United States is far from complete. To the contrary, in cities where local populations populate multiple, overlapping diasporas, the work of social and cultural healing vis-à-vis placemaking and community development has just begun.

Notes

Introduction

1. See Robertson-Rehberg, *Housing*.

2. See Mike Pare, "Walnut Commons Project Defies Building Trends," TimesFree-Press.com, September 7, 2012, http://www.timesfreepress.com/news/local/story/2012/sep/07/walnut-commons-project-defies-building-trends/87268/.

3. See Mike Pare, "Study: VW Plant's Impact on Chattanooga Area Better than Projected," TimesFreePress.com, June 5, 2013, http://www.timesfreepress.com/news/local/story/2013/jun/05/vw-plants-impact-better-than-projected/109956/. It should be noted that, in the wake of Volkswagen's fuel efficiency scandal, there have been rumors of layoffs at the Chattanooga Volkswagen facility.

4. "GeekMove: Move to the Gig City," GIG Tank 365, accessed March 14, 2013, http://www.thegigtank.com/geekmove/.

5. See Kneebone, *Great Recession*, and Petrilli, "50 U.S. Zip Codes."

6. The 38-acre, 440-unit site was constructed in 1952 and was originally known as the Boone-Hysinger Homes. The property was constructed as an African American–only public housing project for low-income residents displaced from the Westside by the Golden Gateway urban renewal project. In 2011, the Chattanooga Housing Authority estimated that $35 million was needed to repair the Harriet Tubman development. The CHA shuttered the sixty-year-old development in late 2011 and, in spring 2014, the City of Chattanooga purchased the property from CHA for $2.6 million. Presently, there is a struggle going on between local residents who want to see the site redeveloped into affordable housing and those who want to see it used for economic development and/or industrial expansion.

7. The Chattanooga Housing Authority's 2012 Annual Plan states that 1,477 applicants had been blocked out of their closed waiting list. For more information, see Chattanooga Housing Authority, *2012 Annual Plan*.

8. The Westside Community Association reported in October 2012 that 125 families with vouchers could not find landlords to accept them as Section 8 tenants.

Chapter One

1. See McCollough et al., *Moccasin Bend*.

2. Tennessee Writers' Project, *Chattanooga City Guide*, 15. This is a non-circulating reference book housed at the local public library: http://catalog.lib.chattanooga.gov/polaris/search/title.aspx?ctx=1.1033.0.0.5&pos=1.

3. See J. Brown, *Old Frontiers*.

4. See Govan and Livingood, *Chattanooga Country*.

5. The Anglo-Cherokee War, 1758–1761 (in the Cherokee language: the "war with those in the red coats" or "War with the English"), was also known from the Anglo-European perspective as: the Cherokee War, the Cherokee Uprising, or the Cherokee Rebellion.

6. Although Dragging Canoe is widely cited as one of the premier leaders of late eighteenth-century Native anticolonial resistance, there are few things written about him. For the most comprehensive biography, see Cox, *Heart of the Eagle*.

7. Dragging Canoe's famous statement foretold the subsequent forced removal of the southeastern tribes to territories west of the Mississippi River. See Rozema, *Footsteps of the Cherokees*.

8. Dragging Canoe is widely accepted as one of the first Native American warriors and political actors to organize a united front against Native removal from the southeastern frontier. His actions inspired many subsequent pan-Indian leaders, including Tecumseh (Shawnee), who joined Cherokee forces during the Chickamauga Wars and went on to organize the largest tribal confederacy against the United States.

9. Between 1812 and 1840, the ABCFM sent convoys to British India, the Bombay area of India, northern Ceylon (present-day Sri Lanka), the Sandwich Islands (present-day Hawaii), East Asia (China, Singapore, and Siam/Thailand), the Middle East (Greece, Cyprus, Turkey, Syria, the Holy Land, and Persia/Iran), western and southern Africa, and the Tennessee frontier to interact with and convert the Cherokee. See Maxfield, "Formation and Early History"; Govan and Livingood, *Chattanooga Country*; Perdue and Green, *Cherokee Removal*; and Miles, *Ties That Bind*.

10. Walker, *Torchlights to the Cherokees*, 23.

11. Today, the Eastgate Town Center resides on the site of the Brainerd Mission. A one-acre piece of the Mission's cemetery, as well as the earthen levee constructed to protect the site from high creek waters, is all that remains of the original property.

12. For a full account of the daily activities that occurred at the Chickamauga/Brainerd Mission during the first six years of its operation, see Phillips and Phillips, *Brainerd Journal*.

13. Ibid., 67.

14. Ibid., 195.

15. Ibid.

16. Walker, *Torchlights to the Cherokees*, 23.

17. Phillips and Phillips, *Brainerd Journal*, 209.

18. Boudinot and Ridge went on to become members of the five-person treaty party, which was responsible for negotiating the Treaty of New Echota (1835). This treaty facilitated the forced removal of the Cherokee to Oklahoma following the passage of President Andrew Jackson's Indian Removal Act by accepting land grants in "Indian Territory" in exchange for surrendering their rights to sovereign land in the southeast. Considered traitors by the majority of the Cherokee and forced to relocate, both were violently murdered in Oklahoma in the wake of the Trail of Tears. See Perdue and Green, *Cherokee Removal*.

19. See, especially, Perdue, *Slavery and the Evolution*; Perdue and Green, *Cherokee Removal*; and Miles, *Ties That Bind*.

20. This popular resistance to political and cultural assimilation has been well documented by social historians. See Perdue and Green, *Cherokee Removal*, and Miles, *Ties That Bind*.

21. For a full text version of this law and others that came after it, see the Cherokee Advocate Office's *Laws of the Cherokee Nation*.

22. Over the past decade, several edited collections and a handful of monographs have been published on the topic of black-Native interconnectedness in the United States. These stories complement a more substantial canon of black-indigenous cultural history in Latin America and the Caribbean and represent a growing field focused on the socio-spatial interactions between multiple and overlapping diasporic communities. See Miles, *Ties That Bind*, and Tayac, *IndiVisible*.

23. Govan and Livingood, *Chattanooga Country*.

24. Jackson, *Indian Removal Speech to Congress*.

25. Norgren and Nanda argue that these three legal actions—the Indian Removal Act (May 28, 1830), Cherokee Nation v. Georgia (1831), and Cherokee v. Worcester (1832)—are crucial because they set contradictory legal precedents with respect to Native Americans' 'sovereign' nations and the United States federal government. Though each appears to advocate for Native American rights, framing the relationship between the two nations in terms of mutuality and respect, in reality, the federal government and courts codified a legal structure that rendered tribal sovereignty conditional, at best. Norgren and Nanda contend that this paradoxical legal relationship has been the driving force behind all subsequent U.S.-Native American law and public policy over the past one and one-half centuries. For more information, see Norgren and Nanda, *American Cultural Pluralism and Law*.

26. See Perdue and Green, *Cherokee Removal*.

27. Ross and Moulton, *Papers of Chief John Ross*, vol. 1, *1807–1839*.

28. See Wiltse, *History of Chattanooga*, 1:31.

29. W. Scott and Wirth, *Orders No. 25*.

30. Wiltse, *History of Chattanooga*, 1:29.

31. Ibid., 35.

32. Tennessee Writers' Project, *Chattanooga City Guide*, 20.

33. See Parham, *Chattanooga, Tennessee*, 7.

34. United States Census Bureau, *Slavery Schedule*.

35. Although the precise location of the slave market has been debated, it is known to have been located near the intersection of Market and Ninth Streets, close to the Union Passenger Terminal. One can find colorful descriptions of pre-Civil War Market Street in several recent books. See Evans and Herzogenrath, *Contributions by United States Colored Troops*; Hubbard, *African Americans of Chattanooga*; and M. Scott, *Blues Empress*.

36. Parham, *Chattanooga, Tennessee*, 5.

Chapter Two

1. For accounts of these sixteenth- through eighteenth-century encounters, see Govan and Livingood, *Chattanooga Country*, and Miles, *Ties That Bind*.

2. Tayac, *IndiVisible*.

3. Kappler, *Treaty with the Cherokee 1817*.

4. United States Census Bureau, *Slavery Schedule*.

5. Henry Wiltse compiled his manuscript in the early twentieth century and conducted these interviews between 1900 and 1901.

6. See Hubbard, *African Americans of Chattanooga*; Evans, *Contributions by United States Colored Troops*; and United States Census Bureau, *Slavery Schedule*.

7. See M. Scott, *Blues Empress*.

8. Wiltse, *History of Chattanooga*, 2:3.

9. Ibid., 2:3.

10. The First Battle of Chattanooga (June 7–8, 1862) involved a minor artillery bombardment by Union Brigadier General James S. Negley against Confederate Maj. Gen. Edmund Kirby Smith. During the Second Battle of Chattanooga (August 21, 1863), a Union artillery bombardment convinced General Braxton Bragg to evacuate the city. The Chattanooga Campaign, or the "Battles for Chattanooga" (November 23–25, 1863), are often cited as the battles that secured the Union's victory and enabled Major General Ulysses S. Grant to defeat Confederate General Braxton Bragg and allow Union general William T. Sherman to continue this campaign to Atlanta and, ultimately, the "March to the Sea." See Wiltse, *History of Chattanooga*, and Govan and Livingood, *Chattanooga Country*.

11. See Evans, *Contributions by United States Colored Troops*, and Evans, *Bright Memories*.

12. Evans, *Contributions by United States Colored Troops*.

13. Ibid., 52.

14. Ibid., 75.

15. Ibid., 109; "Wanted Immediately Any Number of Carpet-Baggers to Come to Chattanooga and Settle," advertisement printed on front page of the *Chattanooga Daily Republican*, Chattanooga, TN, December 8–January 8, 1868.

16. United States Census Bureau, *Manufacturing Statistics Summary Report*.

17. See Scott, *Blues Empress*, 35.

18. United States Census Bureau, *Manufacturing Statistics and Population*.

19. See Hubbard, *African Americans of Chattanooga*, and Scott, *Blues Empress*.

20. See Evans and Hubbard, *Historic African American Places*.

21. Ibid., 101.

22. No source listed. Retrieved from the Chattanooga Public Library's Local History archive on African American-related news clippings, Chattanooga, TN.

23. See Hubbard, *African Americans of Chattanooga*, and Scott, *Blues Empress*.

24. *Chattanooga Times*, October 27, 1880.

25. Chattanooga City Ordinance No. 84, January 24, 1871.

26. Chattanooga City Ordinances 132–134, May 29, 1878.

27. See Evans, *Contributions by United States Colored Troops*, 109.

28. *Chattanooga Times*, June 8, 1880.

29. *Chattanooga Times*, February 21, 1885.

30. *Chattanooga Times*, July 22, 1885.

31. Tennessee Writers' Project, *Chattanooga City Guide*, 52.

32. The first person lynched in Chattanooga was Charlie Williams on September 6, 1885. Additionally, Alfred Blount and Ed Johnson were dragged from the city jail and lynched from the Walnut Street Bridge on February 14, 1893 and March 19, 1906, respectively. Both men were accused of raping white women, and both maintained their innocence even as they were brutally and publicly murdered. The Walnut Street Bridge was completed in 1891 and was the first bridge connecting the historically black town of Hill City to downtown Chattanooga. Several local historians claim that the local Ku Klux Klan chapter publicly vowed to lynch an African American from every one of the bridge's 100-plus iron trusses as a threat to keep blacks from crossing the river and entering the city. See Chris Brooks, personal communication with the author, August 6, 2012.

33. Chattanooga Chamber of Commerce, *Report, 1890*, 82.

34. Connor, *Historical Guide to Chattanooga*, 16.

35. Chattanooga Chamber of Commerce, *Report, 1890*, 22.

36. *Chattanooga Times*, February 28, 1885.

37. *Chattanooga Times*, August 3, 1887.

38. *Chattanooga Times*, April 30, 1889.

39. *Chattanooga Times*, May 8, 1886.

40. *Chattanooga Times*, December 5, 1887.

Chapter Three

1. Tennessee Writers' Project, *Chattanooga City Guide*, 8–9.

2. Ibid., 8.

3. White, *Biography and Achievements*, 1.

4. Most scholars locate the origin of Jim Crow laws in the 1881 Tennessee passenger train code, although some legal historians argue Chapter 130 (1876), which permitted race-based discrimination in public and private establishments across the state, set the first legal precedent. For more information, see State of Tennessee, *Jim Crow and Disfranchisement*.

5. See *Chattanooga Daily Times*, November 10, 1915.

6. See Hubbard, *African Americans of Chattanooga*, and Scott, *Blues Empress*.

7. Hubbard, *African Americans of Chattanooga*, 25.

8. See Steinberg, *And to Think, It Only Cost*.

9. *Chattanooga Daily Times*, May 17, 1921, as quoted in ibid., 2.

10. See *Chattanooga Times*, May 16, 1911.

11. *Chattanooga Times*, September 13, 1930.

12. Sidney Shalett, "Women Want 'Hell's Half' Rechristened," *Chattanooga Times*, March 18, 1936.

13. Sidney Shalett, "Case Histories of Some Dwellers," *Chattanooga Times*, March 28, 1937.

14. Authorized by President Franklin D. Roosevelt as part of the New Deal/WPA urban housing program, the United States Housing Authority (USHA) allocated

$29.615 million to provide 5,863 low-cost rental units to as many as 23,000 slum dwellers nationwide.

15. See "College Hill Housing Work Given President's Approval," *Chattanooga Times*, October 22, 1938.

16. Ibid.

17. "College Hill Apartments Open," *Chattanooga Times*, June 18, 1940; see also "Condemnation Board to Inspect 'Unfit' Chattanooga Dwellings," *Chattanooga Times*, September 15, 1940.

18. See "Acting in Good Faith," *Chattanooga Times*, October 14, 1955.

19. See "City Will Be Asked to Bar Mixed Crowds at Dances," *Chattanooga Times*, February 1, 1956.

20. See "Preach against Violence," *Chattanooga Times*, February 1, 1956.

21. See Springer Gibson, "Negroes Request Integration Now in City's Schools," *Chattanooga Times*, March 12, 1958.

22. "Seating Rule on Buses Off," *Chattanooga Times*, January 8, 1957.

23. Springer Gibson, "Negro Students Stage Sit-Downs," *Chattanooga Times*, February 20, 1960. See also "Counter Sit In's at Four City Stores," *Chattanooga Times*, May 1, 1960.

24. See "Brief Entered in School Case," *Chattanooga Times*, May 4, 1960.

25. See Springer Gibson, "$1,000 Is Added to Reward Funds for Blast Cases," *Chattanooga Times*, August 24, 1960.

26. Freeman, personal communication.

27. Denying whiteness as a racial category, neglecting to see that whiteness has a history and geography—as Americans have long done—allows whiteness to stand as the norm. "Whiteness never has to speak its name," Lipsitz wrote, "never has to acknowledge its role as an organizing principle in social and cultural relations." Despite its pervasiveness, the stability of whiteness as a form of social power is quite fragile, depending "not only on white hegemony over separate racialized groups, but also on manipulating racial outsiders to fight against one another, to compete with one another for white approval, and to seek the rewards and privileges of whiteness for themselves at the expense of other racialized populations." See Lipsitz, *Possessive Investment in Whiteness*.

28. Hughley, personal communication; Rankins, personal communication.

29. Hughley, personal communication.

Chapter Four

1. Freeman, personal communication.

2. See Parham, *Chattanooga, Tennessee*; Hubbard, *African Americans of Chattanooga*; and Scott, *Blues Empress*.

3. See Sanborn Fire Insurance Company, *Chattanooga, Tennessee, 1889* (Fire Insurance Maps for Chattanooga).

4. See ibid., maps for 1917 and 1954.

5. The southward and westward migration of Jewish immigrants is well documented. See Franklin, *African Americans and Jews*, and Webb, *Fight against Fear*.

6. See United States Census Bureau, *Population Statistics, 1820–1940*.

7. *Chattanooga City Directories, 1871–1901*, 1.

8. See ibid., plus *Chattanooga City Directories, 1920–21*.

9. See Dunne, *Gastonia*.

10. Chuck Hamilton, "Chattanooga's Radical History," Chattanoogan.com, March 25, 2013, http://www.chattanoogan.com/2013/3/25/247459/Chattanooga-s -Radical-History.aspx.

11. *Chattanooga Times*, February 2, 1930, 2.

12. Brooks, personal communication.

13. Schecter quoted in ibid.

14. "Leaders Denounce Communists," *Chattanooga Times*, February 1, 1930.

15. Although the newspaper's byline stated it was published in Birmingham, Alabama, the *Southern Worker* was actually published and printed in Chattanooga as CPUSA organizers printed "Birmingham" to mislead anti-communists who might try to target and destroy the office and printing press (Brooks, personal communication).

16. "The Bond of Solidarity Grows Stronger," *Southern Worker*, vol. 1, no. 12, November 8, 1930.

17. Clark White, "Blues Culture and Black Experience in the River City," *Chattanooga Pulse*, February 6, 2014, http://www.chattanoogapulse.com/features/blues -culture-and-black-experience-in-the-river-city/.

18. *Chattanooga City Directories, 1871–1901*. See also Hubbard, *African Americans of Chattanooga*, and Scott, *Blues Empress*.

19. J. White, *Biography and Achievements*, 2.

20. Freeman, personal communication.

21. United States Census Bureau, *Population Statistics, 1950–2010*.

22. Freeman, personal communication.

23. Hughley, personal communication.

24. Robert R. Church Park (1899), in Memphis, was financed by businessman and civic leader Robert R. Church, who, for many decades, was the wealthiest African American living in Memphis. Church was dedicated to providing urban amenities and institutions to the black community in the absence of governmental support. See Lommel, *Robert Church*.

25. "Lincoln Park Opens June 1," *Chattanooga Times*, April 12, 1918.

26. Sanborn Fire Insurance Company, *Chattanooga, 1889*, maps for 1901, 1917.

27. "Remembering Citico Hotel," *Rockmart (GA) Journal*, April 1, 1998.

28. *Chicago Defender*, September 26, 1936, 3.

29. "First Ground Broken Today for Colored Swimming Pool," *Chattanooga Times*, August 3, 1937.

30. Jasper Duncan, "Chattanooga Dedicates New $60,000 Swimming Pool for Negroes," *Pittsburgh Courier*, July 9, 1938.

31. For more information about Chattanooga's significance to the Southern Negro League and professional baseball, see Jenkins, *Baseball in Chattanooga*.

32. "Dedication Is Set at Lincoln Center," *Chattanooga Times*, December 12, 1946.

33. Hughley, personal communication.

Chapter Five

1. A number of sociologists have demonstrated how the shift from a manufacturing-based to a service-based economy disproportionately impacted communities of color. See Hong, *Ruptures of American Capital*.

2. United States Census Bureau, *Population Statistics, 1950–2010*.

3. Freeman, personal communication.

4. United States Census Bureau, *Population Statistics, 1950–2010*.

5. Freeman, personal communication; Littlefield, personal communication.

6. Freeman, personal communication.

7. Libby Wann, "Merchants Fight Razing of 900 Block of Market," *Chattanooga Times*, December 8, 1976.

8. Clarence Franklin Scaife, "Upgrading Not Slated on East 9th," *Chattanooga Times*, February 24, 1977.

9. "Klansmen Dealt Blow by $535,000 Verdict," *New Pittsburgh Courier*, March 20, 1982.

10. "Klan Charges Dropped," *Washington Post*, September 16, 1980.

11. "Chattanooga Police Arrest Three Armed Klansmen," *Washington Post*, July 27, 1980.

12. Brooks, personal communication.

13. "Blacks Relive KKK Incident," *New Pittsburgh Courier*, May 9, 1981.

14. The four women who were shot, as well as a fifth who was injured by broken glass during the shootings, filed a civil suit against the Ku Klux Klan. On March 19, 1982, a U.S. District Court civil jury ruled in favor of the women. Collectively, they were awarded $535,000 in civil damages. This trial marked the first time a civil rights suit had been filed against the Ku Klux Klan.

15. Chattanooga Venture, *Untitled Promotional Material*.

16. Lorrie Burke, "Downtown Community Gets a New Look," *News Free Press*, May 11, 1986.

17. Editorial, "M. L. King Key to New Downtown," *Chattanooga Times*, May 13, 1986.

18. See United States Census Bureau, *Population Statistics, 1950–2010*.

19. Kathy Gilbert, "Inner City Businesses Battle to Survive," *Chattanooga Times Free Press*, September 6, 1999.

20. Yolanda Putnam, "City, Foundations Celebrate M. L. King Area Successes," *Times Free Press*, December 17, 2003.

21. Yolanda Putnam, "More Upscale Housing, Diversity Expected on MLK," *Times Free Press*, May 4, 2003.

22. See Denver Foundation, "Moving Forward," 5.

23. Jason Reynolds, "King-Size Investment—$28 Million Will Build or Renovate More than 100 Homes in Area," *Chattanooga Times Free Press*, May 4, 2003.

24. Jason Reynolds, "MLK Ripe for Development," *Chattanooga Times Free Press*, June 21, 2004.

25. See University of Tennessee–Chattanooga, *Master Plan, 2012*.

26. Ibid., "Executive Summary."

27. University of Tennessee–Chattanooga, *Comprehensive Housing Master Plan*, 1.

28. Ibid., "Executive Summary."

29. Tyree, personal communication; Gursakal, personal communication.

30. University of Tennessee–Chattanooga, *Master Plan, 2012*, 58.

31. Ibid., 80.

32. See United States Census Bureau, *Population Statistics, 1950–2010*.

33. University of Tennessee–Chattanooga, *Master Plan, 2012*, 40.

34. Davis, personal communication.

35. Associated Press, "City Sings the Blues: Chattanooga's Bessie Smith Hall; A Star That Never Was," *Washington Post*, June 21, 1994.

36. Davis, personal communication.

37. Ibid.

38. Mark Making, *Vision Statement*.

39. McDonald, personal communication.

Chapter Six

1. See the Sanborn Fire Insurance maps in Sanborn Fire Insurance Company, *Chattanooga, Tennessee, 1885* and *Chattanooga, Tennessee, 1889*.

2. See Coulter, *Documentation of the Art*.

3. Watson, personal communication.

4. Rushing, personal communication.

5. Watson, personal communication.

6. See Urban Land Institute and Chattanooga-Hamilton County Regional Planning Commission, *Moccasin Bend, Chattanooga, Tennessee*.

7. Clark, personal communication.

8. See Chattanooga-Hamilton County Regional Planning Commission and Carr/Lynch Associates, *Tennessee Riverpark Master Plan*.

9. Chattanooga Venture, *Untitled Pamphlet*.

10. Littlefield, personal communication.

11. Chattanooga Venture, *Untitled Pamphlet*.

12. Littlefield, personal communication.

13. Richard Mullins, "Chattanooga to Show Off for Visions '86 Conference," *Chattanooga Times*, March 15, 1986.

14. Carolyn Mitchell, "Look Back, Look Ahead," *Chattanooga Times*, March 18, 1986.

15. Judy Frank, "In-Fighting May Endanger Venture Project Albright Says," *Chattanooga Times*, February 21, 1986.

16. Judy Frank, "City Studying Venture Plan for Rights Group," *Chattanooga Times*, August 29, 1986.

17. David Miller, "Visions '86 to Feature Governor, Rouse," *News Free Press*, February 2, 1986.

18. Ibid.

19. John McGee, "Homecoming '86," *News Free Press*, December 1, 1986.

20. John McGee, "Venture to Open Office Here to Make City's Assets Visible," *News Free Press*, January 1, 1988.

21. Chattanooga Venture, *Annual Report.*

22. Michael Davis, "Forum Seeks Answers to Racial Relations," *Chattanooga Times,* May 17, 1989.

23. James Bennett (J. B.) Collins, "Tenants Group Sees Venture Offer as Move to Interfere," *News Free Press,* December 12, 1990.

24. Duane Gang and Dave Flessner, "Fund Raising for City Project Nearly Complete," *Times Free Press,* December 15, 2002.

Chapter Seven

1. Duane Gang, "Riverfront Makeover," *Times Free Press,* February 2, 2002.

2. Editorial, *Times Free Press,* February 13, 2002.

3. Editorial, *Times Free Press,* March 24, 2002.

4. See Hargreaves Associates, Inc., *21st Century Chattanooga Waterfront Plan.*

5. Duane Gang, "Mayor Unveils Trust for Riverfront," *Times Free Press,* March 23, 2002.

6. Ibid.

7. Duane Gang, "Waterfront Plan Has New Approach in Fundraising," *Times Free Press,* November 25, 2002.

8. See Duane Gang, "City Sells Bonds for Waterfront Projects," *Times Free Press,* October 11, 2002, and Mike Pare, "$105 Million in Riverfront Work Readied," *Times Free Press,* September 28, 2002.

9. Angie Herrington, "Trail of Tears History in Waterfront Plans," *Times Free Press,* September 26, 2002.

10. Ibid.

11. Trevor Higgins, "A Grand Finale," *Times Free Press,* May 8, 2005.

12. Coulter, *Documentation of the Art,* 5.

13. Mike Pare, "Pedestrian Tunnel Would Link River to Downtown Area," *Times Free Press,* May 13, 2003.

14. Duane Gang, "Panel Approves Funding for Waterfront Artwork," *Times Free Press,* July 18, 2003.

15. Townsend, personal communication.

16. Team Gadugi, *Passage.*

17. Coulter, *Documentation of the Art,* 14.

18. Townsend, personal communication.

19. Mike Pare, "Reviving the Riverfront," *Times Free Press,* May 2, 2004; see also C. Hamilton, "Chickamauga, Tennessee."

20. Editorial, "Beyond the Orange Barrels," *Times Free Press,* September 21, 2003.

21. Coulter, *Documentation of the Art,* 13–15.

22. Team Gadugi, *Passage.*

23. Trevor Higgins, "Passage Dedication Heeds City's Cherokee Culture," *Chattanooga Times Free Press,* May 13, 2005.

24. Angie Herrington, "Fire across the River," *Times Free Press,* May 14, 2005.

25. Coulter, *Documentation of the Art,* 20.

26. Gadugi artists quoted in Ann Nichols, "Debut of Waterfront Public Art," *Times Free Press,* March 20, 2005.

27. Coulter, *Documentation of the Art*, 15.

28. Mike Pare, "City Plans $13 Million Park for Roper Site," *Times Free Press*, April 6, 2004.

29. Hussey, *Ascending Path*.

30. City of Chattanooga, *Memorandum of Understanding*.

31. Littlefield, personal communication.

32. Clark, personal communication.

33. Hughley, personal communication.

34. Herman Wang, "What Price Success?," *Times Free Press*, July 24, 2005.

35. Brooks, personal communication.

36. Cousins, personal communication.

Chapter Eight

1. Lance, personal communication, August 10, 2012.

2. Ibid.

3. Ibid.

4. Ibid.

5. Ibid.

6. Ibid; Brooks, personal communication.

7. Chattanooga Organized for Action, "How Does COA Staff Work?"

8. See Kretzmann and McKnight, *Building Communities*.

9. Chattanooga Organized for Action, *COA, Personal Assessment Survey*.

10. Chattanooga Organized for Action, *Support Internal Plan*.

11. Grove Street Settlement House, "Guiding Principles, 2012."

12. Chattanooga Organized for Action, "How Does COA Staff Work?"

13. Chattanooga Organized for Action, *SPARC Initiative*.

14. Planning Free School of Chattanooga, "Who We Are."

15. See Knapp, "Experimenting with Anarchistic Approaches"; Kozol, *Free Schools*; and Morrison, *Free School Teaching*.

16. Lance, personal communication, June 6, 2013.

17. Planning Free School of Chattanooga, *Transportation and Mobility*.

18. Planning Free School of Chattanooga, *Developing a Neighborhood Assessment Toolkit*.
19. Ibid.

20. Planning Free School of Chattanooga, *Employment and Workforce Development*.

Chapter Nine

1. See City of Chattanooga, *Ralph Kelley Profile*.

2. "Conrad Opposes Engineers on Closing of Lincoln Park," *Chattanooga Times*, November 10, 1974.

3. Pat Wilcox, "Site in Glenwood to Become Park," *Chattanooga Times*, November 3, 1979.

4. Hamilton County Regional Planning Agency, *Erlanger-UTC Area Study*, 9.

5. "Lincoln Park: On the Move," *Chattanooga Times*, April 4, 1980.

6. Ibid.

7. Ibid.

8. Hughley, personal communication.

9. Ibid.; Tiffany Rankins, personal communication.

10. Wade Rawlins, "After Home Improvement Work, Lincoln Park Regains Its Pride," *Chattanooga Times*, August 20, 1989.

11. Ibid.

12. The 2000 Decennial Census is the first census where block-level data is available for Chattanooga. Because of its small size, historic Block Group-level data does not offer an accurate picture of social life and trends in Lincoln Park. See United States Census Bureau, *Population Statistics Report on the Block Level*.

13. See Ellis Smith, "Central Avenue Extension to Change Downtown Chattanooga Traffic Patterns," *Chattanooga Times Free Press*, accessed March 15, 2013, http://www .timesfreepress.com/news/news/story/2011/nov/05/central-avenue-extension -change-downtown-chattanoo/63174/.

14. Rankins, personal communication.

15. Yolanda Putnam, "Lincoln Park Residents Oppose Chattanooga Plan to Extend Central Avenue," *Chattanooga Times Free Press*, accessed March 13, 2013, http://www .timesfreepress.com/news/local/story/2013/mar/19/lincoln-park-residents-oppose -extension/102834/.

16. Rankins, personal communication.

17. Ibid.

18. Ibid.

19. Ibid.

20. I was the facilitator of the Planning Free School and therefore played an instrumental role in these early organizing efforts. This chapter is based on personal field notes, Planning Free School Workshop transcripts, and interviews with Chattanooga Organized for Action (COA) staff members and leaders from the Lincoln Park Neighborhood Association between March and June 2013.

21. City of Chattanooga, *Central Avenue Extension*, 3.

22. Planning Free School of Chattanooga, *Arts and Cultural Development*.

23. Planning Free School of Chattanooga, *Housing Workshop Transcript*.

24. See Chattanooga Organized for Action, "Victory for Lincoln Park." Six months later, Jeff Cannon left his position with the City of Chattanooga. Lincoln Park leaders were never provided these drawings, as was promised by City staff.

25. "Mayor Andy Berke to Lincoln Park Residents: We Want and Need Your Input," *Chattanooga Times Free Press*, accessed May 25, 2013, http://www.timesfreepress .com/news/2013/may/28/andy-berke-to-lincoln-park-residents-we-want/.

26. James Rojas's "Place It!" model was developed to engage workshop participants in discussions about their emotional attachments to place. Rojas is often credited with developing the term and idea *Latino Urbanism*, and runs his Place It! workshops for diverse audiences across the United States.

27. Hughley, personal communication; Rankins, personal communication.

28. Rankins, personal communication.

29. Yolanda Putnam, "Lincoln Park Residents Developing Community Plan," *Chattanooga Times Free Press*, accessed June 23, 2013, http://www.timesfreepress.com /news/local/story/2013/jun/23/lincoln-park-residents-developing/111528/.

30. Joy Lukachick and Yolanda Putnam, "Chattanooga Mayor Andy Berke Outlines Plans for Lincoln Park Land," *Chattanooga Times Free Press*, accessed August 23, 2013, http://www.timesfreepress.com/news/local/story/2013/aug/23/chattanooga -mayor-andy-berke-outlines-plans-lincol/116861/.

31. Joy Lukachick, "Erlanger Land Swap a Win for Lincoln Park Neighborhood in Chattanooga," *Chattanooga Times Free Press*, accessed October 22, 2013, http://www .timesfreepress.com/news/local/story/2013/oct/22/land-swap-is-win-for-lincoln -park/121961/.

32. See G. Brown, "Vision for Lincoln Park."

33. Joy Lukachick, "As Details Emerge on a Central Avenue Expansion, Lincoln Park Residents Say They Aren't Happy," *Chattanooga Times Free Press*, accessed March 17, 2014, http://www.timesfreepress.com/news/local/story/2014/mar/15/as -more-details-emerge-on-a-central-avenue/134388/.

34. See City of Chattanooga, *Central Avenue Extension*.

35. For more information about the redevelopment of the Cumberland site, see Shelley Bradbury, "New Multi-Family Units Proposed near Erlanger and UTC," *Chattanooga Times Free Press*, accessed July 20, 2014, http://www.timesfreepress.com /news/business/aroundregion/story/2014/jul/10/new-multi-family-units -proposed-near-erlanger-utc/251887/.

36. Chattanooga-Hamilton County Regional Planning Association, *Third to Riverside Neighborhood Plan*, 79.

Conclusion

1. Woods, *Development Arrested*, 261.

Appendix One

1. Woods, *Development Arrested*, 260.
2. Lefebvre, *Production of Space*, 60.
3. Ibid., 10.
4. Ibid., 34.
5. See Massey, "New Directions in Space," and Massey, *For Space*.
6. Massey, "New Directions," 8.
7. Ibid., 12.
8. Ibid., 18.
9. Ibid., 11.
10. Soja, "Spatiality of Social Life," 90.
11. Soja, *Thirdspace*. For explorations into the multi- and inter-disciplinary nature of the "spatial turn," see the essays in Gregory and Urry, *Social Relations*, especially Massey's "New Directions in Space" and Soja's "Spatiality of Social Life." See also

Soja's *Postmoderm Geographies* and *Seeking Spatial Justice*. For interdisciplinary accounts of the "spatial turn," see Warf and Arias, *Spatial Turn*.

12. Soja, *Thirdspace*, 103.

13. Massey, "New Directions in Space," 10.

14. Ibid., 18–19.

15. For early works, see Du Bois, *Black Reconstruction*, and Drake and Cayton's *Black Metropolis*. More recent works include Kelley's *Race Rebels*, Woods's *Development Arrested*, Inikori's essay "Wonders of the African World," and McKittrick and Woods's *Black Geographies*. Du Bois's *Black Reconstruction* is arguably the most comprehensive account of the racialization of space. Du Bois illustrated how racist attitudes toward African Americans prior to, during, and following the Civil War precluded the success of Negro emancipation in the wake of chattel slavery. Despite these overt hostilities, African Americans managed to relocate families, settle farms and towns, build schools, and participate in politics in significant numbers. Unfortunately, these gains were quickly arrested. In 1871, the Freedman's Bureau was systematically dismantled by racist legislators; six years later, federal troops were withdrawn from southern communities. With virtually no mechanisms to hold them accountable for their actions, conservative whites unleashed waves of terror against African Americans. By the twilight of the Reconstruction period (1865–1880), a combined rural sharecropping-urban New South socio-spatial order had taken hegemonic root in the Delta and across the American South. For the next fifty years, this logic dominated spatial development across the South, producing a variety of locally- and regionally-specific uneven geographies and spaces of cultural belonging, including those found in historic and contemporary downtown Chattanooga.

16. Braziel and Mannur, *Theorizing Diaspora*.

17. Most studies, the authors contend, take one of three disparate units of analysis: the body, economic/historical materialist, or metaphoric. Each of these scopes has the effect of "reducing black geographies into geographic determinism, the flesh, or the imagination. . . . In short, a black sense of place and black geographic knowledges are both undermined by hegemonic spatial practices (of say, segregation and neglect) and seemingly unavailable as a worldview" (McKittrick and Woods, "Nobody Knows the Mysteries," 7).

18. Ibid., 5.

19. Ibid.

20. See Inikori, "Wonders of the African World."

21. See Inikori, "Slavery and the Rise of Capitalism."

22. R. Hamilton, *Routes of Passage*, 7.

23. Boyce Davies and M'Bow, "Towards African Diaspora Citizenship," 15.

24. Fanon, *Wretched of the Earth*, 44.

25. Woods, *Development Arrested*, 56.

26. R. Hamilton, *Routes of Passage*, 408.

27. See Patterson and Kelley, "Unfinished Migrations," 41.

28. Miles, *Ties That Bind*; Miles and Holland, *Crossing Waters, Crossing Worlds*; Tayac, *IndiVisible*; Forbes, *Africans and Native Americans*.

29. Hall, "Thinking about Thinking."

30. Patterson and Kelley, "Unfinished Migrations." For example, work that excavates and reconstructs overlapping Native American-African American cultural development—both in the Southeast and later west of the Mississippi River—have led some contemporary scholars and political activists to employ a language of "indivisibility" when discussing black-Native relations in the United States. The concept of *indivisibility* is rooted in notions of kinship, common socioeconomic experience, and political solidarity, and establishes ethical and epistemological foundations for imagining radically new forms of political solidarity and community togetherness, and are direct rejections of the "divide and conquer" strategies of racial formation, categorization, and division exercised by colonial powers across the globe, including in and around the site of present-day Chattanooga. For more information about diasporic indivisibility, see Forbes, *Africans and Native Americans*; Miles, *Ties That Bind*; and especially Tayac, *IndiVisible*.

31. McKittrick and Woods, "Nobody Knows the Mysteries," 6.

32. Jacobs, *Life and Death*.

33. Lynch, *Image of the City*, 2.

34. Whyte, *Social Life*.

35. See Fleming, *Art of Placemaking*, and Markusen and Gadwa, *Creative Placemaking*.

36. World Archaeological Congress, *Archaeologies of Placemaking*.

37. Schneekloth and Shibley, *Placemaking*, 1.

38. Ben-Joseph, *Code of the City*.

39. Schneekloth and Shibley, *Placemaking*.

40. Martin, "'Place-Framing' as Place-Making," 740.

41. Beauregard, "From Place to Site."

42. Arefi, *Deconstructing Placemaking*, 6.

43. See Blomley, *Unsettling the City*.

44. McKittrick and Woods, "Nobody Knows the Mysteries," 4.

45. Ang-Lygate, "Everywhere to Go but Home," 377.

46. Hong's discussion of "propertied subjects" adds theoretical depth to historic transnational and trans-regional migration trends. Propertied subjects are both gendered and racialized, which leads to vast socioeconomic disparities along gender and racial lines. Hong describes the intersection of race and gender for women of color as the "profound impossibility of ownership" (*Ruptures of American Capital*, 236). Despite this profound impossibility, Hong demonstrated how communities of color have formed alternative, "subterranean" economies and communities throughout modern history. Subaltern conceptualizations of property and ownership serve as ruptures in the hegemonic processes and structures of capital accumulation and urban development.

47. See Woods, *Development Arrested*, and Scott, *Blues Empress*.

48. McKittrick and Woods, "Nobody Knows the Mysteries," 5.

49. Ibid., 4.

50. See Nguyên, "Vietnamese Diasporic Placemaking." Nguyên was the first scholar to use the term *diasporic placemaking* in the context of Vietnamese immigrant community building.

51. Blomley, *Unsettling the City*, 51.

52. Ibid., 53.

53. Ibid., 114.

54. Sandercock, *Making the Invisible Visible*.

55. Lightweis-Goff, *Blood at the Root*, 160.

56. Ibid., 174–76.

57. Sandercock, *Making the Invisible Visible*, 20.

Appendix Two

1. Sandercock, *Making the Invisible Visible*, 37.

2. Sandercock, *Towards Cosmopolis*, 35–36.

3. McKittrick and Woods, "Nobody Knows the Mysteries," 7.

4. Bruner, *Actual Minds, Possible Worlds*.

5. See Hayden, *Power of Place*.

6. There is a rich literature dedicated to the relationship between planning practice and storytelling. See especially Bruner, *Actual Minds, Possible Worlds*; Mandelbaum, "Telling Stories"; Throgmorton, *Planning as Persuasive Storytelling*; Chase, "Narrative Inquiry"; Forester, *Learning from Practice Stories*; Sandercock, *Making the Invisible Visible*; Forester, *Deliberative Practitioner*; and Eckstein and Throgmorton, *Story and Sustainability*.

7. Chase, "Narrative Inquiry," 660.

8. Forester, *Deliberative Practitioner*; Forester, *Dealing with Differences*, 12.

9. See Seidman, *Interviewing as Qualitative Research*.

10. See especially Forester, "Participatory Action Research"; Reardon, "Participatory Action Research"; Reardon, "Enhancing the Capacity"; Jennings, "Urban Planning, Community Participation"; and Corburn, "Reconnecting with Our Roots."

11. See, for example, Jennings, *Blacks, Latinos, and Asians*; Reardon, "Combating Racism through Planning Education"; and Umemoto's works "Walking in Another's Shoes" and *Truce*.

12. Quoted in Forester, *Deliberative Practitioner*, 121.

13. Forester, *Deliberative Practitioner*, 116.

14. In *Free Schools*, Kozol challenged free school educators to become active participants in the struggle for racial and social equity and justice. While he saw the free school model as holding great potential for transformative social change, he maintained that such work required long-term commitment to place, intellectual rigor, and technical competency. He wrote, "There has to be a way to find pragmatic competence, internal strength, and ethical passion all in the same process. This is the only kind of revolution that can possibly transform the lives of people in the land in which we live and in the time in which we are now living. . . . The question, then, in my own sense of struggle, is as follows: How can the Free School achieve, at one and the same time, a sane, ongoing, down to earth, skill oriented, sequential, credentializing and credentialized curricular experience directly geared in to the real survival needs of colonized children in a competitive and technological society; and simultaneously evolve, maintain, nourish, and revivify the 'uncredentialized,' 'unauthoritative,' 'unsanctioned,' 'non-curricular' consciousness of pain, rage, love, and revolution

which first infused their school with truth and magic, exhilaration and comradeship. Few schools up to now seem to have been able to do both; some that I know, however, come extremely close" (44–45, 49).

15. In *Seeking Spatial Justice*, Soja argued that spatial injustices are "situated and contextualized in three overlapping and interactive levels of geographical resolution" (8): (1) the creation and enforcement of political boundaries, which range in scale from the block to the multinational level; (2) endogenous struggles over the distribution of urban benefits and burdens; and (3) on the regional/"meso-regional" scale, which illuminate patterns of uneven geographic development. Considering that spatial in/justices organize themselves on a multitude of scales, Soja called for renewed focus on regional coalition building, regional democracy, and an overall regionalization of the "right to the city" framework.

Bibliography

Newspapers and Periodicals

Chattanooga Daily Times	*Chicago Defender*	*Rockmart (GA) Journal*
Chattanoogan	*New Pittsburgh Courier*	*Southern Worker*
Chattanooga Observer	*News Free Press*	*Times Free Press*
Chattanooga Pulse	*Publication for National*	*Washington Post*
Chattanooga Times	*Textile Workers*	

Books, Interviews, and Other Sources

Ang-Lygate, Magdalene. "Everywhere to Go but Home: On (re)(dis)(un) Location." *Journal of Gender Studies* 5, no. 3 (1996): 375–88.

Arefi, Mahyar. *Deconstructing Placemaking: Needs, Opportunities, and Assets.* New York: Routledge, 2014.

Backus, Meghan. Personal communication with the author, January 3, 2013.

Beauregard, Robert, A. "From Place to Site: Negotiating Narrative Complexity." In *Site Matters: Design Concepts, Histories, and Strategies*, edited by Carol Burns and Andrea Kahn, 39–58. New York: Routledge, 2005.

Bell, Monty. Personal communication with the author, June 1, 2013.

Ben-Joseph, Eran. *The Code of the City: Standards and the Hidden Language of Place Making.* Cambridge, MA: MIT Press, 2005.

Blomley, Nicholas K. *Unsettling the City: Urban Land and the Politics of Property.* New York: Routledge, 2004.

Boyce Davies, Carole, and Babacar M'Bow. "Towards African Diaspora Citizenship: Politicizing an Existing Global Geography." In *Black Geographies and the Politics of Place*, edited by Katherine McKittrick and Clyde Woods, 14–35. Toronto: South End Press, 2007.

Braziel, Jana, and Anita Mannur, eds. *Theorizing Diaspora: A Reader.* Malden, MA: Blackwell Publishing Ltd, 2003.

Brooks, Chris. Personal communication with the author, August 6, 2012.

Brown, Garth. "Vision for Lincoln Park: Proposed Site Plan." Chattanooga, TN, 2014.

Brown, John P. *Old Frontiers: The Story of the Cherokee Indians from Earliest Times to the Date of Their Removal to the West, 1838.* Kingsport, TN: Southern Publishers, 1938.

Bruner, Jerome S. *Actual Minds, Possible Worlds.* Cambridge, MA: Harvard University Press, 1986.

Chase, Susan. "Narrative Inquiry: Multiple Lenses, Approaches, Voices." In *The SAGE Handbook of Qualitative Research*, 3rd ed., edited by Norman K. Denzin and Yvonna S. Lincoln, 651–80. Thousand Oaks, CA: Sage, 2005.

Chattanooga Chamber of Commerce. *Chattanooga, Tennessee Industrial Report.* Chattanooga, TN, 1964.

———. *Report of the Chattanooga Chamber of Commerce, 1890.* Chattanooga, TN, 1890.

Chattanooga City Directories, 1871–1901. Nashville: Tennessee State Library and Archives, 1990.

Chattanooga City Directories, 1920–21. Nashville: Tennessee State Library and Archives, 1990.

Chattanooga Housing Authority. *2012 Annual Plan.* Chattanooga, TN, 2012.

Chattanooga Organized for Action. *Chattanooga: A Home to All.* Chattanooga, TN, 2012.

———. *COA, Personal Assessment Survey.* Chattanooga, TN, 2012.

———. "How Does COA Staff Work?" Chattanooga, TN, Internal Organizational Document, January 21, 2013.

———. *SPARC Initiative.* Chattanooga, TN, 2013.

———. *Support Internal Plan.* Chattanooga, TN, 2013.

———. "A Victory for Lincoln Park." Email distributed via electronic newsletter. Chattanooga, TN, May 29, 2013.

Chattanooga Venture. *Annual Report.* Chattanooga, TN, 1989.

———. *Untitled Pamphlet.* Chattanooga, TN, 1986.

———. *Untitled Promotional Material.* Chattanooga, TN, 1984.

Chattanooga-Hamilton County Regional Planning Association. *Third to Riverside Neighborhood Plan Draft.* Chattanooga, TN, June 2013.

Chattanooga-Hamilton County Regional Planning Commission and Carr/Lynch Associates. *Tennessee Riverpark Master Plan.* Cambridge, MA: The Associates, 1984.

Cherokee Advocate Office. *Laws of the Cherokee Nation: Adopted by the Council at Various Periods, 1852.* Library of Congress. Accessed November 1, 2013. http://www.loc.gov/law/help/american-indian-consts/PDF/28014183.pdf.

City of Chattanooga. *Central Avenue Extension—National Environmental Protection Act (NEPA) Historical/Architectural Assessment,* April 2013.

———. Chattanooga City Ordinance No. 84, January 24, 1871.

———. Chattanooga City Ordinances 132–134, May 29, 1878.

———. *Memorandum of Understanding between the City of Chattanooga and Cherokee Nation,* October 16, 2006.

———. *Ralph Kelley Profile,* 2016.

Clark, Bruz. Personal communication with the author, October 24, 2012.

Connor, George C. *Historical Guide to Chattanooga and Lookout Mountain: With Descriptions of the Battles, Battle-Fields, Climate, Industries, Minerals, Timber, etc.* Chattanooga, TN: T. H. Payne, 1889.

Corburn, Jason. "Reconnecting with Our Roots: American Urban Planning and Public Health in the Twenty-First Century." *Urban Affairs Review* 42, no. 5 (2007): 688–713.

Coulter, Ann. *Documentation of the Art at the Passage at Ross's Landing.* Chattanooga, TN: A. Coulter Consulting, 2006.

Cousins, Maxine. Personal communication with the author, October 29, 2012.

Cox, Brent Alan. *Heart of the Eagle: Dragging Canoe and the Emergence of the Chickamauga Confederacy.* Milan, TN: Chenanee Publishers, 1999.

Crawford, Margaret, Michael Speaks, and Rahul Mehrotra, eds. *Everyday Urbanism: Margaret Crawford vs. Michael Speaks.* Ann Arbor: University of Michigan, A. Alfred Taubman College of Architecture, 2005.

Davis, Carmen. Personal communication with the author, January 11, 2013.

Denver Foundation. "Moving Forward While Staying in Place: Embedded Funders and Community Change." Chapin Hall Discussion Paper, University of Chicago, 2004.

Drake, St. Clair, and Horace R. Cayton. *Black Metropolis: A Study of Negro Life in a Northern City.* New York: Harcourt, Brace and Company, 1945.

Du Bois, W. E. B. *Black Reconstruction in America: An Essay toward a History of the Part which Black Folk Played in the Attempt to Reconstruct Democracy in America, 1860–1880.* New York: Atheneum, 1930.

Dunne, William F. *Gastonia: Citadel of the Class Struggle in the New South.* New York: Workers Library, 1929. Published for the National Textile Workers Union.

Eckstein, Barbara J., and James A. Throgmorton, eds. *Story and Sustainability: Planning, Practice, and Possibility for American Cities.* Cambridge, MA: MIT Press, 2003.

Evans, E. R. *Bright Memories: Beck Farm, Camp Contraband, and Hill City.* Chattanooga, TN: Hill City Association, 2012.

Evans, E. Raymond, and Bernd Herzogenrath. *Contributions by United States Colored Troops (USCT) of Chattanooga and North Georgia during the American Civil War, Reconstruction, and Formation of Chattanooga.* Chickamauga, GA: B. C. Foster, 2003.

Evans, Raymond, and Rita Hubbard. *Historic African American Places in the Chattanooga Area.* Signal Mountain, TN: CASI Publishing, 2009.

Fanon, Frantz. *The Wretched of the Earth.* New York: Grove Press, 1963.

Finger, John R. *The Eastern Band of Cherokees, 1819–1900.* Knoxville: University of Tennessee Press, 1984.

Fleming, Ronald Lee. *The Art of Placemaking: Interpreting Community through Public Art and Urban Design.* London: Merrell, 2007.

Forbes, Jack D. *Africans and Native Americans: The Language of Race and the Evolution of Red-Black Peoples.* Champaign: University of Illinois Press, 1993.

Forester, John. *Dealing with Differences: Dramas of Mediating Public Disputes.* Oxford: Oxford University Press, 2009.

———. *The Deliberative Practitioner: Encouraging Participatory Planning Processes.* Cambridge, MA: MIT Press, 1999.

———. *Learning from Practice Stories: The Priority of Practical Judgment.* Ithaca, NY: Cornell University, Department of City and Regional Planning, 1993.

———. "Participatory Action Research from the Inside: Community Development Practice in East St. Louis." *American Sociologist* 24, no. 1 (1993): 69–91.

Franklin, V. P. *African Americans and Jews in the Twentieth Century: Studies in Convergence and Conflict.* Columbia: University of Missouri Press, 1998.

Freeman, Moses. Personal communication with the author, September 12, 2012.

Gilliland, Michael. Personal communication with the author, September 26, 2012.

Govan, Gilbert E., and James Weston Livingood. *The Chattanooga Country, 1540–1976: From Tomahawks to TVA*. 3rd ed. Knoxville: University of Tennessee Press, 1977.

Gregory, Derek, and John Urry. *Social Relations and Spatial Structures*. New York: St. Martin's Press, 1985.

Grove Street Settlement House. "Guiding Principles, 2012." Accessed February 13, 2013. http://grovestreetsettlementhouse.wordpress.com/our-guiding-principles/.

Gursakal, Baris. Personal communication with the author, November 9, 2012.

Hall, Stuart. "Thinking about Thinking." Afterword to *Culture, Politics, Race and Diaspora: The Thought of Stuart Hall*. "Caribbean Reasonings," edited by Brian Meeks. Kingston, Jamaica: Ian Randle, 2007.

Hamilton, Chuck. "Chickamauga, Tennessee—Part 1 of 3." Chattanoogan.com, May 3, 2012. http://www.chattanoogan.com/2012/5/25/226946/Chickamauga -Tennessee—Part-1-of-3.aspx.

Hamilton, Ruth Simms. *Routes of Passage: Rethinking the African Diaspora*. East Lansing: Michigan State University Press, 2007.

Hamilton County Regional Planning Agency. *Erlanger-UTC Area Study*. Chattanooga, TN, 1985.

Hargreaves Associates, Inc. *21st Century Chattanooga Waterfront Plan*. Chattanooga, TN, 2005.

Hayden, Dolores. *The Power of Place: Urban Landscapes as Public History*. Cambridge, MA: MIT Press, 1995.

Hollenbeck, Megan. Personal communication with the author, August 16, 2012.

Hong, Grace Kyungwon. *The Ruptures of American Capital: Women of Color, Feminism, and the Culture of Immigrant Labor*. Minneapolis: University of Minnesota Press, 2006.

Hubbard, Rita L. *African Americans of Chattanooga: A History of Unsung Heroes*. Charleston, SC: History Press, 2007.

Hughley, Vannice. Personal communication with the author, June 8, 2013.

Hussey, Andres. *Ascending Path: Statement of the Artist*. Chattanooga, TN: n.p., 2007. Printed on a plaque at the site of the sculpture.

Inikori, Joseph E. "Slavery and the Rise of Capitalism." The 1993 Elsa Goveia Memorial Lecture: Slavery and the Rise of Capitalism, Department of History, the University of the West Indies, Mona, Jamaica, 1993.

———. "Wonders of the African World and the Trans-Atlantic Slave Trade." *Black Scholar* 1, no. 30 (2001): 30–31.

Jackson, Andrew. *Indian Removal Speech to Congress, December 6, 1830*. Accessed July 2, 2012. https://memory.loc.gov/cgi-bin/ampage?collId=llrd&fileName=010 /llrd010.db&recNum=438.

Jacobs, Jane. *The Life and Death of Great American Cities*. New York: Vintage Books, 1961.

Jenkins, David. *Baseball in Chattanooga*. Charleston, SC: Arcadia Publishers, 2005.

Jennings, James. *Blacks, Latinos, and Asians in Urban America: Status and Prospects for Politics and Activism*. Westport, CT: Praeger, 1994.

———. "Urban Planning, Community Participation, and the Roxbury Master Plan in Boston." *Annals of the American Academy of Political and Social Science* 594, no. 1 (2004): 12–33.

Kappler, Charles J., ed. *Treaty with the Cherokee, 1817.* Washington, DC: Government Printing Office, 1904.

Kelley, Robin D. G. *Race Rebels: Culture, Politics, and the Black Working Class.* New York: Free Press, 1996.

King, Duane. *Report to the Friends of Moccasin Bend on the Cherokee Removal in the Chattanooga Area.* Chattanooga, TN, 1996.

Knapp, Courtney E. "Experimenting with Anarchistic Approaches to Collaborative Planning: The Planning Free School of Chattanooga." *Journal of Urban Affairs* 39, no. 5 (2017): 1–23.

———. "Flipping the Script: Toward a Transformative Urban Redevelopment Agenda in Chattanooga, Tennessee." *Progressive Planning* 195 (Spring 2013): 14–17.

Kneebone, Elizabeth. *The Great Recession and Poverty in Metropolitan America.* Washington, DC: Brookings Institution, 2010.

Kozol, Jonathan. *Free Schools.* Boston: Houghton Mifflin, 1972.

Kretzmann, John P., and John L. McKnight. *Building Communities from the Inside Out: A Path toward Finding and Mobilizing a Community's Assets.* Evanston, IL: Center for Urban Affairs and Policy Research, Neighborhood Innovations Network, Northwestern University, 1993.

Lance, Perrin. Personal communication with the author, August 10, 2012.

———. Personal communication with the author, June 6, 2013.

Lefebvre, Henri. *The Production of Space.* Oxford: Blackwell, 1991.

Lightweis-Goff, Jennie. *Blood at the Root: Lynching as American Cultural Nucleus.* Albany: State University of New York Press, 2011.

Lipsitz, George. *The Possessive Investment in Whiteness: How White People Profit from Identity Politics.* Philadelphia: Temple University Press, 1998.

Littlefield, Ron. Personal communication with the author, March 14, 2013.

Lommel, Cookie. *Robert Church.* Los Angeles: Melrose Square, 1995.

Lynch, Kevin. *The Image of the City.* Cambridge, MA: MIT Press, 1960.

Mandelbaum, Seymour J. "Telling Stories." *Journal of Planning Education and Research* 10, no. 3 (1991): 209–14.

Mark Making. *Vision Statement, 2014.* http://markmaking.org/mission-public-art-chattanooga/.

Markusen, Ann, and Anne Gadwa. *Creative Placemaking.* Washington, DC: National Endowment for the Arts, 2010.

Martin, Deborah G. "'Place-Framing' as Place-Making: Constituting a Neighborhood for Organizing and Activism." *Annals of the Association of American Geographers* 93, no. 3 (2003): 730–50.

Massachusetts Institute of Technology. *Planning for Environmental Justice.* Cambridge, MA: MIT Department of Urban Studies and Planning, 2002.

Massey, Doreen. *For Space.* London: SAGE, 2005.

———. "New Directions in Space." In *Social Relations and Spatial Structures*, edited by Derek Gregory and John Urry, 9–19. New York: St. Martin's Press, 1985.

Maxfield, Charles A. "The Formation and Early History of the American Board of Commissioners for Foreign Missions." In *The "Reflex Influence" of Missions: The Domestic Operations of the American Board of Commissioners for Foreign Missions, 1810–1850*. Unpublished diss., Union Theological Seminary, 1995.

McCollough, C. R., Quentin Bass, Emanuel Breitburg, and Chattanooga Regional Anthropological Association. *Moccasin Bend, the Pride of Chattanooga: Investigation of the Value of Its Archaeological and Historical Contents as a Public Resource; Preliminary Investigations, Seasons, 1–3*. Chattanooga, TN: Chattanooga Regional Anthropological Association, 1983.

McDonald, Frances. Personal communication with the author, August 18, 2012.

McKittrick, Katherine, and Clyde Woods, eds. *Black Geographies and the Politics of Place*. Toronto: South End Press, 2007.

———. "Nobody Knows the Mysteries." In *Black Geographies and the Politics of Place*, edited by Katherine McKittrick and Clyde Woods, 1–13. Toronto: South End Press, 2007.

Miles, Tiya. *Ties That Bind: The Story of an Afro-Cherokee Family in Slavery and Freedom*. Berkeley: University of California Press, 2005.

Miles, Tiya, and Sharon Patricia Holland. *Crossing Waters, Crossing Worlds: The African Diaspora in Indian Country*. Durham, NC: Duke University Press, 2006.

Morrison, Kristan Accles. *Free School Teaching: A Journey into Radical Progressive Education*. Albany: State University of New York Press, 2012.

Nguyên, Thu Su'o'ng Thi. "Vietnamese Diasporic Placemaking: An Ethnographic Moment in Uneven Geographic Development." *Educational Policy* 24, no. 1 (2010): 159–88.

Nix, William. Personal communication with the author, June 4, 2013.

Norgren, Jill, and Serena Nanda. *American Cultural Pluralism and Law*. Westport, CT: Greenwood Publishing Group, 1996.

Parham, Louis L. *Chattanooga, Tennessee; Hamilton County, and Lookout Mountain: An Epitome of Chattanooga from Her Early Days down to the Present; Hamilton County, Its Soil, Climate, Area, Population, Wealth, etc. Lookout Mountain, Its Battlefields, Beauties, Climate, and Other Attractions*. Chattanooga, TN: Louis L. Parham, 1876.

Patterson, Tiffany Ruby, and Robin D. G. Kelley. "Unfinished Migrations: Reflections on the African Diaspora and the Making of the Modern World." *African Studies Review* 43, no. 1 (2000): 11–45.

Perdue, Theda. *Slavery and the Evolution of Cherokee Society, 1540–1866*. Knoxville: University of Tennessee Press, 1979.

Perdue, Theda, and Michael D. Green. *The Cherokee Removal: A Brief History with Documents*. Boston: Bedford Books of St. Martin's Press, 1995.

Petrilli, Michael. "50 U.S. Zip Codes with the Biggest Increases in White Share of Population: 2000–2010." *Flypaper*. Washington, DC: Thomas B. Fordham Institute, 2012.

Phillips, Joyce B., and Paul Gary Phillips. *The Brainerd Journal: A Mission to the Cherokees, 1817–1823*. Lincoln: University of Nebraska Press, 1998.

Planning Free School of Chattanooga. *Arts and Cultural Development Workshop Transcript*, April 20, 2013.

———. Community Assessment Workshop Transcript, March 21, 2013.

———. *Developing a Neighborhood Assessment Toolkit Workshop Transcript*, March 21, 2013.

———. *Employment and Workforce Development Workshop Transcript*, February 20, 2013.

———. *Housing Workshop Transcript*, May 15, 2013.

———. *Informational Brochure*. Chattanooga, TN, 2013.

———. *Transportation and Mobility Workshop Transcript*, February 10, 2013.

———. "Who We Are," 2013. Accessed January 8, 2013. http://www.freeschoolchatt .blogspot.com.

Rankins, Tiffany. Personal communication with the author, June 8, 2013.

Reardon, Kenneth M. "Combating Racism through Planning Education: Lessons from the East St. Louis Action Research Project." *Planning Practice and Research* 13, no. 4 (1998): 421–32.

———. "Participatory Action Research as Service Learning." *New Directions for Teaching and Learning*, no. 73 (1998): 57–64.

———. "Enhancing the Capacity of Community-Based Organizations in East St. Louis." *Journal of Planning Education and Research* 17, no. 4 (1998): 323–33.

Robertson-Rehberg, Mary E. *Housing: 2010 State of Chattanooga Region Report*. Chattanooga, TN: Ochs Center for Metropolitan Studies, 2010.

Ross, John, and Gary E. Moulton. *The Papers of Chief John Ross*. Vol. 1, *1807–1839*. Norman: University of Oklahoma Press, 1985.

Royce, Charles C., and Smithsonian Institution. *Map of the Former Territorial Limits of the Cherokee "Nation of" Indians: Exhibiting the Boundaries of the Various Cessions of Land Made by Them to the Colonies and to the United States by Treaty Stipulations, from the Beginning of Their Relations with the Whites to the Date of Their Removal West of the Mississippi River*. Washington, DC: Smithsonian Institution, Bureau of Ethnology, 1884. Accessed August 6, 2011. https://www.loc.gov/item/99446145/.

Rozema, Vicki. *Footsteps of the Cherokees: A Guide to the Eastern Homelands of the Cherokee Nation*. Winston-Salem, NC: John F. Blair, 1995.

Rushing, Christian. Personal communication with the author, August 29, 2012.

Sanborn Fire Insurance Company. *Chattanooga, Tennessee, 1885*. Accessed June 11, 2012. http://sanborn.umi.com.

———. *Chattanooga, Tennessee, 1889*. Accessed June 11, 2012. http://sanborn.umi.com.

———. *Chattanooga, Tennessee, 1901*. Accessed June 11, 2012. http://sanborn.umi.com.

———. *Chattanooga, Tennessee, 1917*. Accessed June 11, 2012. http://sanborn.umi.com.

———. *Chattanooga, Tennessee, 1954*. Accessed June 11, 2012. http://sanborn.umi.com.

Sandercock, Leonie. *Making the Invisible Visible: A Multicultural Planning History*. Berkeley: University of California Press, 1998.

———. "Towards a Planning Imagination for the Twenty-First Century." *Journal of the American Planning Association* 70, no. 2 (2004): 133–41.

———. *Towards Cosmopolis: Planning for Multicultural Cities*. Chichester, UK: J. Wiley, 1998.

Schneekloth, Lynda H., and Robert G. Shibley. *Placemaking: The Art and Practice of Building Communities*. New York: Wiley, 1995.

Scott, Michelle R. *Blues Empress in Black Chattanooga: Bessie Smith and the Emerging Urban South*. Urbana: University of Illinois Press, 2008.

Scott, Winfield, and Wirth, W. J. *Orders No. 25, May 17, 1838*. Eastern Division, Cherokee Agency, Tennessee. Accessed June 19, 2012. www.loc.gov.

Seidman, Irving. *Interviewing as Qualitative Research: A Guide for Researchers in Education and the Social Sciences*. New York: Teachers College Press, 2013.

Soja, Edward W. *Postmodern Geographies: The Reassertion of Space in Critical Social Theory*. London: Verso, 1989.

———. *Seeking Spatial Justice*. Minneapolis: University of Minnesota Press, 2010.

———. "The Spatiality of Social Life: Towards a Transformative Retheorisation." In *Social Relations and Spatial Structures*, edited by Derek Gregory and John Urry, 93–95. New York: St. Martin's Press, 1985.

———. *Thirdspace: Journeys to Los Angeles and Other Real-and-Imagined Places*. Cambridge, MA: Blackwell, 1996.

State of Tennessee. *Jim Crow and Disfranchisement of Southern Blacks, 2013*. Accessed September 12, 2013. http://www.tn.gov/tsla/exhibits/blackhistory/jimcrow.htm.

Steinberg, David H. *And to Think, It Only Cost a Nickel! The Development of Public Transportation in the Chattanooga Area*. Chattanooga, TN: David H. Steinberg, 1975.

Tayac, Gabrielle. *IndiVisible: African-Native American Lives in the Americas*. Washington, DC: Smithsonian Institution's National Museum of the American Indian in association with the National Museum of African American History and Culture and the Smithsonian Institution Traveling Exhibition Service, 2009.

Team Gadugi. *The Passage: Statement of the Artists*. Chattanooga, TN: n.p., 2005. Printed on a plaque at the site of the Passage.

Tennessee Writers' Project. *Chattanooga City Guide*. N.p., 1900.

Throgmorton, James A. *Planning as Persuasive Storytelling: The Rhetorical Construction of Chicago's Electric Future*. Chicago: University of Chicago Press, 1996.

Townsend, Peggy. Personal communication with the author, March 26, 2013.

Tyree, Gayle, personal communication with the author, October 5, 2012.

Umemoto, Karen. "Walking in Another's Shoes: Epistemological Challenges in Participatory Planning." *Journal of Planning Literature* 16, no. 3 (January 2002): 397–477.

———. *The Truce: Lessons from an LA Gang War*. Ithaca, NY: Cornell University Press, 2006.

United States Census Bureau. *Hamilton County Comprehensive Population Statistics Report on the Census Tract Level, 1950–2010, SF1 Tables*. Accessed March 15, 2013. http://www.socialexplorer.com.

———. *Hamilton County Manufacturing Statistics Summary Report, 1850–1860*. Accessed March 16, 2013. http://www.socialexplorer.com.

———. *Hamilton County Population Statistics, 1820–1940, SF1 Tables*. Accessed March 16, 2013. http://www.socialexplorer.com.

———. *Hamilton County Population Statistics Report on the Block Level, 2000 and 2010 SF1 Tables*. Accessed March 25, 2013. http://www.socialexplorer.com.

———. *Hamilton County Population Statistics and Slavery Schedule, 1840–1860.* Accessed March 16, 2013. http://www.socialexplorer.com.

———. *Manufacturing Statistics and Population, 1870–1900.* Accessed January 10, 2012. http://www.socialexplorer.com.

University of Tennessee–Chattanooga. *Comprehensive Housing Master Plan,* Chattanooga, TN, 2011.

———. *Master Plan, 2012.* Accessed July 8, 2013. http://www.utc.edu/master-plan/.

Urban Land Institute and Chattanooga-Hamilton County Regional Planning Commission. *Moccasin Bend, Chattanooga, Tennessee: An Evaluation of Land Use and Development Strategies for the Chattanooga-Hamilton County Regional Planning Commission, April 25–30, 1982: A Panel Study Report.* Washington, DC: Urban Land Institute, 1982.

Waite, Maurice, ed. *Pocket Oxford English Dictionary.* New York: Oxford University Press, 2013.

Walker, Robert Sparks. *Torchlights to the Cherokees.* Johnson City, TN: Overmountain Press, 1993.

Warf, Barney, and Santa Arias, eds. *The Spatial Turn: Interdisciplinary Perspectives.* London and New York: Routledge, 2008.

Watson, Stroud. Personal communication with the author, January 29, 2013.

Webb, Clive. *Fight against Fear: Southern Jews and Black Civil Rights.* Athens: University of Georgia Press, 2001.

Westside Community Association. "A Petition to the City Council of Chattanooga." Chattanooga, TN, 2011.

White, J. Bliss. *Biography and Achievements of the Colored Citizens of Chattanooga.* Signal Mountain, TN: Mountain Press, 1904.

Whyte, William Hollingsworth. *The Social Life of Small Urban Spaces.* New York: Project for Public Spaces, 1980, 2001.

Wiltse, Henry M. *History of Chattanooga.* Vols. 1 and 2. Chattanooga, TN: n. p., ca. 1910.

Woodard Henderson, Ash-Lee. *Chattanooga Organized for Action Annual General Assembly,* July 27, 2012.

Woods, Clyde. *Development Arrested: The Blues and Plantation Power in the Mississippi Delta.* London: Verso, 1998.

World Archaeological Congress. *Archaeologies of Placemaking: Monuments, Memories, and Engagement in Native North America.* Edited by Patricia E. Rubertone. Walnut Creek, CA.: Left Coast Press, 2008.

INDEX

CPSIA information can be obtained
at www.ICGtesting.com
Printed in the USA
LVOW11s0551100518
576678LV00007B/371/P